HOW TO
Restore Your C3
CORVETTE

1968-1982

Walt Thurn

S-A DESIGN

CarTech®

CarTech®

CarTech®, Inc.
39966 Grand Avenue
North Branch, MN 55056
Phone: 651-277-1200 or 800-551-4754
Fax: 651-277-1203
www.cartechbooks.com

Edit by Paul Johnson
Layout by Monica Seiberlich

ISBN 978-1-61325-037-2
Item No. SA248

Library of Congress Cataloging-in-Publication Data

Thurn, Walt.
  How to restore your C3 Corvette : 1968-1982 / by Walt Thurn.
     pages cm
  ISBN 978-1-61325-037-2
1. Corvette automobile–Conservation and restoration. I. Title.

TL215.C6T498 2013
629.28'722–dc23

                    2013007443

Printed in China
10 9 8 7 6 5 4 3 2 1

OVERSEAS DISTRIBUTION BY:

PGUK
63 Hatton Garden
London EC1N 8LE, England
Phone: 020 7061 1980 • Fax: 020 7242 3725

Renniks Publications Ltd.
3/37-39 Green Street
Banksmeadow, NSW 2109, Australia
Phone: 2 9695 7055 • Fax: 2 9695 7355

CONTENTS

S-A DESIGN

ACKNOWLEDGMENTS

Writing this book has been a time-consuming but fascinating opportunity to revisit my past Corvette experiences. During my lifetime Corvette journey, I have spent many hours working on my own C3 Corvettes and spent time with a successful L88 Corvette race team. I could not have completed this book without the help and support of my wife Dianne, who encouraged me along the way.

But the real hero in making this book happen is Art Dorsett, owner of Van Steel Corvette Parts and Service, which has been in operation since 1977. The idea to write this book came when he decided to restore his 1980 L48 automatic Corvette coupe. He has owned this car since 1980 and has only put a little over 40,000 miles on it. He offered the use of his car as well as customer cars that came through his shop to assemble this book. He has spent countless hours reading my material, giving me guidance and access to the day-to-day operation of his company. This included letting me photograph his technicians assembling C3 suspension parts for customers and tapping into their extensive C3 rebuilding experience.

Van Steel has an excellent industrywide reputation for quality Corvette suspension components and service. They refurbish and build all driveline components that are fitted into a C3 Corvette. They offer original-equipment-style parts as well as advanced tubular A-arms and coil-over shock systems for this generation. They offer a variety of high-quality early Corvette suspension components at reasonable prices. In addition to providing parts for C3 customers Van Steel specializes in restoring C3 Corvettes for street use. Their work covers service on the frame, suspension, body restoration, and painting for the third-generation Corvette.

Dorsett's son Danny is president and their small and dedicated staff of employees supports the company's daily operations. This includes business manager Paul Lesinski, lead technician Russ Hunt, and technicians Andre Diaz and Jay Johnson.

Also helping complete the book was Tackley Auto Body's owner Mike Tackley. He gave me unlimited access to his busy shop. I made many visits during the time-consuming Corvette paint preparation process. Tackley's painter, Tom Otto, allowed me to enter his domain (his paint booth) to photograph him painting. The rest of his staff was also very cooperative.

Ed Scoppa is the proud owner of a 1969 Corvette coupe that he is restoring in his garage. He has shared his Corvette restoration experiences and photos with me whenever I asked. He removed the body from the chassis at his home and sent the frame to Van Steel for refurbishing. Ed deserves big thanks for giving me an inside look at how a private owner is able to complete this restoration task at home. In addition, Ed connected me with his engine builder, Southern Style Racing Engines. George Pils, owner of Southern Style Racing, has been building Chevrolet racing and street engines since 1972. He allowed me to photograph the Corvette engine rebuilding process in his well-equipped shop and was patient with all of my questions.

The service team at Maher Chevrolet was always willing to provide me with technical assistance and encouragement.

Mike Circle, owner of Circle Products, is an expert at rebuilding Muncie, BorgWarner, and GM Turbo 350 and 400 transmissions. He was happy to share his extensive transmission knowledge with me.

Gear Star provided advice and photos and therefore was helpful in my endeavor to write the transmission chapter. Their knowledge on rebuilding Turbo Hydra-Matic transmissions was invaluable.

Vern Carmack, owner of Vern's Chevy Service has been servicing Corvettes for many years. He always made himself available to answer my questions regarding C3 Corvettes.

I want to thank the many vendors who supply quality parts to the Corvette hobby that allows it to thrive. There are too many to mention here but you can find them in the Source Guide. If you need a part I am sure you will be able to locate it with one of these companies.

I also want to thank my long-time friend Bill Dudley. He is the proud owner of a 1969 red 350/350 Corvette convertible with factory air conditioning. He has owned this Corvette since 1970 and it remains in his care after all these years. He and I have spent many hours working on his car learning about Corvettes and sharing life stories. Thanks, Bill.

Finally I must mention the former R.E.D. Corvette racing team that I was with in the early 1970s. Dana and Toye English were the team owners who campaigned two L88 Corvettes (a 1968 and 1969) successfully in the United States and at Le Mans. It was during my time with this team that I met Zora Arkus-Duntov and Gib Hufstader who both provided technical support to the team. Drivers Dave Heinz and Bob Johnson, who are no longer with us, had the courage to drive the L88 at more than 200 mph on the Mulsanne straightaway at Le Mans. They were great people and great drivers. This race team experience created my passion for Corvettes and for Corvette Racing, which still burns within me today. I have the C3 to thank for fueling this fire.

This was an educational experience and I feel fortunate to have been offered the opportunity by CarTech to take you on this C3 journey. My fingers are crossed that you find this book worthwhile during the restoration of one of my favorite Corvette generations, the C3.

ABOUT THE AUTHOR

Walt Thurn has been interested in Corvettes for most of his adult life. He has owned multiple Corvettes and has written numerous magazine articles on C3, C4, C5, and C6 Corvettes. He also has covered international Corvette racing events in the United States, Canada, and Europe. During the early 1970s, he was responsible for providing public relations for the Toye English L88 C3 Corvette Racing team. Team drivers Bob Johnson/Dave Heinz finished fourth overall and first in GT at the 1972 12 Hours of Sebring endurance race. Only two Ferraris and one Alfa Romeo prototype finished in front of the thundering L88 hardtop. Walt covered this event for the team. This Corvette record stood until 2004 when a Pratt & Miller C5R matched this finish.

During his time with the team, Walt met Corvette chief engineer Zora Arkus-Duntov and lead Corvette engineer Gib Hufstader. Arkus-Duntov and Hufstader provided valuable behind-the-scenes support to the English racing team, especially at the 1972 24 Hours of Le Mans. This private team finished 15th overall at that year's race, which was the first for a Corvette since 1960. English Racing went on to finish third overall at the 1973 24 Hours of Daytona. Walt was there to record and document this important part of Corvette's C3 racing history.

During the early 1990s, Walt wrote stories about the racing successes of the Morrison Motorsports ZR-1 team for *Corvette Fever* magazine. While covering that team's activities he met many of today's industry insiders and race team personnel. These people include John Heinricy, Jim Minneker, Boris Said, Andy Pilgrim, Stu Hayner, Reese Cox, Chuck, and Lance Mallett.

In May of 1997, Walt shadowed the Mallett Motorsports team in a new black C5 Corvette in the One Lap of America. His articles about this wild experience gave readers a firsthand insight into the reliability of the fifth-generation Corvette.

In 2000, Walt joined the Pratt & Miller C5R team as a writer. He spent one year with the factory Corvette team covering the 2000 season. He accompanied the C5/C6 Corvette Registry on three Le Mans trips in Europe and wrote stories about those experiences in their quarterly magazine.

He has been published in magazines such as *VETTE*, *Corvette Fever*, *Corvette Quarterly*, *C5/C6 Registry Newsletter*, and *Corvette Magazine*. He has traveled to Europe extensively to document the construction and racing activities of the C6 Z06 R with Callaway Competition. The Z06 R competes in the European FIA GT3 championship and has won five international championships.

Walt and his wife Dianne live in Florida.

INTRODUCTION

The first Corvette I saw as a young boy was a white 1955 convertible. I closely followed the Corvette's development and became an instant fan of its styling and performance. My first racing experience was at the Sebring 12-hour race. These early Corvettes were fast but faded quickly because of poor brakes. But they were loud and American made. And they made a big impact on the racing scene. I witnessed the Grand Sport leading the first lap at the 1964 Sebring race and was amazed that a Corvette could keep pace with the exotic racers from Europe.

I became acutely aware of Corvette Chief Engineer Zora Arkus-Duntov's struggle to improve Corvette performance while working under a silly corporate performance ban laid down by GM executives. Arkus-Duntov was a fighter and he and his merry band of rebels continued adding special equipment packages to sell to dedicated Corvette racers.

Ford, meanwhile, was full-speed ahead with their "Total Performance" campaign. The Blue Oval fully supported the Ford Shelby Cobra and the Ford GT40 prototype. Arkus-Duntov

kept targeting the Cobras by building bigger engines and refining the Corvette chassis. Four-wheel-disc brakes and the big-block were introduced in 1965. The C2 Corvette was a styling success with customers but had terrible aerodynamics. The Mako Shark–inspired 1968 Corvette solved many of Arkus-Duntov's complaints. It was much more efficient aerodynamically and by 1969 the L88-powered Corvettes were the GT cars to beat.

My first C3 was a Monza-red 427 coupe that I purchased in 1969. It had the rare factory sidepipes and factory A/C, and was a head turner wherever I drove it. Arkus-Duntov's hard work had paid off and that Corvette was as good as any sports car on the road during the time I owned it.

It was during this time I became involved with an L88 Corvette racing team in Tampa, Florida. The team campaigned a 1969 Corvette convertible that was one of four open-chambered L88s built for private race teams. This race team finished sixth overall and second in GT at the 1971 24 Hours of Daytona and tenth overall and second in GT at

the 1971 12 Hours of Sebring. In 1972 they won their class at Daytona and finished fourth overall and first in GT at Sebring. This performance got them an invitation to compete at the famous 24 Hours of Le Mans in France. That Corvette, driven by Dave Heinz and Bob Johnson, was the first Corvette to be classified as a finisher since 1960.

The team disbanded in 1974 and I finally parted company with my 1969 soon after that, but the experience helped me become a lifelong fan of C3 Corvettes. I purchased another C3 in 1979 (on page 48) and had many enjoyable years with that car.

The people I have met in the Corvette industry and hobby—from all over the country and Europe—are the most valuable treasures, not the cars. I have been involved in the Corvette hobby most of my life and my close friends call me a Corvette junkie. Four generations of Corvettes have spent time in my garage and every one holds a special place in my memories. However, the C3 introduced me to the Corvette hobby and that is why I accepted the invitation to write this book.

I hope you have fun with your car. Corvettes are great to drive and a blast to work on. The Corvette hobby is not just about the car; it's about the people who share the same passion for the car that you do. Enjoying owning your C3 includes taking it to major Corvette shows, such as Corvettes at Carlisle, the National Corvette Museum, and even local car shows. It also includes going to the Saturday night drags, autocrossing on Sunday, or driving to work during the week. Corvette ownership is all about enjoying your ride.

I had the good fortune to spend time with C3 Chief Engineer Zora Arkus-Duntov and his lead development engineer Gib Hufstader in the early 1970s. They provided our L88 team with excellent technical advice and attended races to help us through the tough spots. Their active involvement in improving the competition C3 Corvette helped turn this generation Corvette into a fast and reliable sports car.

This book focuses on giving you clear descriptions and procedural instructions for disassembling, inspecting, and then reassembling the Corvette component groups. With this book in hand, you will be able to complete the crucial restoration procedures for your car.

Chapter 1 offers a brief developmental history of the car, including the production numbers and features of each production year.

Chapter 2 provides you with some guidelines on project planning, how to choose the level of restoration you should attempt, and buying the right project car. This chapter also discusses what type of tools and equipment you need.

Chapter 3 discusses how to remove the frame and interior from your project car plus how and where to store components. A materials list for building a body dolly is also provided.

Chapter 4 gives an overview on how to repair and prepare your Corvette's body for painting. This includes minor body repairs as well as panel replacement. The chapter discusses various methods used to strip off the old paint and correctly fill and sand body imperfections. Deciding how to paint your car is also covered. To make the best choice for your particular project, you need to decide whether you have the skills to do this work yourself or whether you should select a professional paint shop to do the work.

Chapter 5 covers how a professional paints a Corvette. You get a firsthand look at what steps are required before the car is put into the paint booth.

Chapter 6 details how to restore your Corvette frame. This includes disassembly, inspection, repair, and final finishing.

Chapter 7 explains how to reassemble your restored C3 Corvette's frame. This includes installing the front and rear suspension and rebuilding the differential.

Chapter 8 discusses reinstalling the braking system and the brake and fuel lines back onto your C3 frame. Reassembly of the rear parking brake system is also covered.

Chapter 9 gives an overview of the various engine options that were installed into C3 Corvettes during their 14 years of production. I also discuss overhauling or replacing your engine with a Chevrolet Performance crate engine.

Chapter 10 explores the various transmissions that were available for C3 Corvettes. This includes the Muncie and BorgWarner 4-speeds and the GM Turbo Hydra-Matic 350, 400, and 700R4 automatic transmissions.

Chapter 11 discusses reinstalling and reconnecting the wiring harness and reinstalling the interior. This includes dash reassembly on 1968–1977 model years and 1978–1982 Corvettes.

Chapter 12 has you finally reuniting your refurbished body and frame.

In summary, this book is designed to give you restoration guidelines on how to buy, inspect, dismantle, refurbish, and reassemble a C3 Corvette. This book is not designed to win you awards for originality and gather awards from organizations such as the NCRS. The intent is to enable you to restore your C3 so that it is reliable, drivable, and a fun sports car to own. It is designed to give you an overview of the car you want to buy or already own. After reading this book, you should possess a greater understanding and the knowledge to restore the fabulous C3 Corvette.

C3 HISTORY

Corvette folks often refer to their cars by generations. So, here is a quick guide on how to identify them:

- C1 (first generation) refers to all Corvettes built from 1953 to 1962 with straight-axle rear suspensions. All future Corvettes were equipped with independent rear suspension (IRS).
- C2s (second generation) were built from 1963 to 1967.
- C3s (third generation) were built from 1968 to 1982.
- C4s (fourth generation) skipped 1983 due to quality problems and were built from 1984 to 1996.
- C5s (fifth generation) were built from 1997 to 2004.
- C6s (sixth generation) were built from 2005 to 2013.
- C7s (seventh generation) began production in 2013 for the 2014 model year.

The first 300 Corvettes were assembled in 1953 at the Warren, Michigan, plant. Production was moved to St. Louis, Missouri, in 1954 and remained at this location until August 1, 1981. A new plant opened at Bowling Green, Kentucky, in July of 1981 and production remains in this location today.

The Pre-Dawn of the C3 Corvette

Before getting into how to restore or refurbish your C3, let's look at some of the reasons this generation has had such a significant impact on Corvette history.

Arkus-Duntov's Racing Efforts

The success of the C3 on the world's racing circuits is due to the efforts of Zora Arkus-Duntov and his engineering team. He was Corvette's first chief engineer and was

There are many things to think about in selecting a project Corvette. The most important to consider is what kind of driving you want to do. For example, Bill Dudley, the owner of this beautiful 1969 small-block enjoys top-down driving near his Florida home. His 350/350 is the perfect ride for his driving requirements.

passionate about racing and high-performance sports cars. He was the son of Russian parents, born in Belgium, and completed his schooling in Europe. He immigrated to New York before World War II and started Ardun Mechanical Company in 1941. The company built precision parts and performed critical engineering services for the war effort. When the war was over Ardun downsized and began moving into the automotive performance market. The company developed an overhead-valve conversion for the very popular flathead Ford V-8. Called the Ardun Head it increased the stock horsepower by 62 percent. This and many other automotive consulting contracts kept the company profitable after the war.

In 1953 Arkus-Duntov visited the GM Motorama car show in New York City and inspected a prototype Corvette on display. It was love at first sight. He applied for a job at General Motors and was hired May 1, 1953, as a junior engineer at Chevrolet. One year after joining General Motors, he was invited to drive a factory Porsche at the 1954 24 Hours of Le Mans. Rather than asking GM's permission, he accepted the offer and flew to Europe. He won his class at the age of

The first Corvette was completed on June 30, 1953, in the Warren, Michigan, assembly plant. There were 299 more 1953 Corvettes built at the Warren plant. The assembly line was moved to St. Louis, Missouri, in time for the beginning of the 1954 Corvette production run. This 1953 Corvette was the 93rd one built in Warren. These Corvettes are worth a lot of money in the collector car market. (Photo Courtesy GM Heritage Center)

Arkus-Duntov spied the first Corvette prototype, called the EX-122, at the January 1953 GM Motorama auto show held at the Waldorf Astoria hotel in New York City. Corvette production began shortly after the show. After seeing the car, Arkus-Duntov applied for a job at Chevrolet and was hired May 1, 1953, as a junior engineer at $14,000 per year. In an attempt to spark sales and performance, Arkus-Duntov's team installed a 195-hp 265-ci V-8 into the 1955 Corvette. A total of 693 Corvettes were sold with a V-8 during the 1955 model year. Seven were ordered with the tame 155-hp 6-cylinder engine, which brought the 1955 production total to 700 units. (Photo Courtesy GM Heritage Center)

Zora Arkus-Duntov joined General Motors as a junior engineer in 1953. He was named Director of High Performance Vehicles in 1957 and became Corvette's first chief engineer December 1, 1968. He retired from this position in 1975 at age 65. Many have called him the father of Corvette. His passion for racing and his engineering ability helped transform the Corvette's performance image.

This is one of the four factory Corvettes entered in the 1956 12 Hours of Sebring endurance race. It finished ninth overall and first in class. This car was used in Chevrolet's successful 1956 ad campaign titled "The Real McCoy." The car has been fully restored and is now in the hands of a private collector.

Chevrolet produced this dramatic ad touting the road racing success of its new sports car. Sales of the revised 1956 Corvette jumped to 3,467 total units. Arkus-Duntov's emphasis on performance was beginning to pay off with an impressive increase in sales.

45, and this victory was the highlight of his racing career.

GM management frowned upon Arkus-Duntov's race activity, but no action was taken against him for participating in this race. It wasn't long before he began developing engineering solutions at Chevrolet to improve Corvette's weak performance and poor sales. Only 4,640 Corvettes were sold between 1953 and 1955. The company had decided to stop production until Ford introduced its two-seat Thunderbird in 1955, which was a huge sales success. Styling worked on a major revision for the 1956 Corvette.

Meanwhile, Arkus-Duntov began looking for ways to improve the car's anemic performance. His first breakthrough was fitting the new 265-ci small-block engine into a Corvette. The change became an option for the 1955 Corvette. The year 1955 was also the first time a customer could order a 3-speed manual transmission instead of the standard 2-speed Powerglide automatic for a Corvette.

The revised 1956 Corvette featured roll-up windows, a power-operated top, and a removable hardtop. Arkus-Duntov was still a racer at heart, and in 1956, he entered four factory-modified Corvettes in the 12 Hours of Sebring. One finished ninth overall and won its class. This victory was used for the successful Corvette ad campaign titled "The Real McCoy." Sales totaled 3,467 units.

In 1957, Arkus-Duntov's team installed an optional 283-hp fuel-injected 283-ci engine with a 4-speed manual transmission in the Corvette. He also surprised the competition by entering a new prototype Corvette at Sebring named the Corvette SS. This radical tube-framed racer was very competitive against the top European sports cars but lack of development sidelined the car early in the race.

Arkus-Duntov planned on going to Le Mans but in the spring of 1957 General Motors banned all racing activities. Undaunted, he began working behind the scenes to provide performance parts to top Corvette race teams. Bill Mitchell, GM design VP, was also a serious sports car racing fan. In 1958 he arranged

Corvette's big news in 1957 was the introduction of the first Arkus-Duntov–designed fuel-injected engine. The new 283-ci engine developed 283 hp and was the first engine at General Motors to produce one horsepower per cubic inch. The high-revving small-block put Corvette on the performance map.

Vice President of GM Design Bill Mitchell bought a 1957 Corvette SS race-car test chassis for one dollar and installed this beautiful body he designed called the Stingray. The Stingray was successfully raced for several years before its retirement. Mitchell made it roadworthy and drove it to work! It is now part of the GM Heritage Collection.

The 1963 Corvette Stingray was a huge sales success. Sales rose from 14,531 in 1962 to 21,513 in 1963. However, Arkus-Duntov was very vocal about its weight, poor rear visibility in the split window coupe, and large frontal area. The horizontal area above the grille made the car lift at high speeds. The split window disappeared in 1964, but the aerodynamic problem remained until the C3 was introduced in 1968. Today the split window is highly sought by collectors.

to purchase the chassis used by Arkus-Duntov to develop the 1957 Corvette SS race car. Mitchell's purchase price was one dollar. Mitchell's design team created a new body for the chassis and named it Stingray. The new racer made the cover of all the major automotive magazines and won numerous races with driver Dr. Dick Thompson. Arkus-Duntov and his staff worked quietly behind the scenes to support Mitchell's Stingray racing efforts. This design was very well received by the public.

Mitchell's Stingray

Development and testing of a new 1963 Corvette began in 1960 and was targeted for the 1963 model year. Mitchell based his design of the new Corvette on his Stingray racer. Arkus-Duntov was unhappy with the Stingray design because of the huge frontal area that made the car lift at high speeds. Mitchell ignored his concern and finalized the design while Arkus-Duntov and his team created a new ladder frame chassis

for the car. The new chassis featured an IRS, a first for Corvette. It was named Stingray and featured a stunning design, but it was very heavy (3,015 pounds) for a sports car.

Arkus-Duntov wanted a lightweight version so it could be raced at Le Mans. He and his team secretly built a lightweight (2,000 pounds) version of the Stingray in 1962 and named it Grand Sport. Production was halted after five cars were built when GM's top management found out about the project and ordered Arkus-Duntov to destroy the cars. He defied the order and sold the cars to private racers, which is why these cars still exist today. This stunt almost cost him his job, but somehow he survived the chopping block.

Shelby's Influence

Carroll Shelby changed the automotive landscape forever when he introduced the Cobra, which combined a light (2,000 pounds) AC Bristol English body with a Ford V-8 engine. This combination crushed the Stingray on the racetrack. The new Corvette sold 21,513 units and was a huge sales success but was a loser in the competition world.

Arkus-Duntov continued to support independent race teams with special parts, but the Ford Cobras were too fast. In 1965 the Corvette became available with four-wheel disc brakes and an optional 396-ci big-block engine. For the first time, the Corvette was able to compete

with its nemesis the Cobra without any visible factory support.

The L88 Engine

Arkus-Duntov and his team immediately began working on a racing version of this engine to sell to private racing teams. The option, called L88, was an all-out 427-ci racing engine designed to stomp the Cobra's. Roger Penske raced a prototype L88 at the 1966 24 Hours of Daytona and

the 1966 12 Hours of Sebring. In both races the Penske team won the Grand Touring category with the help of Arkus-Duntov's chassis engineer Gib Hufstader. The L88 engine entered production in 1967 and race teams quickly began winning races with this engine package.

In 1965 Arkus-Duntov developed a new secret weapon to beat the Cobras, the L88 engine option. This prototype 427-ci engine was installed into a standard coupe and sold to Roger Penske Racing in late 1965. Penske's team finished tenth overall and first in GT at the 1966 Daytona 24-hour race.

To remedy Corvette's weight problem, this 2,000-pound Grand Sport was built in 1962. To be able to race at Le Mans, 100 examples were planned. General Motors banned racing in 1963 and only five examples were completed. General Motors ordered them to be destroyed, but Arkus-Duntov sold them to private racers. They all survived and this Grand Sport (#004) is part of the Collier Foundation museum. Arkus-Duntov built the Grand Sport to compete against the new Ford Cobra. The lightweight Ford featured a body and chassis built by AC Bristol in England that was stuffed with a Ford V-8. The 3,000-pound Corvette was no match against this 2,000-pound rocket. Only the Grand Sport was capable of beating the Cobra but General Motors killed the program.

Gib Hufstader retired after working at General Motors for 45 years. He was a design release engineer for the Corvette chassis and worked closely with Arkus-Duntov, who assigned him to provide engineering assistance to top Corvette racing teams during GM's racing ban that began in 1963. Hufstader is responsible for seven GM patents and was inducted into the National Corvette Museum Hall of Fame in 2001. He loves to vintage race his Corvette.

This was an amazing accomplishment because during the night a crash broke off the entire nose of the racer. The headlights were torn off the car and the radiator was punctured. The remaining fiberglass was wired to the frame and flashlights were taped to the fenders for headlights. The team found a spare radiator in a fan's Corvette in the parking lot. The radiator was removed and installed into the racer. The team left a note on the windshield telling the owner what happened and that he would get his radiator back after the race. He did.

The car was repaired and repainted Sunoco blue for the team's new sponsor. It finished ninth overall and first in GT at the 12 Hours of Sebring. In 1967 the L88 became a factory option and captured many sports car racing records.

The Mako Shark II show car first appeared in 1965 and heavily influenced the design of the 1968 Corvette. It was redesigned in 1969 and became the Manta Ray and traveled the show circuits for several years. It is now retired and housed at GM's Heritage Center. The original Mako Shark sits in the background.

The Mako Shark II

Meanwhile, Bill Mitchell and his staff were working on a new body design for the Stingray. Mitchell finally listened to Arkus-Duntov's disapproval of the Stingray's broad non-aerodynamic nose and began fixing it for the new car. In 1965, the results of the design team's work was displayed at the 1965 New York International Auto Show. A new Corvette show car called the Mako Shark II was unveiled to gauge public reaction to the new design. The car featured a much more aerodynamic design and offered the public an early peek at

the new Corvette that was scheduled to be released for 1967.

Due to high production costs the existing Corvette chassis was retained under the new car with minimal changes. The swoopy new body was filled with high-tech features including hideaway windshield wipers, pop-up headlights, fiber-optic light monitors, and Astro ventilation. The coupe version was designed with two removable panels that could be stored in the back luggage compartment. Its scheduled 1967 introduction was delayed because of quality problems that included engine over-

heating, water and wind leaks in the cabin. The Stingray was hastily refurbished and sold for one more year as a 1967 model.

Finally, the C3

The 1968 Corvette was introduced in the fall of 1967 and immediately made the covers of every major automotive magazine. In spite of early quality problems the 1968 Corvette (nicknamed "The Shark") started a remarkable 14-year production run for Corvette. During these years a total of 542,870 C3 Corvettes were built, but only a small percentage of them can be considered collector cars.

Two societies evaluate and judge Corvettes to determine if they are numbers matching to verify if they were delivered from the factory with the options on the car being judged. These two groups are the National Corvette Restorers Society (NCRS) and Bloomington Gold. The judge-certified cars that win their top awards always hold the highest value. The chrome-bumper cars with the correct rare options usually top

Because of early production problems with the C3 Corvette, the C2 was quickly redesigned and released. Today the last Stingray remains very popular with Corvette collectors. The 427-ci, 435-hp option as shown in this beautiful black convertible in Wezep, Holland, is at the top of the collector list.

The National Corvette Restorers Society and Bloomington Gold have access to extensive original Corvette construction databases. This enables them to judge and award owners with Top Flight or Blooming Gold certificates if they meet the numbers-matching criteria.

the price list. Some even exceed the million-dollar mark!

New federal emissions and crash standards were implemented in 1973 and the C3's weight began increasing while horsepower decreased. This makes them less desirable to collectors. This also means thousands

of good, solid, non-collectible Corvettes are available for the weekend hobbyist.

The purpose of this book is to help locate and restore one of these cars. To that end, the following is information about each one of these 14 model year Corvettes.

Front and Rear Chrome Bumper Cars 1968-1972

The 1968–1972 C3 Corvettes carried small chrome bumpers and plastic fascia. The cars feature the notchback roof design, and most carried the high-compression high-performance

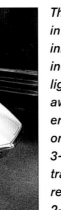

The 1968 Corvette was introduced with many innovative features including fiber-optic light monitors, hideaway windshield wipers, removable T-tops on the coupe, and a 3-speed automatic transmission that replaced the former 2-speed Powerglide. Quality problems plagued the new Corvette and many were not resolved until the 1969s were introduced.

Corvette introduced this T-top feature in 1968, which remained standard for all coupes through 1982. A removable rear window like the one on this coupe was only available from 1968 to 1972. The rear window was fixed in 1973 and remained that way until 1982 when the commemorative edition featured a pop-up rear window.

The 1968 Corvette was the first car in the GM lineup to eliminate conventional door handles. Instead, a push button and grab handle on the top of the door were introduced. To open the door, push down on the upper door flap and the button at the same time to release the lock. This was a one-year-only feature. The button was eliminated in all subsequent C3s and the door was operated with the door flap only.

The 1968 Corvette had a dashboard ignition key slot and no locking steering column. This was a one-year-only feature that did not provide any antitheft protection on the steering column.

This L88 Corvette was one of the first early L88s built for race teams in 1968. Yenko Chevrolet in Canonsburg, Pennsylvania, prepared it, and it raced successfully with the Sunray DX team. It finished sixth overall and first in class at the 1968 12 Hours of Sebring. Corvette Repair faithfully restored this significant C3. A private collector now owns it.

engines. By 1973, performance was on the decline in American V-8 cars and the Corvette suffered the same fate. The 1973–1982 C3s carried the federally mandated 5-mph bumpers. The last year of the big-block was 1974; in 1975 the Corvette featured a fastback roofline.

1968

There were 28,566 units produced (9,936 coupes and 18,630 convertibles). This first design mirrored the 1965 Corvette Mako Shark show car. The new shape was more aerodynamic and featured a new interior. The coupe had removable T-tops and rear window. A vacuum-operated windshield wiper panel was used to keep the wipers from view. This is the only C3 with the ignition key in the dash and push-button door handles. The new body was mounted on the 1963–1967 chassis. Two engine displacements, 327 or 427 ci, were

In 1969 only 4,355 customers ordered the optional N14 side-mounted exhaust system. This option was first offered in 1966 and discontinued in 1967. It was returned to the option list for 1969 and was dropped for the 1970 model year because of new noise regulations. Many C3 owners have installed these very popular systems on later third-generation Corvettes. If this system is installed on a 1969 Corvette, look at the option codes to see if it was originally installed at the factory.

available. The lowest horsepower was 300 and the highest was 435. Eighty high-performance L88 Corvettes were produced for racing. Prices tend to be higher for this year because they were the first C3s built.

The fit and finish of the 1968 Corvette is among the worst for this generation and would be the most expensive to purchase and restore.

It also might be more difficult to run on today's fuels.

1969

Due to a strike, production was extended four months and 38,762 units were produced (22,129 coupes and 16,663 convertibles). Minor outside cosmetic changes appeared, including the name "Stingray" on

Bill Dudley brought this beautiful red 1969 Monza convertible from its original owner in April 1970. Dudley has cared for it ever since and keeps it in sound mechanical condition. It is equipped with factory air, 4-speed, power steering, both tops, and is powered by a 350-hp/350-ci engine. This is one of my favorite C3 designs.

Arkus-Duntov produced four open-chamber 1969 L88s for private race teams. Or Constanzo purchased this car in January 1969 and raced it successfully for two years. It was sold to Race Engineering & Development (R.E.D.) owned by Toye English. Called the Rebel car, it won the 1971 IMSA (International Motor Sports Association) over-two-liter championship and finished fourth overall and first in GT at the 1972 12 Hours of Sebring with drivers Dave Heinz and Bob Johnson. R.E.D.'s #4 1968 second team car that raced at the 1972 Le Mans, France, race sits next to it.

Corvette Repair restored both of these historic Corvettes. Corvette Repair owner Kevin Mackay is a stickler for details when it comes to returning these famous racing Corvettes to their original glory. Private collectors now own both of these classic Corvette race cars.

the front fenders. Factory sidepipes that were an option in 1966 and 1967 were reintroduced for this year only. The chassis received subtle upgrades, including stronger wheel bearings, wider wheels, and improvements to the engine cooling system. The button door handles disappeared, and the interior doorpanels were narrowed to give more passenger room. The steering wheel was reduced from 16 to 15 inches in diameter, and the key switch was moved to the steering column and featured a steering-wheel lock. The small-block was enlarged to 350 ci. Horsepower ranged from 300 to 435. There were 116 high-performance L88s and at least two ZL-1 all-aluminum-engine Corvettes built. These special racers brought Corvette extensive competition successes.

Prices for the special high-performance versions of this car are extremely high. However, prices are more reasonable for standard coupes or convertibles without rare options. This is among the cleanest of the third-generation designs; if you desire an early driver C3 this is my favorite. Like the 1968, they are more difficult to run on today's fuels.

1970

Production was 17,316 units (10,668 coupes and 6,648 convertibles). The 350 small-block remained unchanged but the 427 was enlarged to 454 ci. Horsepower ranged from 300 to 390. The L88 was discontinued, and this was the last year for high-compression engines that ran on leaded fuel. A 370-hp, solid-lifter small-block LT-1 was introduced. The ZR-1 small-block "race only" 'Vette appeared with an LT-1 engine and 4-speed transmission; only 25 were produced. Sidepipes were dis-

continued. A new eggcrate grille and side vents were introduced, along with enlarged fenders to reduce rock damage. Rectangular exhaust pipes were the final external cosmetic changes made in 1970.

Fewer of these Corvettes are available because of low production and they are probably more expensive and harder to find. These cars are also more difficult to run on today's fuels.

This 1970 photo shows the interior of my personal 1969 Corvette. Note the new steering column ignition key and the smaller-diameter steering wheel. My T-top ride was equipped with a 390-hp/427-ci engine with factory sidepipes and air conditioning. It was sold in 1974 and its whereabouts are unknown.

In 1969, Corvette offered the all-aluminum 427-ci engine packages for $4,718. The engine weighed the same as a small-block but produced a huge increase in power and torque. Many race teams replaced their L88 engines with the ZL-1. Only two street cars are known to exist and this is one of them. It was purchased from a government auction in 1991 for $300,000 and is still owned by the same person.

Only 33 ZR-1 special-optioned small-block Corvettes were produced between 1970 and 1971. Arkus-Duntov built them to compete in the Sports Car Club of America (SCCA) B Production racing category. This 1970 convertible is one of only eight built in 1970 and was never raced.

Government safety and fuel standards continued to put pressure on manufacturers to limit or eliminate high-performance engines. Arkus-Duntov's team sold 12 1971 ZR-2 Corvettes that were equipped with the 425-hp/ 454-ci engine with very few options. This 8,700-mile convertible is one of the few original ZR-2s that remain today.

This 1972 convertible, owned by Jim Oliver, is an excellent example of what a C3 can look like with a proper restoration. It is not a numbers-matching award winner, but it features new suspension, engine, and drivetrain. It is a daily driver and all of the goodies work including its air conditioner.

1971

Production was 21,801 units (14,680 coupes and 7,121 convertibles). The base engine was reduced from 300 to 270 hp and fitted with low-compression heads that allowed use of low-octane or unleaded fuels. The LT-1 engine's power was reduced to 330 hp and the base 454-ci was reduced to 365 hp. A new LS6 454-ci was introduced and rated at 425 hp; only 188 were produced. The body was unchanged from 1970. All 1971 Corvettes ran on unleaded fuel.

Because many were produced and they run on unleaded fuel with lower compression engines, the 1971 models are suitable to restore.

1972

A total of 27,004 units were produced (20,496 coupes and 6,508 convertibles). This was the last year for the chrome front and rear bumpers. The fiber-optic light monitoring system was discontinued. This was the last year for the removable rear window in the coupes. The engine horsepower ratings dropped again. The base engine was 200 hp, the LT-1 was 255 hp and the 454 LS5 was 270 hp. This was the last year for the LT-1. Only 20 255-hp ZR-1s were built.

This was the highest production of the 1970–1972 model run. This model looks identical to the previous two and would make a good project car if you want chrome bumpers.

Soft Bumper Cars 1973–1982

The C3s built from 1973 to 1982 came with large, steel-beam bumpers that were integrated into the frame and bodywork. A soft plastic cover adorned the new federally mandated 5-mph bumpers. Gone were the elegant yet fragile chrome bumpers of the previous era.

1973

Production was 30,464 units (25,521 coupes and 4,943 convertibles). In 1973 all new cars were required to pass a 5-mph crash test.

To comply with this rule, all Corvettes were equipped with a 5-mph crash bumper on the front. The bumper consisted of a steel beam bolted to the frame and covered with a soft rubber nose painted body color. The rear chrome bumpers remained. The hood was extended to cover the windshield wipers, and a side-impact beam was added to the door for crash protection. Aluminum wheels were offered, but due to production problems they were quickly withdrawn from the option list. Some sets were delivered to customers but they are very rare. New chassis mounts and sound deadening was utilized to reduce road noise in the cabin. The base engine was reduced to 190 hp, and a 250-hp L82 small-block was introduced.

This was a popular design because of its lack of chrome and sleek new nose. However, chrome bumper fans disliked this new look. Properly restored they are fun cars to own and drive and might be available for a reasonable price.

In 1973 Corvette underwent a mid-generation makeover with the introduction of an injection-molded urethane-covered front 5-mph crash bumper. It still retained its rear chrome bumpers and rear lip spoiler. It featured new front fender vents, badging, and domed hood. Some consider this one of the C3's cleanest overall designs. A new hood was introduced that eliminated the troublesome pop-up windshield wiper door. This door sometimes failed to open and burned out the windshield wiper motor.

1974

A total of 37,502 units were produced (32,028 coupes and 5,474 convertibles). This was the last year the 270-hp/454-ci big-block was offered. The 5-mph front and rear crash bumpers painted body color were now standard. The base 350-ci engine was increased to 195 hp. The rear bumper had a seam down the middle that distinguished it from 1975-and-later Corvettes. This was the last year the Corvette was built without a catalytic converter and retained factory dual exhausts. Early rubber bumpers have a tendency to crack and change color.

Overall, this is a good project car if you can find a rust-free example with no body damage.

1975

There were 38,465 units produced (33,836 coupes and 4,629 convertibles). The biggest news of 1975 was the retirement of Corvette's first chief engineer, Zora Arkus-Duntov. He was replaced by Dave McLellan. Corvette was now equipped with a catalytic converter and High-Energy Ignition (HEI) ignition system. The HEI was installed to produce a hotter spark to help the engine burn emissions in the converter. The exhaust blended into one converter under the passenger compartment and split back out into dual exhausts at the rear. The base engine was reduced to 165 hp and the L82 was reduced to 205 hp. This was the last year for convertibles. This new technology that included a catalytic converter and HEI ignition produced very low horsepower.

Personally, I would prefer a 1974 if they are the same price.

In 1974 the rear chrome bumpers were replaced with this 5-mph two-piece injection-molded urethane rear bumper cover. The exhaust tips were removed and fitted with hidden curved pipes that exited underneath the rear of the car. The split in the rear cover was eliminated when the 1973 Corvette was introduced.

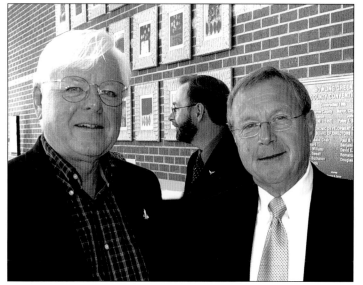

Dave McLellan (left) replaced retiring Zora Arkus-Duntov in 1975 to become Corvette's second chief engineer. Dave worked closely with GM designer Jerry Palmer (right) who helped him freshen the look of the aging third-generation Corvette. C7 designer Kirk Bennion is in the background.

In 1975, Chevrolet offered a Corvette convertible for one last model year until it was reintroduced in 1986. Only 4,629 were delivered to customers. The 1975 Corvette was the first to be equipped with a single catalytic converter for emissions control. The dual exhaust was routed into one pipe that fed into the converter and exited into dual mufflers. An air pump forced air into the converter to help burn hydrocarbons; its connector was attached to the right side of the converter. The system created a lot of backpressure and hurt performance.

1976

Production consisted of 46,567 coupes. The base engine was bumped back up to 180 hp and the L82 now produced 210 hp. The 1976 was fitted with a Vega GT steering wheel, much to the dismay of many enthusiasts. Aluminum wheels returned to the option list and could now be ordered.

This car featured more horsepower, but the interior is not among my favorites; however, it probably would be inexpensive to purchase.

1977

A total of 49,213 coupes were produced. For 1977, horsepower remained the same as 1976, but the car received interior and trim upgrades. Leather trim became standard, and this was the last year for the small, fixed rear window. All trim was painted satin black. A new center console, steering column, and three-spoke steering wheel were added.

This year had a very nice interior and a lot of them were built. If you do not want a fastback this is a desirable project car.

1978

There were 46,776 coupes produced. For its 25th anniversary, General Motors introduced a new fixed fastback rear window on the Corvette. A black/silver Indy pace car replica was produced (6,502) and set off a buyer frenzy. The pace cars featured front and rear spoilers and special bucket seats. A two-tone silver, 25th Anniversary model (RPO B2Z) also became available. A new dash was featured with a lockable glovebox on the passenger side. The base engine was bumped to 185 hp and the L82 produced 220 hp. All 1978 cars had special 25th Anniversary badges.

In 1976, all Corvettes were fitted with a Vega GT steering wheel. This wheel only lasted for one model year and was replaced (in 1977) with a new three-spoke design that was better accepted by Corvette buyers.

The YJ8 aluminum wheel option was added to the 1976 order list. The four wheels were supported with a steel temporary spare tire. The anti-theft alarm key can be seen in front of the Stingray emblem.

This is a desirable year to own and has many standard creature comforts. Many were produced and if the price is right would be worthwhile to restore.

1979

A total of 53,807 coupes were produced, a record for Corvette. Pace car seats became standard and pace car spoilers became an option (RPO D80). Base horsepower was increased to 195 and the L82 rose to 225 hp.

This model year is identical to the 1978 except the 1978 clamshell pace car seats became standard in all 1979 Corvettes. This was the last year for the L82 4-speed manual transmission. Any of these 1979 Corvette automatic or manual cars would be desirable to restore at the right price.

1980

A total of 40,614 units were produced. New front and rear bumper caps were introduced that resulted in an improvement in the car's aerodynamics. The new front bumper also improved engine cooling. The 4-speed manual transmission was no longer available with the L82, and 85-mph speedometers were mandatory. Base horsepower dropped to 190 and the automatic transmission L82 was increased to 230 hp. A 305-ci/180-hp engine was fitted to all Corvettes sold in California due to emissions regulations. This is the first year that Corvette featured a modified frame at the rear. It was redesigned to accommodate the all-aluminum rear axle housing. The 1963–1979 frames are very similar in design and provide a wider variety of available parts.

The 1980 cars are very comfortable to drive, and the new front and rear bumper caps give the car a sleeker, more aerodynamic look. This was the last year that the higher-performing L82 engine option was available (automatic only). For me it is the most desirable of the 1980–1982 cars.

Jerry Palmer and his design team made a major change to Corvette's rear cabin for its 25th anniversary. They added a large rear window supported with special paint options to this limited-edition pace car. Many pace cars were purchased as an investment, but when 6,502 were produced it reduced their collectability.

The D80 pace car spoiler package was added to the 1979 option list. Both spoilers were made from flexible rubber and over time showed a lot of waves in the finish especially at the rear when they were exposed to the sun.

1981

Production consisted of 40,606 coupes, including 8,995 built in Bowling Green, Kentucky. Corvette production moved to Bowling Green in July 1981. For two months, Corvettes were built simultaneously in Bowling Green and St. Louis, Missouri. St. Louis built solid colors with lacquer while Bowling Green did two-tones with enamel and clearcoat. The L82 option was dropped, and the only engine available produced 190 hp. A new computer system adjusted the ignition and a new electronic carburetor for better emissions performance. Tubular stainless-steel exhaust headers and a fiberglass single-leaf rear spring became standard.

New front and rear aerodynamic bumpers were added to the 1980 Corvette and remained to the end of production in 1982. The front bumper improved cooling, reduced its aerodynamic drag and improved gas mileage.

Federal regulations required all cars, including Corvette, to be fitted with 85-mph speedometers. It was very easy to peg these speedometers if the owner wasn't careful. The 1980 Corvettes featured several weight-reduction changes, including thinner window glass, lighter fiberglass, and aluminum rear-end housing and support. This weight reduction was designed to improve fuel mileage. The rear frame from behind the door to the rear bumper was revised to accommodate the new rear end. The frame rails were thinner. This was the first major change to a Corvette frame since it was introduced in 1963.

In 1982 only one engine was available for Corvette, with the Cross-Fire fuel injection system. It was fitted with a 4-speed overdrive automatic transmission and was a comfortable cruiser. A similar engine was installed into the new 1984 C4 Corvette, but was only offered for one year. It was replaced with the L-98 tuned port injection engine in 1985. (The system featured two injectors that provided more precise fuel metering to the computer system. It was the least popular engine offered in a C3 Corvette.) The 4-speed automatic overdrive was the only transmission available for 1982, and it helped control emissions while improving fuel economy.

This was a transition year for Corvette as its production was divided between assembly plants. I would prefer an 1980 over a 1981 unless one could be found at a very low price.

1982

There were 25,407 units produced, including 6,759 Collector's Editions. The 200-hp Cross-Fire injection intake system became standard and was only available with an automatic transmission. A new two-tone silver/beige Collector's Edition was introduced with a lift-up rear window.

The new Cross-Fire engine was not well received because of its low power output and bulky running characteristics. I would prefer a previous model for a restoration project unless you find one that you cannot pass up.

In 1981 Corvettes were built in St. Louis, Missouri, and Bowling Green, Kentucky. All of the 1981 cars built in Bowling Green had two-tone paint schemes. Solid-color 1981 Corvettes were built in St. Louis. The two-tone paint on this 1978 pace car is very similar to the paint that was offered from the new Bowling Green assembly plant in 1981. It is easy to identify 1981 Corvettes that were built in Bowling Green if they are carrying a two-tone paint scheme code on their VIN.

PLANNING AND EVALUATION

The more time you spend inspecting and evaluating a project Corvette at the front end, the less time you need to spend locating hard-to-find replacement parts. Remember to take plenty of photographs and notes during your inspection.

Choosing the Correct Level of Restoration

In order to decide which year to target for a restoration, you need to determine which year fits into your budget. Here are the various types of restorations, from the least expensive to the most expensive.

If you are looking for a daily driver that presents itself well, this is the least expensive restoration. Usually these cars are in good mechanical and cosmetic condition. They only require some tender loving care to put them in tip-top condition. This kind of Corvette costs more, but repairs are easier to budget.

Minor Cosmetic Repairs

A well-maintained Corvette might require a complete cleaning of the exterior and interior. Road grime around the door openings and the hood surround should be inspected and cleaned. All of the rubber should be coated with a good silicone to keep the rubber pliant and preserved.

The two seats can be easily removed by unbolting the four retaining bolts that secure each seat to the floor. A good vacuuming and a high-quality carpet cleaner can remove many stains and grime that might exist on the carpet. A toothbrush can remove accumulated dirt in many of the interior seams. When the interior is cleaned, reinstall the seats and cover the interior parts with a good preservative.

Clean all of the window glass with window cleaner and dry with a lint-free towel. Ammonia and water also make an effective window cleaner. Mix both into a spray bottle

The more time you spend inspecting and evaluating a project Corvette at the front end, the less time you need to spend locating hard-to-find replacement parts. Remember to take plenty of photographs and notes during your inspection.

It is always a good idea to start off with a fresh battery. I recommend writing the purchase date on a piece of tape and sticking it onto the battery case. This is good information to have in the case of any future warranty claims.

The best place to start looking for body damage is the flooring under the seats. Once the seats are out of the car it is easy to peel the carpet back to inspect the flooring. To remove the four 9/16-inch retaining bolts holding the seat, slide the seat forward to gain access to the two rear bolts. Next, slide the seat all the way to the rear to remove the two front bolts. Once the bolts are removed, the seat can be taken out of the car.

and apply to the window surfaces. When this part of the cleaning is completed, remove the wheels and use a low-pressure washer to remove

Expect surprises when removing seats. This car had old coins, a plastic spoon, and a cigarette lighter. The carpet is badly faded and needs to be replaced.

all of the dirt and grease that has accumulated in the wheel wells.

The paint might require minor touch up to cover any chips. After all of this is completed run your hands over the paint surfaces and if roughness is felt use a Clay Bar over all the painted surfaces to smooth it out and then apply a high-quality wax.

Minor Mechanical Repairs

A well-maintained Corvette usually requires very little mechanical restoration. However, always change all of the fluids and the engine drive belts.

Depending on the age of the battery, it is always cheap insurance to

The best way to uncover previous body damage is to look closely from underneath the car. This car was involved in a collision in the rear and was not repaired very well. Damage to the front and rear of this generation Corvettes is very common.

install a fresh one. Put a piece of tape on the battery and write the installation date on it with a marker.

Inspect the tires and brake pads and replace as necessary.

Major Cosmetic Repairs

If the restoration project car has body and interior damage, it requires a complete stripping of the body hardware and interior. The body needs to be repaired and the old paint removed to see if the car has had prior damage from an accident.

All damaged body areas need to be repaired, sanded, primed, and readied for painting. All damaged interior components, such as torn seats, stained carpets, and damaged dash components, need to be removed.

All serviceable items need to be cleaned, cataloged, and stored for future use.

Major Mechanical Repairs

The car might require complete frame, engine, suspension, transmission, and driveline repair or replacement. Depending on the budget, savvy car shopping and inspection

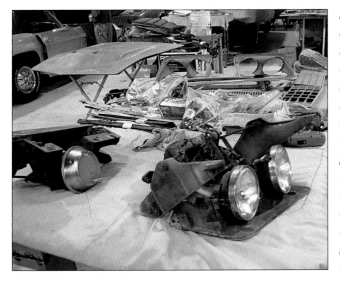

Any trim items that are removed should be inspected and cleaned. A list of the broken parts should be made and new ones purchased. Keep the old parts to compare to the new parts to make sure they are the same. Serviceable parts should be bagged and tagged, photographed, and stored for future use.

prior to purchase can save time and money. However, sometimes a car is found at a low enough price that allows enough room to put major dollars into these repairs.

Do-It-Yourself or Professional

Early on, you need to decide how you're going to get the project done: doing all the work yourself, having a shop do all the work, or a combination of the two.

Shop labor charges at a professional facility are usually quoted at an hourly rate. Any disassembly and restoration work that can be completed in a home shop can save bundles of money.

If the car requires major cosmetic and mechanical restoration, you can disassemble many mechanical, exterior, and interior components yourself. You may need some friends to help you with the heavy lifting, but anything that can be removed at

home will be a big savings to your budget.

Removing the exterior trim including bumpers, chrome, and lights yourself is a fairly easy, but time-consuming process. Each part and attaching hardware should be cleaned, inspected, and repainted if necessary for possible reuse. If the parts can be reused, they need to be cataloged with all of the attaching hardware. Include a note with the part that tells you where it was located.

After removal is completed the parts need to be stored in a safe location for reassembly. All of the interior trim can be removed with the same method, including the seats, seat belts, carpet, console cover, etc. Each part should be inspected and cleaned to determine if it can be reused. Any part that can be reused should be packed carefully.

Seeking outside professional assistance for disassembly and reassembly of major components depends on the way your home shop is equipped. If you decide to remove

A large wooden dolly was built to support this Corvette body when its frame was removed. (See sidebar "Build Your Own Body Dolly" on page 36.) The body can now be moved around the shop or transported back to the owner's house to complete the body restoration. Any work that can be completed at home helps reduce your overall budget.

Removing the frame from a C3 body requires the right equipment and skills to ensure that your Corvette body is not damaged. A sturdy dolly needs to be constructed so the body can be transported to a location where it can be repaired and painted. Always support the front overhang of the body. The nose is prone to cracking when it is free from its frame. The rear of a convertible body is another weak area that requires extra support when transferring it to a body dolly.

Frame rust is not uncommon for C3 Corvettes. These defects should be repaired before the frame is reinstalled.

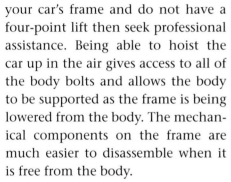

Forty percent of your budget and time should be devoted to restoring the frame and mechanical running gear in your Corvette. Every frame is stamped with the vehicle identification number (VIN) to match it with its original body. It usually can be found on the top of the driver-side frame rail near the seats.

your car's frame and do not have a four-point lift then seek professional assistance. Being able to hoist the car up in the air gives access to all of the body bolts and allows the body to be supported as the frame is being lowered from the body. The mechanical components on the frame are much easier to disassemble when it is free from the body.

Remove all mechanical parts before the frame is repaired, media blasted, and powdercoated. Once the frame is out of the car is a perfect time to remove all of these components.

Budget and Timeline

The faster the Corvette is restored the more expensive it becomes. Professional shops are trained to work quickly because they get paid for each job they complete. Their hourly shop rates allow them to pay their shop expenses (including payroll) and leave enough money for a profit.

On the other hand, most enthusiasts can complete a majority of the restoration. Taking your time, learning as you go, and doing most of the disassembly and reassembly provides big savings. For a do-it-yourselfer,

speed is not a friend; learning and quality should be the goal. If this is your first time disassembling a Corvette, take digital photos at each step. This provides a great reference during reassembly.

Disassembly is usually the shortest part of the restoration process.

Cleaning, refurbishing, cataloging, and storing parts is time consuming. Always remember to "tag and bag" all parts. The impact on your restoration budget is small if you do it yourself. Expect to devote about 10 percent of the total project time and budget to cleaning, painting, and buying new parts, storage bags, and storage containers.

Body preparation is the next part of the project. Removing the frame requires some heavy lifting but you (and some buddies) can do it pretty quickly and without cost. Body repair and paint is time consuming and costly.

For the best job, all of the door, window glass, and trim should be removed and stored. If the frame is being removed, a rolling dolly must be constructed to transport the body to the paint shop. The body must be inspected for damaged or worn panels

and those need to be replaced where necessary. The body must be stripped of its paint and all gaps and cracks must be repaired. Finally the body is sanded and painted. Expect to devote about 40 percent of the total project time and budget to body preparation.

Once the body has been removed from the frame, restoration of both can take place at the same time. This is the perfect time to remove the Corvette's running gear. This includes the front suspension, steering gear, fuel lines, engine, transmission, driveshaft, rear differential, rear suspension, and gas tank.

Most frames of this Corvette generation require repairs for damage caused by rust or road damage. A damaged frame should be bead blasted to remove all grime and surface rust. Finally, after it is repaired it should be powdercoated to preserve the metal.

While the frame is being repaired is a perfect time to refurbish and/ or replace various mechanical components. The engine, transmission, and differential should be inspected and repaired or replaced as necessary. When all of the mechanical parts are refurbished or replaced they need

Should Your Numbers Match?

The C3 early models (1968-1972) are more popular with collectors. Add a documented rare optional equipment to one of these cars and the price can soar. The restoration cost for any of these models in similar condition is very close. Original parts for earlier cars are more expensive, but overall the restoration costs are similar for all models of the 14-year production run. The biggest difference is the initial purchase price, which trends higher for the early cars.

Fortunately the Corvette community has a great resource available that enables an owner to confirm a Corvette's originality: the National Corvette Restorers Society (NCRS). It was founded in 1974 and began documenting and cataloging what original equipment was fitted to each Corvette when it left the factory.

This documentation includes factory options, paint (frame, engine, suspension, and all body components), and location of the vehicle identification number (VIN). In the late 1960s, General Motors introduced several anti-theft measures, and Corvettes left the factory with their VIN stamped on all of their major components to deter thieves and help in the recovery of stolen cars. The NCRS coined the term "numbers matching" to confirm the pedigree of a collector Corvette.

Today the NCRS has a large group of volunteer judges who inspect and evaluate Corvettes that are 20 years old or older to confirm their authenticity. If a car meets their standards, the car is awarded a "Top Flight" certificate that enhances its value.

Another resource group, Bloomington Gold, performs the same function; a Corvette that meets their criteria can become "Gold Certified." This certificate also adds to the value of a Corvette.

To earn either of these certifications, each car must be completely original from front to back, top to bottom, and side to side. This includes the correct hose clamps, hoses, belts, markings, and everything else a Corvette had when it left the factory. Expect to pay top dollar for a numbers-matching Corvette.

Also restoring a numbers-matching Corvette is more expensive and time consuming. You must locate all of the correct parts that were installed in the car the year it was built. Proof that a car is original and has not been altered in any way must be made available during the judging process.

This book is not intended to take you down this path; for that you need to do a lot more research into NCRS or Bloomington Gold requirements.

The intention of this book is to help you restore a third-generation Corvette to the point that it drives and looks like a new car. Even if some things spoil its numbers-matching pedigree, it will be a joy to drive. My advice: Hold on to any original part that was on the car, no matter what the condition. Collectors can always restore a part to make it look original. These original parts add value to your car when you sell it.

Trained NCRS judges determine if a Corvette is fitted with its original factory equipment. Nothing is left to chance during the judging process. Everything, including nuts, bolts, screws, hose clamps, markings, decals, etc., must match original factory specifications for a car to earn a "Top Flight" certificate. This 1969 convertible is being judged at an NCRS event. These C07 and C08 (vinyl covering) auxiliary hardtops were available for convertibles from 1968 to 1975.

to be reinstalled onto the finished frame. Expect to devote 40 percent of the restoration time and budget to body and frame restoration.

After all of this work is completed, expect to spend the remaining 10 percent of your time and budget finishing your new pride and joy.

A project like this, working nights and weekends, usually takes about a year and a half. Count on reaching an occasional snag that could extend this timetable, but this is a good rule of thumb.

Evaluating a Corvette for Restoration

Selecting a project Corvette depends on the size of your restoration budget and the amount of time available to complete the job. Many C3 Corvettes are approaching the half-century mark since they left the factory. Many have had a hard life, and an expert could hide many blemishes under that beautiful bodywork. I have observed many 1968–1982 Corvettes during my many projects and have learned that they all have some very common concerns and routine trouble spots. A full inspection is worth completing prior to buying a Corvette (or any car).

Once the year is determined, the best place to get pricing information is in local newspapers, at Corvette shows, at specialty Corvette stores, or on the Internet. Some valuable resources are mecumauctions.com, ebay.com/motors, and corvetteforum.com. Each offers a lot of information about the price of various years that are for sale in the current market. They are also good places to find out how options and condition impact the final price.

Once you find a Corvette that fits your budget, verify the car's ownership records by studying its VIN and evaluating its mechanical and cosmetic condition. Take a friend on your inspection trip; the more eyes the better. Spend extra time inspecting underneath the car to look for rust or repaired damage. Count on some problems lurking underneath the fiberglass body. Trim and badges are expensive to replace, so it is a good idea to pay a little more for a car that has undamaged trim components. This will save your budget in the future.

Many people do not realize that C3 Corvettes are built around a steel birdcage that is bolted onto a steel ladder frame. If the car you are looking at has spent much of its life in snowy or rainy climates some level of rust is highly probable. The frame can be easily checked for rust by

Throughout this book I will refer to the "steel birdcage" that is underneath every C3 Corvette. This is what the birdcage looks like in a coupe. The convertible is similar but does not include the rollover roof bar behind the driver. Rust is a common problem with C3 birdcages. The two body mounts that are next to the driver's and passenger's feet are where water from a leaking windshield frame will pool and eventually rust the area out. It is important to check this area before purchasing a C3 Corvette. Repairs can be expensive.

Corvette Repair created this impressive see-through 1969 L88 Corvette display car. This gives a clear visualization of how the steel birdcage sits on the frame without any body panels.

Inspection Points

Here are some, but not all, of the things to look for during your buying inspection:

Underhood

- Open the hoods grab a fan blades and pull it backward and forward to observe movement in the fan clutch and water pump bearings. Water pumps go from loose to leaking quickly. Start the engine and listen for any howling noises coming from the pump or fan pulley.
- Check the clearance between the fan blades and the fan shroud. Loose belts or bent brackets could cause contact with the shroud. Weak or broken motor mounts also cause the fan to contact the shroud.
- This one is a little difficult to check at a private home or dealer lot, but it is important to find out if the steering box is filled with clean grease. These boxes are expensive to rebuild so this is worth checking.
- Inspect the flexible coupling (or rag joint) on the steering coupling. Look for splitting of the rubber and signs of wear or contact on the heads of the bolts.
- Have someone turn the steering wheel and look for movement on the steering shaft to see if the splines are loose. Powder or red rust is another sign the bolts are loose or worn.
- On cars with a manual transmission check to see if the end of the shift rod that is located underneath the steering shaft is secured with a spring clip. Many times these rods are held in place with a cotter pin, and they are prone to breaking.
- Check the hood bolts for excessive play or any that are missing. Make sure the bolts are not too long.
- Look for missing or torn rubber weather stripping used to seal the radiator and radiator support.
- Note the number stamped on the engine block. Learning whether the engine is original helps determine the price you are willing to pay.
- Find out how high the belts ride on the pulleys. Belts that ride too high are prone to be thrown off. Correct replacement belts for a Corvette can be hard to find and may need to be ordered from a Corvette aftermarket supplier.

- Engine compartment wiring and ground wires are always worth inspecting. One ground wire is located on the driver's side of the radiator support. Headlight supports are also grounded.
- Feel on the underside of the radiator hoses to determine if they are leaking.
- Check to see if the A/C hoses on the passenger's side near the exhaust manifold are hard and brittle.
- Look at the outer steel ring on the harmonic balancer for signs of shifting. Telltale signs include paint that is rubbed off the timing cover or a wobble when the engine is running.
- Check to see if the heater hoses on the passenger's side of the engine compartment are secured with a bracket. If these hoses are resting on the upper control arm, the constant rubbing could wear a hole in the hoses.

Front Suspension

- If you can get the car up on a lift grip the front and bottom of the tire to check for wheel bearing play. If it feels rough when it is spun, the bearing might be excessively worn.
- Check the rubber bushings on the upper and lower control arms. If they are cracked, worn, or missing the car does not handle properly.
- Inspect for missing or worn sway-bar endlink bushings.
- Look at the upper A-arms to see how many alignment shims are in place (front and rear) on each side. Excessive shims could indicate a bent frame.

Steering

- Push up and down on the idler arm to check for excessive movement.
- Check the power steering hoses when the wheel is fully turned to make sure they are not binding. Also check the hoses for leakage around their fittings.

Frame

- Locate the two frame brackets that secure the rear of the lower A-arms to the frame. These are prone to bending, cracking, breaking, and rusting.

Inspection Points *CONTINUED*

- Check the frame underneath the engine for pothole or collision damage. This is usually the first part of the frame that is affected by road contact.
- Look for any sign of damage repair on the two front frame extensions. These are the first to get damaged in a frontal impact.
- Check the frame underneath both doors for any damage from road impacts or collisions.
- To see if the frame shows any signs of rust damage, use a flat-blade screwdriver to poke the metal and verify its integrity. Also reach around the frame behind the rear of the doors to feel the top of the frame for any rust or damage.
- Be sure the exhaust pipes are secure and not hitting any part of the frame.

Engine
- Check the starter bolts for tightness.
- Inspect the rubber on both motor mounts.
- If the fuel pump and lower hose are covered with grease the front main seal might be leaking.
- Check the engine pan gasket for leaks and use a flashlight to inspect the bottom of the valve cover gaskets, which are prone to leakage.
- Have a mechanic remove the spark plugs and test each cylinder for pressure. The target is 160 to 180 and the readings should all be very close.

Rear Suspension
- Pull on the top and bottom of the rear wheels to check for bearing clearance.
- Look at the condition of the rear shock absorber rubbers.
- Check to see if the front of the rear trailing arms have adjustment shims.
- Inspect the overall condition of the trailing arms for excessive rust or damage.

Differential and Springs
- Watch the movement of the yoke on the differential while an assistant pulls back and forth on the lower

part of each wheel. Movement should be less than 1/8 inch. Worn yokes are a common problem on C3 Corvettes.
- The front of the differential is secured to the frame with one bolt and a rubber cushion. This cushion should not be missing or cracked, as it will cause a clunk when shifting the car.
- Inspect the condition of the spring and the shackle bolts, washers, and rubber bushings at the end of the spring.
- Check to see if any leaks are coming from the differential.

Underside Checks
- Use a flashlight and check underneath both front fenders to determine if the fiberglass has been repaired.
- Pull on the inner fenderwells to see if they have broken loose from the fender.

Passenger Compartment
- Remove the two lower front side vent covers and use a flashlight to determine if any rust has accumulated in the lower wells around the body mount. If rust is present this indicates a leaking windshield frame.
- Check the operation of all the instruments by starting the engine to make sure they are in operating condition.
- Turn on the heater and fan.
- Turn on the A/C and fan and test both inside and outside air selections. The duct temperature should be 45 to 50 degrees F for inside air with maximum fan. Blend the heat while the A/C is running to make sure the heater door is working correctly.
- Test the radio and speakers for volume, static, and clarity.
- If equipped, test the power windows, seat, and door locks for proper operation.
- If equipped, test the tilt-telescopic steering wheel.
- If equipped, test the cruise control during a road test.

The steel birdcage serves as the structure that holds the body together. This structure is prone to rust and can be very expensive to repair. The windshield frame is hollow and if rust has penetrated around the upper frame it drips water and pools around the No. 2 body mount (see illustration on page 161). The best way to check this condition is to remove the driver and passenger lower cowl panels and visually inspect them.

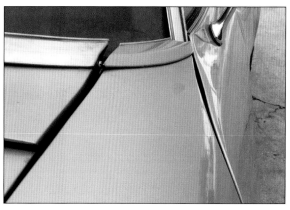

When performing your visual inspection of a Corvette, look closely for panel fit and gaps between various panels such as fenders and doors. These are all areas that need to be corrected during your restoration if you decide to buy that particular car.

putting the car on a four-point lift. Use a flashlight and screwdriver to inspect the frame by tapping it to see if it has any weak spots.

A rusty birdcage is the most difficult to spot because it is covered with body panels and window trim. Removing the inside lower kick panels on the driver and passenger sides of the car is a quick way to find out if the birdcage windshield frame area has been leaking and shows rust. Because repairing the birdcage is time consuming and expensive, it's best to find a car with an undamaged unit.

Project Planning

Before you begin any disassembly, write down any flaws you discovered during the buying process. This includes visual flaws that were spotted such as in the birdcage, frame, leaks, noises, and mechanical or accessory parts that don't work.

It's important to take detailed photographs and make notes of any body flaws that the car might have. Inspect the body from every angle.

It is best to do this in shaded light, which shows the flaws much better than in bright sunlight. Include photos of the front/rear, interior, engine bay, and both sides of the car so you have a complete assessment of the car's condition.

If you have access to a lift, take detailed photos of the underside of the car including the exhaust, engine, rear end, and any exposed frame parts. This is a good time to do a visual inventory of damage on the underside of the body and look for repaired fiberglass damage.

This detailed inspection gives a quick reference when creating a "to do" list and is helpful during reassembly. Placing the photos in an album makes a handy catalog to refer to during reassembly. This catalog also lets you show potential paint/body shops the condition of the car during your selection process.

This is also a great time to begin separating the restoration project plan into four major areas: disassembly, body/paint, frame/mechanical, and reassembly. Disassembly and reassembly are the smallest and least

costly of the four restoration areas. However, correct disassembly can save thousands of dollars over the entire project.

Parts Storage

As part of your project planning, it is important to locate a safe and secure storage location for all the parts you are going to remove. A variety of small plastic food containers with lids, and industrial-grade plastic bags work well. Use large storage bins to hold groups of bags, and wood pallets for large items such as exhaust pipes. This system allows the removed items to remain inventoried and safe until they are reinstalled.

Several storage options are available. A large storage space at your home, such as a shed, trailer, or garage, suffices. Another option is to rent a commercial storage unit. A third option is the mechanical shop you select for the heavy part of your restoration; it might be willing to rent some storage space for your parts.

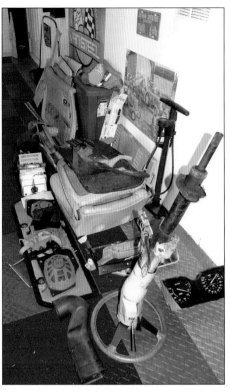

When beginning the disassembly process, it is very important to tag and bag every part. The best way to do this is to use plastic trays, plastic containers, and food storage bags. Remember to use a marker to write on every container to indicate what location the parts were removed from. This makes reassembly much easier.

It is always safer to store removed parts at your home or a rented storage space so that you have total control over them at all times. Many of the removed parts are very expensive to replace. Taking time to organize a safe storage location saves time and money when reassembly is started.

Whatever option you choose make sure the area is secure, clean, dry, and easily accessible. My preference is to secure my parts where I have total control of them at all times, as they are very expensive to replace.

Tools and Equipment

Having the correct tools to do any job saves time and aggravation. Before beginning, check your tool inventory. Safety should always be the top priority when undertaking a project like this. Always wear safety glasses and disposable industrial-grade rubber gloves. Heavy shoes should be worn when removing heavy parts such as the engine, brakes, or suspension components to protect your feet. Use ear and eye protection when doing any high-speed grinding work. Work gloves are also

recommended if pulling heavy components off the car. Large tool sets that include many of the tools on the following list can be purchased for a big savings. Sears Tool Club, Lowe's, or Home Depot usually offer a lifetime warranty on their tools; these are good places to compare prices and quality.

Art Dorsett and his company, Van Steel Corvette Parts and Service, specialize in disassembling and restoring Corvettes of all generations, especially C3s. Throughout this book, I lean heavily on Art and his staff's expertise. I asked Art to assemble the following basic list of tools that he commonly uses to disassemble and reassemble a C3 Corvette.

Ratchets
- Include all of the three basic ratchet sizes for this project: 1/4, 3/8, and 1/2 inch

This moisture encounter plus tool is made by Tramex. It is the perfect device to determine if one of your fiberglass body panels is contaminated with oil or water. A panel that is contaminated and then painted will blister and bubble after several weeks, which will require it to be repainted.

Having the correct tool on hand makes the project go much faster and easier. A good assortment of air-driven grinders, ratchets, and impact guns such as these helps break stubborn bolts loose quickly.

Sockets
- All SAE and metric socket sets should have 6- and 12-point grips
- SAE sockets, both regular and deep well
    - 1/4-inch-drive: 1/4 to 9/16 inch
    - 3/8-inch-drive: 7/16 to 1 inch
    - 1/2-inch-drive: 7/16 to 1⅛ inch
- Metric sockets, both regular and deep well
    - 1/4-inch-drive: 3 to 13 mm
    - 3/8-inch-drive: 5 to 22 mm
    - 1/2-inch-drive: 5 to 22 mm

Internal and External Torx Wrenches
- T-15 to T-55

Hex Key Wrenches
- Standard, .05 to 3/8 inch; Metric, 1.5 to 8 mm

Screwdrivers
- A selection of Phillips and flathead screwdrivers from 2- to 12-inch lengths

Pliers
- A variety of 6- to 9-inch lengths including long-nose, high-leverage, channel lock, and cutter pliers

Combination Wrenches
- 6- and 12-point
    - Standard, 3/8 to 1 inch
    - Metric, 10 to 22 mm

Adjustable Wrenches
- One each in 6-, 8-, and 10-inch sizes

Hammer/Mallet
- One 5-pound hammer/mallet is all that is necessary

Long-Handled Floor Jack/Safety Stands
- 1.5- to 2-ton capacity is sufficient
- Four 2- to 3-ton safety stands

Electronic Torque Wrench
- 1/2-inch drive, adjustable from 20 to 200 ft-lbs

Tap and Die Set
- National coarse and fine
- Metric
- Bolt removal kit

Sandblast Cabinet
- A small portable unit is good for cleaning rust and grime off small parts

Penetrating Oil
- Good for removing rust-encrusted parts

Trim Removal Tools
- Window and trim removal reveal tool
- Window crank and door lock removal tool

Optional
- Air compressor (4 hp or bigger) with 14.8 SCFM at 90–175 max psi
- Portable low-height roller stool
- Air impact guns
    - sizes: 3/8 and 1/2 inch
    - types: air gun, air ratchet, air cutoff wheel, air grinder
- Black impact sockets
    - SAE 3/8-inch-drive from 5/16 to 13/16 inch and 1/2-inch-drive from 5/16 to 1¼ inch
    - Metric 3/8-inch-drive from 7 to 19 mm and 1/2-inch-drive from 9 to 32 mm
- Rental hydraulic engine lift (cherry picker)
- Sawzall reciprocal saw
- Small acetylene torch

DISASSEMBLY AND STORAGE

For disassembly, the trim and interior can be removed before or after removing the frame and mechanical components. Your choice depends on your access to a trailer and towing vehicle. If one is available, I recommend removing the frame first,

which allows you to disassemble the body, interior, and frame at the same time in separate locations.

Once the frame and body are separate, work can begin to disassemble the body and remove the frame's mechanical components.

Remember to always bag and tag all removed parts.

Body/Frame Removal

Removing the frame from a C3 body is a critical part of the restoration process. Over the years these frames have accumulated a lot of wear and tear. Some might even have rust damage or be bent from a previous accident or abuse.

C3 coupe and convertible bodies are bolted to a steel ladder frame with 8 (coupe) or 10 bolts (convertible). Newer Corvettes have their frames molded into the body structure and are not easily removed without extensive work. This C3 design feature makes the body very heavy and requires care not to damage it during the removal process. It is important to ensure the body is properly supported to prevent damage or cause any personal injury during removal.

While many enthusiasts remove the body and frame in their home garage, I turned to Van Steel to perform the task for this book. To illustrate how to remove a C3 frame, Van Steel offered the well-maintained

As you proceed with your disassembly it is very important to store and mark items that can be easily lost such as grilles, trim, bumpers, and bolts. You will save money and time if you follow this advice during this part of your restoration journey.

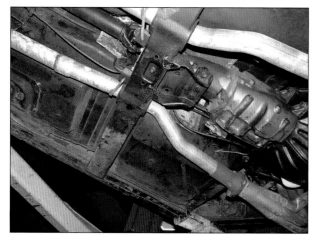

It is very important to visually inspect a Corvette's frame from the underside. It provides a lot of clues as to how the car has been treated. Things to look for are rust, bent or damaged frame rails, and missing parts. Always take photos and make notes of what you discover as you inspect various Corvettes.

Art Dorsett, owner of Van Steel Corvette Parts and Service, has owned this 1980 L-48 automatic coupe since 1980. It has only a little over 40,000 original miles, but he decided to restore it with fresh paint and over-hauled frame and drive components.

care must be taken when the body is lifted off the frame to prevent damage to this connector. Tapping it with a mallet helps break it free from the steering box as the body is raised off the frame. The three steering box bolts that secure it to the frame should be loosened before the frame lift can begin.

7 All wiring that is connected to the body must be unplugged. Bright-colored stickers should be affixed to each side of all engine-wiring connectors and numbered with a black marker. Do this before unplugging any connectors. This greatly eases the burden of reassembly.

Every wire that is unplugged from the harness should be marked with color-coded stickers or masking tape with a description and a number. This eliminates any cross-wiring connections during reassembly. If you are planning to replace your wiring harness with a new one, order the new harness before disassembly, and match and mark the new connectors with the harness currently in your car. This makes reinstallation much easier.

1980 coupe that has served as their project car for the past 30 years. It only has a little more than 40,000 miles on it, but age has faded its interior and exterior. This car and others in Van Steel's shop were used to illustrate the proper disassembly method described here.

1 Remove the rubber or steel bumpers and brackets.

2 Disconnect the battery cables and remove the battery.

3 Remove the hood. This provides better access to engine components that need to be disconnected.

4 Disconnect the flexible steering joint coupling from the steering box.

5 Remove the two 7/16-inch steering shaft spline bolts from

the steering box. Use a deep-well 12-point socket to aid in loosening these bolts.

6 Disconnect the transmission lock-out cable next to the firewall on the steering column. Great

Loosen the three 9/16-inch bolts that secure the steering box to the frame. This provides enough slack so that the steering column rod can be freed during the body lift.

Build Your Own Body Dolly

A body dolly serves several purposes: it provides a platform to secure the body to, allows the body to be transported around the work area, and enables you to transport to another location. Van Steel builds its dollies for all these purposes. The staff constructs them with lumber and industrial-grade bolts. Heavy metal casters are attached to the dolly to enable it to be mobile. Any dolly should be completed before attempting to remove the body from the frame.

If the dolly is needed for another project, you can move the body onto large pieces of wood that sit on four metal castor plates and industrial rollers. Simply place the wood underneath the rear battery/storage compartment and the front driver/passenger footwells.

Here is a list of materials that were used for construction of Van Steel's body dolly:

- 1/2-inch-thick plywood 32 x 18 inches
- Six 4-inch-diameter steel casters
- Four pieces of 2 x 4 x 53-inch wood
- Four pieces of 2 x 4 x 55-1/2-inch wood
- Four pieces of 2 x 4 x 41-inch wood
- Two pieces of 2 x 4 x 33-inch wood
- Six pieces of 4 x 4 x 14-inch wood
- One pound of 8-penny nails
- Eighteen 5/16 x 3 x 1/2-inch lag bolts
- Eight 5/16 x 3-inch lag bolts
- Six 5/16 x 1-inch NC hex bolts
- Six 5/16-inch flat washers
- Six 5/16-inch lock washers
- Six 5/16-inch NC nuts
- Fifty 3/16 x 2-1/2-inch wood screws

8 Move the car to a suitable jacking area. A four-point lift has two towers on each side that support adjustable legs on each tower. Hydraulic pressure lifts the legs by turning a worm gear. A four-point lift is very handy for this kind of project.

9 Remove the rocker arm covers or sidepipe covers if equipped.

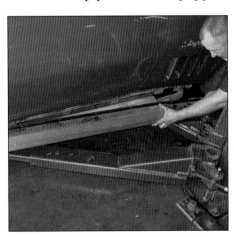

Remove either the sidepipe or rocker arm covers; store them and their retaining hardware in a secure location.

10 Disconnect the master cylinder brake lines.

11 For cars with a standard transmission, disconnect the wire clip on the clutch pedal.

12 Drain all fluids including the radiator and gas tank.

13 Disconnect any vacuum hoses that are attached to the body and frame.

14 Disconnect the accelerator rod from the carburetor throttle lever by removing the cotter key. Remove the accelerator rod and ground strap.

15 Disconnect the oil pressure line from the engine block.

16 Undo the distributor tachometer drive unit.

17 Remove the shifter ball and T-handle if equipped.

18 Remove the license plate and trim cover.

19 Take the rear exhaust panel off the car if so equipped.

20 Disconnect the gas tank sending unit and mark with a sticker and number.

21 Remove the antenna ground strap.

22 Undo the emergency brake cable located on the driver's side of the transmission crossover. Removal of the adjusting nuts allows the cable to be disconnected.

23 Take off the rear access body mount doors on the front side of each rear wheel well.

24 Remove the ground strap from the left front body mount.

25 Take off the lower radiator core support bolts.

26 Remove all 5/8-inch body-mount bolts and rubber doughnuts (8 for 1968–1982 coupes, 10 for convertibles 1968–1975).

Two are located in the engine compartment. One is under the master cylinder and the other is under the heater box.

Two body bolts are located inside the passenger compartment on the side of the footwells.

Removing the small panel on the wheel well allows access to the two body bolts at the end of the doors.

Two body bolts are located behind the rear wheels. These can be seen when the wheel is removed.

A four-point lift is the best way to remove the body from the frame of a C3 Corvette.

Two are at the bottom of each windshield post. To access them remove the interior kick panels from each side of the front lower cabin. Two are located in the rear inner fenderwells behind the doors and covers provide access to these frame bolts. Finally, two are located behind each rear wheel well.

Convertibles have two additional body bolts located under the door trim panels.

27 Both coupe and convertible bodies are constructed with a steel birdcage frame. (See photo on page 28 in Chapter 2 to review the construction of a birdcage frame.) The fiberglass panels were bonded to this frame when the car was originally built. It is strong enough to support lifting the body off the frame if it is not badly rusted. This is the advantage of using a four-point hydraulic lift. It allows the pads to be placed where they support the body behind the front and rear wheel wells. The birdcage is very narrow and correct pad placement is critical so that the body is not damaged. Other removal methods are available but I chose the four-point lift for safety and speed.

After double-checking the correct placement of the pads, slowly raise the lift while someone checks to make sure the frame is clearing the body. Check for electrical plugs and connections that have not been disconnected and confirm that the steering gear is free from the steering box. Also check the engine compartment to make sure everything is disconnected and all components have enough clearance.

28 When everything is clear, raise the body high enough to allow the frame to be rolled away. The frame can be moved out of the way and replaced with a wooden body dolly.

29 When the dolly is in place lower the body onto the dolly and remove the lift pads. The body is now free and can be moved as necessary. Before moving the body make sure all of the loose hanging wires are secured with plastic zip ties or tape. If they are not secured properly they could be ripped or damaged during transit.

30 Return the body to your work area to remove its components.

31 The body can now be transported to the paint facility.

A four-point lift makes the job of removing the body from the frame much easier. The pads should be placed directly on the steel channel of the birdcage that runs beneath each door. After the body bolts are removed and everything is properly disconnected the body can be lifted off the frame. Make sure to raise it high enough so there is ample clearance between the mechanical components and the body before the chassis is removed.

Confirm that all body wiring is secure and not attached or snagged on the frame or mechanical components. When everything is clear roll the frame out from beneath the body and store it in a safe location away from the body. Once the frame is clear, move the dolly under the body and position it so the body rests on the cross braces of the dolly frame. Van Steel has modified their dolly to provide support to the front and back parts of a C3 body.

Body Assessment

The fiberglass body has always been a unique and consistent design aspect of the Corvette. Along with the fiberglass body panels, the Corvette also has a steel birdcage frame and other plastic panels that must be inspected. The fiberglass body is much lighter and less expensive to repair than a sheet-metal body, but it is also somewhat fragile.

You need to closely evaluate the condition of the body before buying a particular car and certainly before you restore one. Significant damage to these areas can be quite expensive. Large cracks, holes, and other damage take substantial time and effort to repair. Replacing a heavily damaged body panel comes at a significant price.

Inspecting Exterior Body Panels

Now is the time to carefully examine the exterior body panels for damage to be added to your repair list. The 1968–1972 Corvette body panels were formed with a looser weave of fiberglass-reinforced plastic, and require a layer of gel coat to prevent the fiberglass weave from showing through the paint. The 1973-1982

Cracks in the fiberglass can appear anywhere on the body. Be sure to give the car a very careful and close inspection. This crack was discovered under the passenger-side bumper and needs to be re-bonded to prevent further cracking. If you locate a crack like this, drill a small hole at the end of the crack to prevent it from spreading.

panels were formed with a tighter compression process using sheet-molded composites (SMC), which eliminated the need for gel coat.

Cracking is common around the front and rear upper fender seams. This is also a problem around the headlights and upper front fenders. Body cracks must be repaired prior to any paint preparation. Grind them out and then fill them in with the correct body filler. (See Chapter 4 for more details.)

This crack is between the bottom of the headlight and the top of the rubber bumper. This area has very little support and is prone to cracking especially if the bumper has received a moderate hit.

Inspecting the Inner Body

At this time, raise your Corvette up on a four-point lift and carefully inspect all of the body panels from underneath. A strong flashlight is the perfect tool for this task. Factory body panels are smooth on the underside and are held together with bonding strips. If you find large swaths of fiberglass over an area, it is strong evidence of a crash repair. To prevent cracking a new paint job, repair these areas before any final paint is applied.

If you spot obvious damage such as a broken or badly cracked panel it

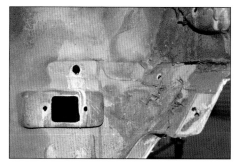

When this Corvette was placed on a lift and inspected with a flashlight, this past damage and sloppy repair work was discovered. Fiberglass repairs were discovered on the underside of the left rear fender. We ground this area down and installed an aftermarket replacement body panel. (See Chapter 4 for more details.) This is a perfect time to fix this kind of damage to prevent the body from cracking in the future.

Due to age and exposure to sunlight, some C3 interiors might show wear and tear as on this 1980 coupe. These seat covers have to be replaced, as they are not repairable. Aftermarket suppliers offer exact replacements for most C3 interior parts.

The dash pads are very similar on all 1968–1977 Corvettes with minor exceptions. This photo of my 1969 Corvette interior was taken in 1970. This is what the standard interior looked like when delivered new from the St. Louis Assembly Plant.

In 1978, all Corvettes were fitted with this new dash panel that included a locking glovebox. This interior was retained until the end of production in 1982.

might be cheaper to replace it. However, until the exterior paint has been removed it is difficult to make the final decision on subtle damage that might be covered up by its exterior paint. (See Chapter 4 for more details.)

Evaluating Frame and Birdcage

Closely inspect the exposed steel birdcage components that have been uncovered by the frame and interior removal. Common rust spots are on the top and sides of the windshield header. The windshield header is hollow and any rust holes enable water to seep into this area and run into the bottom of the birdcage. Over an extended period of time the bottom of the birdcage rusts around the body mount area and breaks away from the frame. This is a critical inspection point that needs to be repaired before any reassembly of the car takes place.

The frame also needs to be closely evaluated for rust. The most common areas are behind the doors where the frame bends up over the rear wheels. Check all of the body mount areas for rust. (See Chapter 6 for more details.)

Interior Removal

Most C3 Corvettes need some interior restoration because the cars have been subjected to wind, rain, and sunlight for more than 30 years. Plastic, cloth, and leather interior components simply deteriorate with age. Many parts can be cleaned, but torn seat cushions need to be replaced. Panels that are brittle should be replaced. If you are able to repaint these panels they should be stored where they are seldom touched to prevent scratches.

Dash panels are very similar on all 1968–1977 Corvettes. They feature

Van Steel's 1980 Corvette body was transported to the owner's garage on its dolly. The paint was stripped off most of the body at Van Steel's shop. The interior had been removed before it was returned to the shop for the next step in its restoration.

Any parts that have been removed are put into plastic bins and marked. This is a great way to quickly find these parts during reassembly.

a separate dash pad, passenger storage unit, auxiliary instrument panel in the center, and a speedometer/tachometer cluster in front of the driver. The 1968 driver-side panel includes the ignition switch on the upper right. The fiber-optic light monitoring system was standard on all 1968–1971 models.

All 1978–1982 dashes are very similar in design and feature a one-piece dash pad with a locking glovebox.

All 1968–1977 manual windows and lock models have door panels with a door lock button and window crank handle.

Before beginning this removal process be sure to select a well-lit area with plenty of room to move around the car.

Once the frame had been removed from the 1980 Corvette at Van Steel, it was returned to the owner's personal garage for interior disassembly. All of the screws and parts that had been removed were marked or tagged and then placed into bags or containers for ease of reassembly.

1 Remove the eight bolts under the front and rear of each seat that secures the seat to the floor.

2 Remove and disassemble the two door panels of the door

assembly. If the car has manual windows use the window crank retaining spring tool to release the window crank from the door. The door lock on 1968–1977 Corvettes must be removed the same way.

3 Remove all attaching screws on the panel, including the

Corvettes equipped with manual roll-up windows must have their cranks removed before the panel can be removed. This special tool makes removing the window crank much easier.

Two different door panel designs were used in C3 Corvettes. The 1968–1977 Corvettes used manual door locks and manual or power windows. The 1978–1982 Corvettes came standard with power windows and door locks. The manual door lock is held in place with a clip that is similar to the window crank clip. Use this same tool to remove the lock knob.

three armrest screws (if equipped). If equipped with a remote mirror, remove the mirror retaining cover screws. Loosen the setscrew on the mirror adjustor. Carefully pull the door panel off the door by starting at the bottom and prying off the door clips.

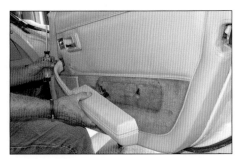

Remove the Phillips screws on the door panel that secure the 1978–1982 armrest. When all of the attachments are removed pull the panel out from the bottom to release the lower clips and pull up to detach it from the window frame. This panel removal method is the same for 1968–1982 panels once the hardware has been removed.

4 Once everything is loose pull up on the panel to release it from the window opening on the door. If the Corvette is equipped with power door locks and windows, disconnect the switches from the panel prior to removal.

5 Remove the door kick plates that secure the driver- and passenger-side compartment carpets to the floor. Use a #45 Torx to remove the driver and passenger seat belt hardware. These must be taken out before the carpet can be removed.

6 The driver-side seat belt warning light is standard on all 1978–1982 Corvettes and must be unplugged under the console. Place stickers or tape on both sides of the plugs and write a brief description to ease reinstallation.

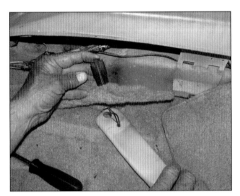

The driver's seat belt warning light is standard on all 1978–1982 Corvettes. The warning light wire must be unplugged from under the driver's side of the console prior to removing the buckle from the car. The side panel must be removed prior to this step.

When the console cover is loose, carefully lift it and unhook the attached wires. If the car is equipped with an automatic transmission, unhook the gear selector loop that is attached to a wire lever on the transmission tunnel. This plastic piece breaks easily, so be careful when unhooking it. After the panel is free, turn it over and unscrew the heating and ventilation switch screws, and reinstall the screws after the switch has been removed so you do not lose them.

7 Three Phillips screws secure the side carpet to the console. They are located in the front, middle, and rear of the panel. They are buried in the carpet so you must feel around to locate them. The carpet is secured to fiberboard so it is important to remove the screws so the panels are not damaged.

8 The console cover and armrest can now be removed. The front of the console is secured by two 1/4-inch nuts that must be removed. Unscrew the accessory plug and unsnap the wire lead. Remove two

The front of the console is secured with two 1/4-inch nuts that must be removed before the console cover can be taken out of the car. It is best to locate these nuts with a mirror before attempting to loosen them.

screws that secure the armrest cover to the console cover.

9 The armrest cover can now be taken out of the car. Carefully lift the console cover; if the car has power windows carefully pry the connectors off the cover with a flat-bladed screwdriver. The cover can now be lifted off, but if it has an automatic transmission the shift lever has a plastic hook that connects to a steel rod on the transmission tunnel. Be careful not to break this plastic retainer by lifting the cover too high.

10 Unplug the heater and A/C control wires and lift the cover clear of the tunnel. Turn the cover over and remove the three 9/32-inch bolts that secure the control unit to the console cover. After removing these three bolts, reinstall them into the cover.

11 Take out the rear cargo compartment carpet. (This car is equipped with optional rear speakers and brackets. Both must be removed

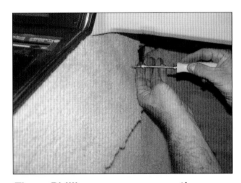

Three Phillips screws secure the console carpet covers on both sides of the interior. The screws are hidden in the carpet and need to be carefully searched out by tapping the carpet with a screwdriver. One screw is in the rear, one in the middle, and one in the front. Be careful when removing this panel as the carpet is mounted on flimsy fiberboard that can be easily broken.

before proceeding.) Remove the Phillips screws that fasten the cargo compartment cover. This cover also secures the carpet. The compartment houses the battery, jack, and storage tray. This plastic cover breaks easily so be careful when removing it from the carpet.

12 Unclip the rear carpet from the upper rear rod that runs horizontally under the rear window. If the car is equipped with optional rear speakers they must be removed prior to removing the cargo carpet. Start at one end and push up the end of the carpet to release it from the rod. Lift the rear carpet from behind the seats; it usually is not secured to the car with any connectors. Slowly pull the carpet out from under the rear cargo compartment trim, toward the passenger door, and out of the car.

The 1968–1977 rear cargo compartment has three bins; the 1978–1982 has two bins. These bins are held in place with up to 10 Phillips screws. They must be removed before the rear carpet can be taken out of the car.

The very back of the rear cargo compartment is held in place with a U-shaped retainer that must be unclipped from a rod that runs across the back of the cargo compartment. Once it is unclipped on one end it can be removed. It is difficult to get it unclipped, but be patient, because once it's started it's easy to remove. On 1968–1977 Corvettes the rear carpet comes in five separate pieces, left/right fenderwells, rear bulkhead, cargo area, and the piece behind the rear seats. These all must be removed as individual pieces.

The front of the cargo compartment is form fitted to the car behind the seats. The carpet is held in place with the console cover. Carefully pull the carpet up and away from the console. Then pull the carpet out of the car by starting at the back of the compartment and working it forward until it can be removed. This is what the rear cargo compartment carpet looked like after it was removed from the 1980 Corvette.

13 In 1968–1977 Corvettes, the rear cargo compartment is par-

titioned into five separate pieces that must be removed individually.

14 Remove the passenger- and driver-side one-piece carpets out of the car.

Both passenger and driver carpets can now be removed. Again, they are only held in place with the lower door trim cover.

15 Slip the sunvisors off their rods. (This car was equipped with the optional passenger vanity mirror, which must be detached before removing the visor.) To release

The 1978-1982 Corvettes equipped with optional remote door mirror controls include an adjuster held in place with a metric setscrew. This setscrew must be loosened prior to removal.

the mirror, place a reveal tool between the top of the visor and underneath the base of the plastic mirror. Use the tool to release the two tabs that secure the mirror and then remove it.

16 Remove the glovebox, then disconnect the vanity mirror. The power source plug is not on the mirror. A single wire is connected to the mirror and snakes behind the windshield molding and ends underneath the dash. It has to be unplugged at this location; be careful not to damage it.

17 Remove the Phillips screws that secure the windshield trim pieces. At the upper rear part of the passenger compartment, remove the screws that secure the left and right roof trim pieces; when they are free, thread the seat belts through the openings.

The windshield pillar trim is attached with Phillips screws. After all of the screws are removed, gently pry off the top and the two side trim pieces.

18 Snap off the center light cover and remove the two bolts that secure the light assembly to the roof. The wire is usually soldered and cannot be unplugged. Work the light through the trim opening and resecure it to the roof T-bar with the two bolts.

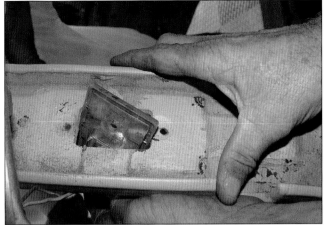

19 Remove the headlight panel cover under the steering column. To do this, unplug the attached vacuum lines. The 1968–1972 Corvettes have two lines (one for the headlight door and the second for the headlights) on this panel. Cars built from 1973 to 1982 have only one headlight line.

20 The steering column is held in place with four bolts. Two 9/16-inch nuts are directly under the speedo/tach instrument panel. The other two 1/2-inch nuts are located on the firewall above the brake pedal. These two are difficult to remove, but a ratchet with a long extension is the best way to reach them.

21 Be careful when unplugging the steering column wires and be aware that various columns have minor wiring connector differences depending on the car's optional equipment. This includes cruise control, tilt wheel, telescopic steering column, etc. However, the basic design of the column is the same.

22 This is a good time to tag and number each connector to help future reassembly. The 1968–1977 instruments are stamped with the correct color-coding that is visible on the metal on the back of each cluster.

After the upper rear trim pieces are removed, unscrew the two bolts that hold the coupe's overhead light on the crossbar. The power wire cannot be unplugged and must be carefully worked through the trim opening. After it is free reattach the light's two bolts.

23 Remove the steering column.

24 Remove the bracket on the firewall located inside the engine compartment.

25 Reinstall the two 1/2-inch nuts onto the bracket, and properly store this bracket until it is time to reassemble the interior.

To remove the steering column, first take out the four screws that hold the headlight override switch located underneath the steering wheel. Unscrew the vacuum valve from the panel. This now exposes the bolts that secure the steering column to the dash. Begin removing the steering column by removing the 9/16-inch nuts that are located under the headlight panel that was just removed. Again tag and bag these nuts as soon as they are removed.

All 1969–1982 Corvettes are equipped with a transmission lock-out cable. This cable prevents the key from being removed unless the car is in Park or Reverse on a standard transmission car. The cable is attached to the steering column near the firewall and must be unhooked before the body is removed.

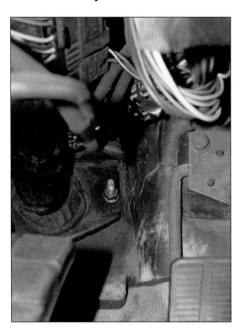

Locate the two 1/2-inch nuts that are on the inside firewall above the brake pedal. Using a long extension, remove them, and set them aside.

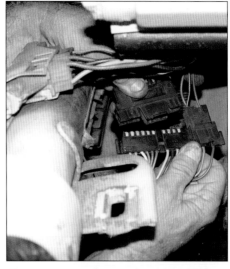

The steering column should now be free enough to lower it so that the wires plugged into the side of the column are exposed. Each bundle of wires must be unplugged and marked with color-coded stickers.

When all of the wires are unplugged, gently rock the column back and forth to work the shaft out of the firewall. When it is free remove it from the car.

This is a good time to remove the steering column bracket that is resting on the firewall inside the engine compartment. Once the bracket is free, reinstall the two 1/2-inch nuts that were removed from inside the car, and store the bracket.

26 When the steering column is out of the way, reach up behind the speedometer and push down on the retaining clip to release it. Take out all of the Phillips screws and remove the instruments from the dash.

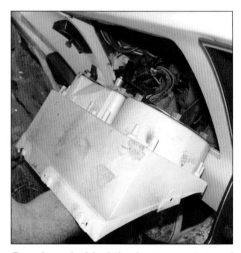

Reach up behind the instrument panel and disconnect the speedometer cable, which is held in place with a clip. It can be released by pushing on the bottom of the clip. Remove the Phillips screws that hold the instrument panel in place and pull it out of the dash after unplugging the instrument wires.

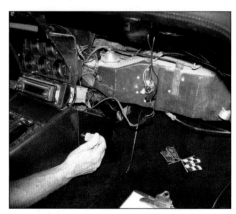

The 1968–1977 instrument panel is taken apart by removing the passenger's side first, the center next, and the driver's side last. The top dash pad is separate and is easier to remove if the lower dash is dismantled.

When the screws are removed from the driver's side of the instrument panel, slowly pull it back to expose the headlight switch. Unplug the wire connector and push the button switch to release it from the panel. Once the panel is loose, unplug the wires, speedometer cable, and tachometer drive. The panel should now be free to take out of the car. Look on the back of the two clusters and notice the color-coded wire markers on each connector. This is helpful during reinstallation.

27 On all 1968–1977 dash panels, remove both passenger- and driver-side instrument panels as separate units. It is best to remove the passenger-side panel first, the center panel next, and the driver-side panel last.

28 On all 1978–1982 panels, unscrew and remove the center console after unplugging the wiring harness.

29 Remove the two screws securing the glovebox shell.

30 Leave the remaining dash panel in place until the windshield is removed.

The one-piece dash pad is the last part to be removed. Leave this panel in place if you are not removing the windshield during the restoration. The clips that hold this panel in place are prone to breaking with the windshield in place. Leave the panel in place if it is undamaged.

Trim and Glass Removal

If the body needs complete restoration, and that includes repainting and body repair, it is necessary to remove all of the trim and body glass. This allows a thorough preparation and restoration of all painted surfaces on the body.

If the glass is reusable, it should be stored in an upright wooden rack that is lined with a soft felt material to avoid breakage. The rack should be stored in an out-of-the-way location to prevent the glass from being damaged or broken.

Windshield

All C3 windshields are held in place with a pliable rubber bond and chrome or black-painted reveal trim pieces. Both windshield wiper arms and blades must be removed or taped out of the way before beginning this procedure.

The windshield door seal is the first part to be removed. Starting at the bottom of the windshield frame check to see if the rubber is held in place with a Phillips screw. If so remove the screw.

Gently pry the rubber seal away from the windshield post starting at the bottom and working up to the top. When you reach the metal clip near the top, work the rubber from underneath the metal clip. The metal clip holds the door glass in place when the window is rolled up. If the rubber is reusable, try not to tear it. These seals are expensive. A dull plastic scraper can help release the rubber.

Once the rubber is clear of the clip, continue working it out of the top windshield frame.

Remove the Phillips screw located at the top of the windshield frame that secures the rubber gasket. Once the screw is released, the gasket can be removed. Store the gasket in a safe place, so it can be reinstalled. If it is torn or damaged this is a good time to replace it with a new gasket.

The windshield pillar post trim frame is held in place with four Phillips screws. Each has to be removed in order to pull the trim off the car. Once the screws have been removed, carefully pull the side trim piece away from the windshield. Store the trim and screws for reinstallation.

A series of clips attached to the windshield frame hold the top windshield reveal trim panel in place. Slide a reveal tool under the trim to release it from the clips. The roof panel or convertible top must be

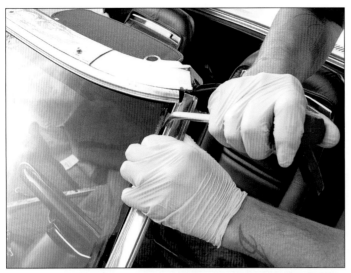

Phillips screw at the bottom of the side window pillar weather strip. The rubber can be gently pulled out of the frame and up toward the top of the windshield. Remove the screw at the top of the windshield to free the weather strip.

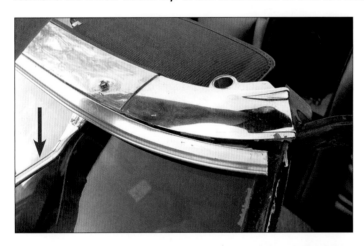

bottom of the windshield. Water was sprayed around the inside bottom of the windshield to help break the adhesive bond.

If your windshield is unbroken and free of nicks you have three choices: leave it alone, take it out yourself, or let a professional remove it. This customer car had a chip in the windshield so it had to be removed. The process begins by removing the

Use a reveal tool (arrow) to unsnap the clips that attach the top trim to the windshield header. This trim is held in place with 8 or 10 clips.

The installer used a special T-handled tool with a curved blade in one hand. He used his other hand to pull the T-handle around the windshield to cut the adhesive. Next a large powered paddle cuts the adhesive at the

removed to perform this task. Take extra care during this process, as it is easy to break the windshield. Pop rivets secure the clips to the windshield frame. Replace them if they are rusty. If they are not rusty it is safe to reuse them for reinstallation.

Removing this glass can be very tricky. Try a professional windshield removal/replacement company. They perform this task daily, and use special tools to do it easily and safely.

After the trim is removed, a special cutting tool is used to separate the glass from the adhesive that holds it in place. Next they spray water around the lower part of the windshield. Then they use a motorized paddle to loosen the adhesive from the windshield. Once completed, two large suction cups are used to remove the glass from the car.

Side Window Glass

After the door panel is removed, lower the window to the full open position. Remove the plastic liner by peeling it along the edge of the adhesive bead.

Remove one weather strip screw and pry back the rubber in front of the window seal.

Remove the two screws that hold the window seal to the door. Remove the seal from the door.

Next remove the one hex bolt that secures the anti-rattle cushion.

Position the window to line up the two sash screws that hold the window in place. Remove the two sash bolts by holding the nuts with a wrench inside the door. Carefully pull up the window making certain to clear the roller assemblies by using the openings in the inner door panel to hold the glass.

Adjust the front and rear channels to their extreme outboard

Two large suction cups were attached to the windshield and two people removed the windshield from the car.

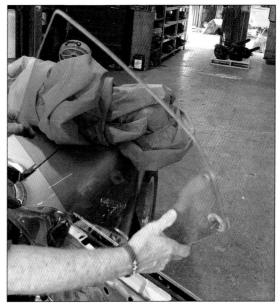

Lift the window out of the door by lifting up on the rear of the glass and working it out of the door at the front. The two screws that hold the glass in place must clear the door panel before the glass can be removed.

Remove the door side glass by taking out the 7/16-inch anti-rattle guide. This provides clearance when removing the window from the door. The glass must be unbolted from the window channels in the front and rear of the door. Remove the 7/16-inch window adjustment nuts at the front and rear of the glass. Now push the glass out of the front and rear track. Keep a firm grip on the glass to prevent it from falling to the bottom of the door and possibly breaking.

All 1968–1972 Corvettes are equipped with a removable rear window. It is held in place with two clips at the top that secure it to the body of the car. The 1973–1977 cars were equipped with fixed rear windows that could not be removed.

positions to allow clearance for the window.

Pull the window up and forward to remove it from the door.

Rear Glass

Corvettes built from 1968 to 1972 are equipped with a flat, removable rear glass panel. These are easily removed. The 1973–1977 models are equipped with a flat, non-removable rear glass held in place with a urethane adhesive. The large one-piece rear window found in 1978–1982 Corvettes is also held in place with urethane adhesive. The only exception is the pop-up rear hatch found on the 1982 Anniversary Edition.

I used a professional glass company to remove the rear window. They followed the same removal procedure that they used to remove the windshield.

If you remove the window yourself, first take off the reveal molding. If you do not have a professional adhesive-cutting tool, use a piece of piano wire tied to two medium screwdrivers. Tie one end of the wire to one screwdriver. Push the other end

The 1978–1982 large rear window is held in place with adhesive just as is the front windshield. In order to remove this glass the reveal molding must taken off and the adhesive has to be cut to free the glass. Many Corvettes are equipped with a heating element that must be unplugged prior to removal. This is the case on the author's 1979 Corvette.

of the wire through the lower end of the window adhesive. Secure this end to a second screwdriver. A helper can grab one end of the wire inside while you use a sawing motion to cut the adhesive around the window.

Attach two suction cups to the window and have your assistant help you carefully separate the window from the body. Be sure to properly store the window in a safe area.

Parts Inventory

At this point in the disassembly you should have a detailed list for each of the following areas:

- Replacement parts to be ordered
- Reusable parts that have been taken off and can be refurbished
- Reusable parts that have been taken off and do not require any action
- Photos taken during the disassembly process to be used for reassembly

Keeping the parts that need to be restored in one place makes it much easier to budget repair costs. All of these suspension parts are going to be overhauled or replaced depending on their condition. Gauges that are in perfect working order should be placed into airtight plastic bags and stored in a dry area until it is time to reuse them.

BODYWORK AND PAINT PREPARATION

If you have followed the procedures in the previous chapters, your Corvette body has been separated from its frame and mechanical components. The body has been mounted onto a dolly that allows it to be moved and transported around the shop or to another location.

The interior has been completely removed (as it was in the 1980 subject car because a new interior from Corvette America was going to be installed). If reusing the interior, it is a good idea to remove as much of it as possible to avoid getting paint overspray on the interior parts. This also affords the opportunity to replace any worn or broken parts before the car is reassembled.

This is a good time to completely clean all of the removed parts including carpet, seat cushions, and all plastic trim pieces. If the plastic trim is nicked or scratched, repair it at this time. If this is the case, get the correct factory interior paint and fix the damage while the parts are out of the car. Remember to take extra care when reinstalling these easy-to-scratch parts.

This is also a good time to re-inspect the exterior and the under-side of the body for hidden damage. If the car shows evidence of prior crash damage, the damage might need to be repaired or a panel might have to be replaced. A strong flashlight is a great way to closely inspect these areas before setting the body onto a dolly. Light damage to panel surfaces distracts from the car's appearance but does not cause structural damage.

Once the paint is removed and damage is found on the fiberglass laminate, it can be filled with an epoxy adhesive and sanded smooth. A damaged panel has to be removed and replaced with a replacement part

The most time consuming and labor intensive part of painting a Corvette is body preparation. The amount of time you spend on filling and smoothing the fiberglass panels directly relates to the quality of your final paint finish. So take the time to do it right.

from a Corvette supplier, such as Corvette America.

Once the inspection is completed, lower the Corvette body onto the body dolly so it can be moved to a suitable area to prepare it for painting. Remember to install large, steel industrial wheels that are on castors so the heavy body can easily be moved around the work area.

Don't forget that removing paint, fixing broken panels, filling imperfections, and sanding the body is extremely messy work. Find an area that has plenty of light and a floor area that is easy to clean to help keep the dust to a minimum. A powerful shop vacuum is a great tool to clean up sanding debris on the floor and inside crevices in the body.

Inspect the underbody shortly after the frame is removed from the body while it is still on the lift. Roll the frame away from the lift area and place it to one side. This gives you enough room to closely inspect the car and look into all small places. Look for holes the beneath flooring especially around the rear storage compartments where the battery may have leaked or a halfshaft came loose and broke the floor. Inspect the firewall for any cracking or non-factory holes that may have been drilled for an aftermarket application. These need to be added to your fiberglass repair list.

The left rear fender on this 1972 Corvette shows evidence that it has experienced a crash. The repair work is visible in the corner of the bodywork. The owner wants this left rear fender refurbished before it is repainted. This area might need to be repaired or cut out and replaced with a new fiberglass section.

Photograph any damage and take notes on exactly what is discovered during the inspection while the car is in the air. This work must be completed before it goes into the paint booth.

Once the underbody inspection is completed it is time to lower the body onto its movable dolly. The dolly gives you flexibility to work on the frame and body in separate areas. The body will be on this dolly for quite awhile so make sure it is secured correctly before removing the lift pads off the birdcage.

Windshield Frame Replacement

Chapter 2 included a diagram of a C3 Corvette's steel birdcage structure that supports the body panels (see page 28). The upper windshield frame was constructed with five major components when it was built at the factory: two main pillar posts, the upper header, and two reinforcing corners. They were spot welded together to form the upper windshield frame.

The left front wheel well on this 1972 Corvette is being closely inspected to determine if any of the inner panels are broken or cracked. This includes any separation of panels, cracked fiberglass, or evidence of fiberglass patchwork that has been applied to the underside of a panel. It is also important to determine if your car has been involved in an accident and has undergone shoddy repairs. It is always a good idea to correct these flaws during the paint preparation process.

The pillar posts and the header are constructed from hollow steel, and usually only the outside surfaces were painted. If a hole develops in the header, water flows down the frame and into the footwell kick panels on both sides of the passenger compartment. Cars that have spent years in moist climates are very prone to having large buildups of rust on the surfaces of their metal windshield frames. The way these frames were constructed makes them prone to rust. The upper frame was spot welded to the ends of the pillar posts. Then the corners were spot welded to both sections, but these overlapping joints were never sealed. Deterioration of the frame usually begins in these areas.

The windshield frame is covered with metal trim, and a large enough gap allows leaves and debris to collect in the channel under the chrome trim. This traps moisture allowing rust to form and it takes awhile for the area to dry out. The most troubling is that this moisture runs down the side of the windshield frame and collects in the lower No. 2 body mount area in wells beside the driver and passenger compartments. Unless these leaks are corrected quickly, the birdcage and frame rust badly and need to be repaired.

After removing the trim and discovering the windshield frame is severely rusted, you may be able to repair it. If the windshield frame is so badly rusted that it needs to be replaced, a reproduction windshield frame replacement pieces can be purchased from a Corvette aftermarket supplier.

If you decide to restore this part you have a couple of options. The first method requires a ton of patience and time. It also requires a 220-volt spot welder and a spot-weld drill. The spot welder has a center drill bit with an outer cutting tip built into it. This enables you to drill out all of the original welds. Then you use a hammer and chisel to cut the frame apart.

The second method is quicker. As an example, the 1977 Corvette in these photos had a very rusty windshield frame that could not be repaired. The owner took the car to Van Steel, where they removed the trim and confirmed that the frame had to be replaced.

An undamaged steel windshield frame was located at a swap meet at a local Corvette show. The VIN was carefully removed from the rusted birdcage and set aside until the repair was finished. Measurements were carefully recorded so the new frame could fit perfectly. Technicians used a reciprocating saw to cut the old frame out of the car. The seams were ground smooth and repainted in black to keep them from rusting. After about three hours of labor, the replacement frame was welded in place. The original VIN number was installed, and the repair looked good as new.

Windshield Frame Replacement

1 Windshield Frame Assessment

This 1977 Corvette came to Van Steel with a badly rusted windshield frame. The frame needed to be replaced before any body repairs or painting. A stock windshield has been set in place to verify that the frame is not bent.

Rust caused severe damage to this Corvette's steel birdcage windshield frame. This damage is not visible when the windshield and the trim are installed. This is a fairly common problem with Corvettes that have spent most of their lives in humid parts of the country.

2 Measure Windshield Frame

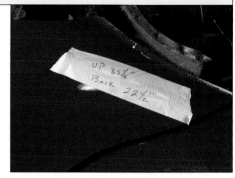

It is very important to take accurate measurements of the windshield frame prior to removal. The best way to measure a convertible frame is from the rear bulkhead to the top of the frame. On coupes, measure from the rear roof to the windshield frame. Also measure from the floor to the top of the windshield frame on both coupes and convertibles. These measurements must be duplicated when the damaged frame is replaced.

This is an easy way to remember the driver- and passenger-side windshield frame measurements (providing your fenders are still attached). It provides a handy guide during reassembly of this critical component.

3 Inspect Replacement Windshield Frame

This used windshield frame was found at a Corvette swap meet and was in excellent condition. It even had the VIN plate attached. However, it will be removed and discarded. The VIN plate from the original, rusted frame will be removed and reattached to this frame.

4 Cut Out Old Windshield Frame

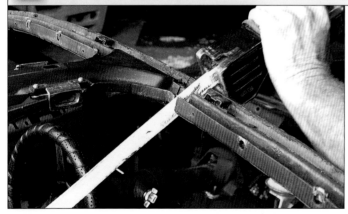

Use a reciprocating saw to cut through the windshield frame on either side of the T-bar on coupes. The T-bar support needs to be chiseled off once the remainder of the frame is removed. This is not necessary on convertibles.

Measure the length of the new windshield frame before you cut out the old unit. This replacement frame extends below the original lower weld joint. The original windshield frame was removed at the lower joint. The new frame needs to be cut at the same location. It is welded onto the lower joint here. Take extra care when making this cut so it lines up correctly with the lower weld joint.

4 Cut Out Old Windshield Frame
(continued)

The front of the T-bar is spot welded to the upper windshield frame. The windshield glass sits in a trough, and the T-bar is spot welded to the frame in the center. Cut the windshield frame near the edge of the trough to gain access to the welds. Once the welds are exposed, use a grinder to grind through the welds so the old frame can be pried off the T-bar.

5 Straighten T-Bar

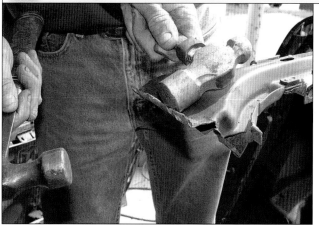

Once the old frame is removed, straighten and smooth the bent T-bar metal before the new frame is attached to it. This is very lightweight stamped metal. It is very easy to straighten by gently tapping two hammers together.

6 Remove T-Bar Attachment

Before the new frame can be installed into the car, remove the T-bar attachment from the replacement windshield frame. Cut it off with a reciprocating saw at the end of the T-bar. Use an air-driven grinding wheel to cut the welds on the T-bar side to remove the remaining pieces of T-bar metal that is secured to the new frame. All remnants of the frame must be ground away in order to fit the old and new parts together successfully.

7 Install New T-Bar

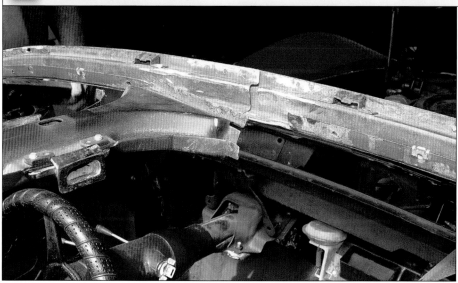

The T-bar has been successfully removed from the new windshield frame and is now being fitted to the existing T-bar that was left in the car. The new frame is secured to the two lower frames that were left intact when the old frame was removed. The original T-bar is put in place as shown in the photo. Once it is lined up correctly it is clamped in place.

8 Confirm Fit

With the new frame resting correctly on the two lower windshield frames, compare the height and rake measurements to the ones written down before the original frame was removed. The new frame sits on top of the two lower frame sections; they do not overlap. They need to be completely welded on all sides to secure the replacement frame to the car. Make any adjustments that are necessary before welding the frame into place.

9 Weld Frame into Place

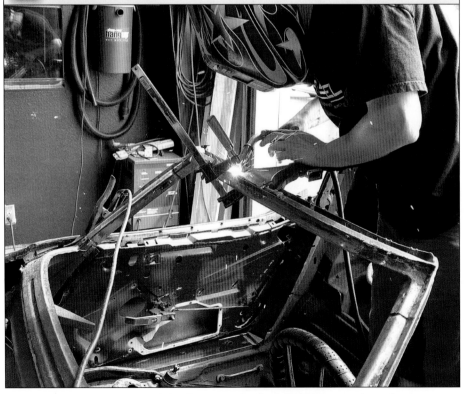

Tack weld the lower part of the frame on both sides of the car in order to recheck the fit. Place a tack weld on the inside and outside of each frame to hold it place. Once everything is confirmed, run a bead of weld completely around the lower frame on each side of the car.

10 Inspect Final Fit

Here, the welds have been completed, ground down, and painted. The windshield has been laid in place, and the roof panels have been attached to confirm that everything fits correctly. This job took about three hours to complete.

Body Panel Type

This is a good time to discuss more details about the kind of fiberglass material beneath your old paint.

From 1953 to 1972, factory body panels were formed by a chopgun blowing fiberglass-reinforced plastic (FRP) strands and resin into metal molds. The molds were pressed together using high pressure and heat to keep the panel thickness consistent during the panel curing process.

Starting in 1973, Corvette body panel construction methods changed to use sheet-molded composites (SMC). These panels were formed with a mix of fiberglass, resin, a catalyst, and a release agent. The mix was inserted into a high-pressure mold until it was cured. The finished panels were smoother than the previous FRPs and provided a better finish on the production line.

There are many products on the market that are available to repair fiberglass body panels. One example is Vette Panel Adhesive by Evercoat. Type 1 is for FRP Corvettes and Type 2 is for SMC Corvettes. Type 2 can be used to bond SMC and FRP panels together. If using another product make sure it is compatible with FRP or SMC fiberglass panels.

Fiberglass Repairs

C3 Corvette owners are very fortunate because numerous aftermarket suppliers offer both types (FRP and SMC) of high-quality duplicate replacement body panels. They include fenders, door panels, hoods, and front and rear body clips. Common damage areas usually found in the front and rear of the car include the front nose, fenders, and under the front valance panel. In the rear the bumper and taillight areas are also common places to find damage.

Many of these areas can be repaired instead of replacing them prior to painting. Epoxy filler can be used to quickly repair small nicks or gouges on the body that have not gone through the fiberglass.

Fiberglass resin, hardener, 1/2-pint mixing container, wooden mixing stick, fiberglass sheet, metal roller, food wrap, and tape are some of the basic fiberglass repair tools and materials. This combination of products can repair cracked bonding seams and small cracks or gouges that sometimes occur in the body from road use.

Corvette front body panels No 1, 2, 3, and 4 are bonded together on all 1973-1982 cars. The remaining panels are secured with bolts. The 1968 to 1972 front assemblies are very similar and include the same bonding strips.

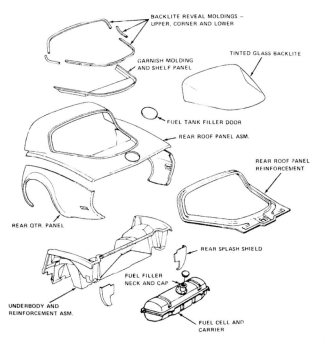

BACKLITE REVEAL MOLDINGS – UPPER, CORNER AND LOWER

TINTED GLASS BACKLITE

GARNISH MOLDING AND SHELF PANEL

FUEL TANK FILLER DOOR

REAR ROOF PANEL ASM.

REAR ROOF PANEL REINFORCEMENT

REAR QTR. PANEL

REAR SPLASH SHIELD

FUEL FILLER NECK AND CAP

UNDERBODY AND REINFORCEMENT ASM.

FUEL CELL AND CARRIER

These components are required for a complete rear body assembly on all 1978–1982 Corvettes. The 1968–1973 models use several different parts that are not shown here. In addition, 1974–1977 Corvettes use several different parts in their rear body area, but the basic number of components is similar.

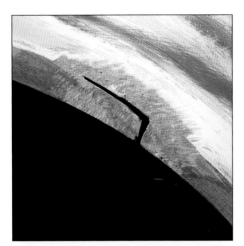

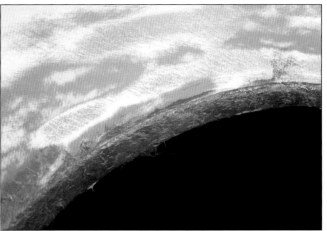

Body panels that have cracks or holes completely through the fiberglass are structurally damaged. The fender lip on this Corvette was split so this part suffered structural damage and an extensive repair was required. The lip was ground down to expose the break and to determine exactly where the break ended.

Structural repairs require a backing strip attached behind the damaged area to restore strength to the area.

First, strip the paint from the damaged area. Then use a 3-inch air grinder with a 100-grit paper disc to cut a groove all along the crack. (Hold the wheel at a 45-degree angle on the top and bottom of the crack.) This provides a good bonding surface for the repair.

Clean the area beneath the crack. (Photo Courtesy Ed Scoppa)

Use a scrap piece of fiberglass to make a bonding strip. If that is not available make one with fiberglass sheet, resin, and hardener. Secure the backing strip underneath the damaged area with resin and hardener. Form the fiberglass sheet around the damaged lip of the fender and impregnate it with resin to secure it to the lip.

After allowing the area to cure correctly, the material can be ground down so the fender lip can be correctly duplicated. Use a 3- or 6-inch air grinder with 100-grit paper disk. Then use a sheet of sandpaper on an orbital sander. Finish the area by hand with a sanding block. (Photo Courtesy Ed Scoppa)

The resin comes in a large container, and the MEK hardener is packaged in a small bottle. Use a disposable marked plastic cup to mix the resin and hardener together with a disposable paint stick. You can also use throwaway paintbrushes to mix and apply the resin to the body. Use rubber gloves during this procedure. The recommended mixture is two drops of hardener for every one ounce of resin. This material gets hard quickly so it best to work with small amounts at a time. The fiberglass sheets are laid onto the damaged area and the resin is applied to the sheet and rolled onto the body. Once it gets hard it can be ground down, finished, and painted.

Several disposable work gloves are also handy to have when working with these materials. The resin sets up quickly and is difficult to remove from your hands.

Structural Damage or Broken Parts

Doing these repairs yourself before the car goes to the paint shop (as long as the paint shop agrees beforehand) saves a lot of money.

A panel that's suffered from a serious collision can completely split or rip. You need to repair this damage because road vibration causes such a crack to grow.

First, drill a small hole at the end of the crack to prevent it from spreading. Then grind the entire area out so that the crack is completely exposed. Depending on where the damage is located you may or may not be able to insert a bonding strip behind the damage. If the crack is ground out enough, you can force in enough fiberglass sheet, resin, and hardener to properly repair the damage. When the repair is completely cured, it can be easily sanded and shaped so that no repair is visible.

Body panels that are broken in two require a backing strip or patch to be placed behind the damaged area. Scrap pieces of fiberglass work well for these repairs if they have the correct contour of the area that needs to be repaired.

If the pieces don't have the correct contour, a new patch can be created by placing a piece of polyethylene film material over the area that needs to be repaired. This film is the same type that is used to wrap food. Make it large enough to extend at least 3 to 4 inches beyond the repair area.

Cut a piece of fiberglass sheet, saturate it with resin and hardener, and place it on the film. After it hardens, remove the plastic sheet. After it cures, it can be used as a patch on the inside of the damaged panel.

Adhesive filler may be needed to restore the correct curvature of the fender. Use a low-cost disposable plastic spreader to add the filler and to restore the curvature of the work area. These disposable spreaders can be custom cut to the curvature of the area you are working on. They make this type of corrections easy to complete.

Use an angle grinder with a 3-inch, 100-grit paper disc to grind down the area. Use primer as a guide coat to check the work. You may need to sand the area again and add more filler until the fender looks original. (Photo Courtesy Ed Scoppa)

The door key area is a common repair area for 1969-1982 C3 doors. When you open the door, you push down on the upper handle and put your thumb around the door lock area. Over time this continuous pushing fatigues the fiberglass in the area, so repair is necessary. The fiberglass may be cracked or broken.

The 1968 Corvettes had a push button in this area and are also prone to cracking. Do not add more fiberglass than absolutely needed or the door lock mechanism cannot be secured to the door. Grind and reglass the cracked areas and build them up to the original thickness. Sand them smooth. (Photo Courtesy Ed Scoppa)

With either kind of patch, use a grinder or sander to make the inside of the broken area rough, and cut the patch so that at least 2 inches overlaps the damaged area. Drill two small holes in the patch and thread wire through it to hold it in place. Cover the patch with resin/hardener and use the wire to keep it tight against the panel. After it cures, remove the wire.

Now clean the area around the damage, place fiberglass sheeting over the area, add resin, hardener, and let it cure. Once the resin is cured, sand and feather the repaired area into the rest of the panel.

Broken parts, such as a fender, can be cut out of the car along their factory bonding seams and replaced with aftermarket parts that duplicate the original units. Use a power grinder to cut along the factory-bonding strip, and then remove the damaged panel. Scuff and sand the front surfaces of the replacement panel and the adjacent panel about 3 to 4 inches from where it is attached.

Also scuff the bonding strip and the underside of the replacement panel, and wipe them clean with a cleaning solution. Bevel the attaching edges 30 degrees to form a V-joint. Apply an epoxy adhesive and clamp the parts into place. Fill any open spots and finish the area by grinding, sanding, filling, and priming the repaired area.

Cracked Bonding Seam

If the car has a cracked bonding seam on the front or rear, grind it out and fill it with a new resin and fiberglass section. Remove all of the paint around the cracked area before starting this repair.

Use a grinding wheel or a belt sander to form a shallow V along the crack of the bonding seam. Scuff above and below the area to provide an adequate surface for the repair materials to adhere. If the seam is completely cracked, adding a bonding strip on the underside for strength may be required. Fill the seam with two-part epoxy filler to bond the crack back together. After it cures grind it smooth.

Place small strips of fiberglass sheet that are impregnated with resin over the repaired seam. After the repaired area has had adequate time to cure, sand, fill, and prime the area. A heat lamp can reduce the curing time dramatically.

Fiberglass Crack Repair

1 Identify Cracked Fender

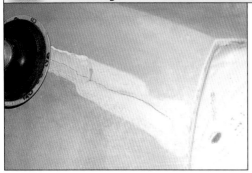

Both rear fender-bonding seams on this Corvette were cracked from age and needed repairing. Before a repair can begin, grind down the seam using an angle grinder with an 80-grit, 5-inch abrasive wheel. This removes a majority of the old bonding material (shown).

Next, use a 3- or 6-inch air grinder with 100-grit sanding wheel to grind the crack out. Make a groove with the sanding wheel so the repair material has a good bonding surface. Tape and paper off the area to be repaired to prevent excess resin dropping onto other parts of the panel that are not being repaired.

2 Pour Resin into Mixing Cup

Pour a small amount of resin into a mixing cup. Don't forget to add two drops of hardener for every one ounce of resin.

3 Add Hardener to Resin

Add the correct amount of MEK hardener drops to the container. Use a disposable stick to quickly mix the two together before the resin sets up. Make sure the hardener and resin are thoroughly mixed so the resin correctly and effectively bonds to the fiberglass. You don't want to redo the work.

4 Soak Fiberglass Strands

Pull apart the straight edges of a fiberglass sheet to help blend the fibers into the existing panel. Use the mixing stick (shown) to be sure the the fiberglass strands are thoroughly soaked with resin.

5 Apply Fiberglass to Panel

This step is a very rapid process because the resin sets up quickly. Be sure you have all necessary items nearby before starting. Place some resin-saturated fiberglass onto the repaired panel (shown). The mixing stick or a paintbrush are good tools to use. Notice how the resin drips onto the taped-off area.

6 Squeegee Resin into Repair Area

Use a metal squeegee to force the resin into the repaired area. The squeegee also eliminates any air bubbles that may have gotten underneath the resin. It is important to flatten the resin into the repaired area.

Wait 8 to 10 hours before proceeding with the next step. If using a heat lamp to speed the set process, keep it at least 12 inches from the repair and wait one hour before moving to the next step.

7 Trim Along Repair Area

Once the resin is hard, use a razor blade to carefully cut along the edges of the tape to remove it from the panel.

8 Allow Time for Repair Area to Cure

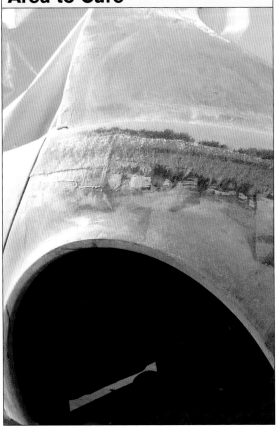

The bonding seam on this Corvette rear fender has been repaired. It is usually best to wait the appropriate amount of time according to the package directions to allow the resin to harden correctly. You can speed up the process by applying a heat lamp to the area.

9 Choose and Apply Filler

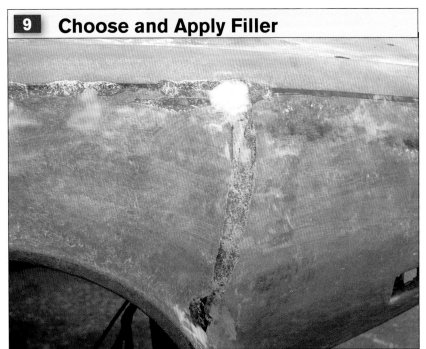

This Evercoat adhesive filler is especially made for SMC and FRC panels. It has enough flex to prevent cracking when the panels flex under load and provides a smooth, durable surface when paint is applied. Sand the repaired area with a sanding block and 220-grit paper to remove small imperfections that have been filled with fiberglass filler. It is very important to create a very smooth surface prior to applying primer and paint to the finished surfaces.

C3 doors are prone to striking the rear of the front fender if the hinges are weak. This chips the rear seam on the fender. To repair this area, apply fiberglass resin to the seam (left). The repair needs to be sanded and shaped for a perfect fit (right). The door should be installed to ensure the final fit is a perfect match.

Excessive Door Gap

A common area that usually needs bodywork attention is where the front fender ends at the door opening. If the door is improperly adjusted or a door hinge breaks, the front of the door can damage the seam at the door opening on the front fender. The door could break off part of the fender or crack a large area. Also, depending on how well the car was built, the fender-to-door seam gap might be excessive.

One method of repair is to break the front fender loose and move it into the correct position.

Another repair method is to use fiberglass sheet, resin, and hardener to make a new seam. This repair is easier with the door removed, but take careful measurements before taking the door off. Make sure you have a correct fit when you reinstall the door on its hinges.

Damaged Body Panel

Corvette fiberglass body panels are extremely strong, but flexible. They can take high impacts and not break; however, if they are hit hard enough they separate. Aftermarket body panels are available to complete any repairs.

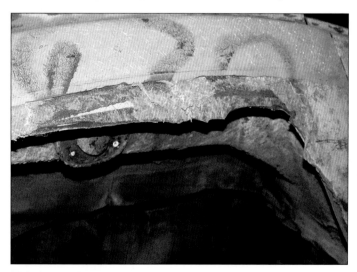

This lower right rear fender has been torn away from the rear upper deck during a collision. It exposed the bonding seam that holds the panels together.

Apply a coat of primer to the damaged area to better visualize the area that needs to be repaired. Clamp a replacement fender in place and mark the bonding seam with tape. Grind out the remnants of the old lower fender with a sanding wheel along the entire length of the bonding seam on the fender.

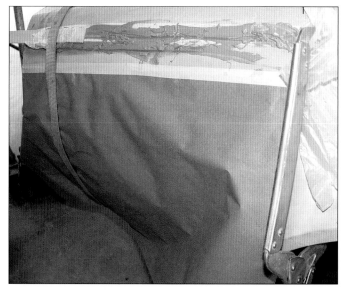

Apply a two-part bonding epoxy to the complete bonding strip. Fit the replacement fender panel onto the bonding strip and push it into the adhesive. This adhesive secures the replacement fender panel to the upper rear deck of the Corvette.

Hold the panel in place with screws or clamps and straps (shown). Use plastic wrap to protect the clamps so they can be easily removed once the adhesive has cured.

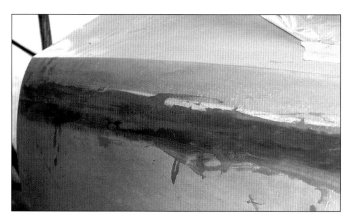

When the fender panel has bonded to the upper deck it can be sanded. Fill and sand smooth any blemishes before primer is applied and the car heads to the paint booth.

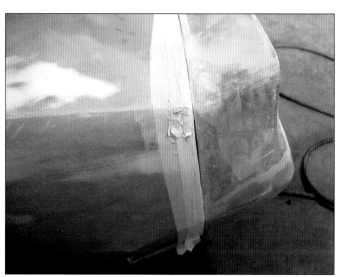

Over time the factory bumper covers deteriorate and crack from sun exposure. Fortunately, aftermarket fiberglass replicas are available as replacement units. This cover is being filled and sanded until it is a perfect match. Put the fiberglass bumper on the car and mark all of the gaps with tape. Add or remove fiberglass fillers from the bumper until the proper fit is achieved by sanding the area until it is even.

A Corvette was brought into Van Steel's shop with severe damage to its right rear fender. A large part of the lower fender was missing, and it broke along the bonding seam. The old fender had to be ground away from the car's upper rear deck-bonding seam. The remaining fender was ground away, and all of the adhesive on the bonding strip was removed.

A new lower rear fender was ordered and upon its arrival the fender was prepared for attachment. The inside of the new fender was roughed up with a rotary sanding wheel to help the adhesive bond to the fender.

Van Steel used clamps rather than screws, which is a more common method to secure the new fender while the bonding epoxy cures. Once the fender cured, the bonding seam was sanded and any small imperfections filled and prepared for painting.

Bumper Covers

In 1973, Corvette introduced a soft front bumper cover (made of injection-molded urethane) to comply with the federal 5-mph-crash bumper and it covers the standard metal beam attached to the frame. The semisoft cover conforms to the body. A two-piece rear cover was added in 1974 for that year only. The rear cover became one piece in 1975 and remained that way until the end of C3 production in 1982.

Over time sun exposure created waves or cracks in the rubber surface of the cover. It is relatively common for large hunks of rubber to break off. If your car is going to be a daily driver and not a show car, replacing a cracked or worn bumper cover with a fiberglass replica is often the best choice.

Fiberglass covers do not come with attachment brackets. You may have to adjust the holes to make the bumper cover fit (this one belongs to the 1980 Corvette in the background). The holes might have to be elongated to provide enough adjustment to correctly fit the new cover. Once the fit is verified, secure the bracket with pop rivets. Reinstall the cover onto the car to make sure nothing has shifted during this process.

With all of the correct holes added to the cover, it is ready to be prepared for painting. After the covers have been sanded and primed, they are sent to the paint booth. The mirrors are painted at the same time.

Each Corvette has a little variation in the way each body panel fits. The rubber bumper cover conforms to those differences. Fiberglass covers do not, so be prepared to do some grinding and filling during the fitment of one of these replacement panels. Once they are fitted and painted they give the car a smooth, finished look that cannot be duplicated with a rubber bumper cover.

Final Sanding and Filling

The body of your Corvette is now nearing the end of the paint preparation process. Before moving the car to the paint shop, every panel on the car should be closely inspected for any small nicks or gouges. Run your hands over every surface and repair any imperfections with filler. Sand the body until you are sure it is smooth.

Once sanding is completed, use an air gun to blow all of the dust and sanding material off the surfaces of the car.

Finally, use a spray bottle of water and a paper towel to hand wash the surface of the body.

Who Will Paint the Car?

Before any paint work is started, you need to decide who is going to do the work. The painting process requires patience and time to get top-quality results. Now is the time to think about how to proceed. You can choose to paint your car yourself or select a quality paint shop to perform the work.

Painting It Yourself

Paint preparation requires a lot of labor to make sure the foundation of the Corvette body is smooth and blemish free. Body preparation and sanding all body surfaces are also time consuming and require a lot of patience. Anything missed during this step will glare at you through your finished paint job, so be sure the

body filler, primer, and other chemicals are properly applied. If not, you could end up repainting your car.

When done right, the sanded surface has a smooth gloss. Panels are ripple and blemish free. Body and paint preparation consumes about 80 percent of the total time it takes to paint a Corvette. You can save yourself a lot of money if you have prior painting and body repair experience.

It is important to have access to an environmentally approved paint booth before starting. Paint is very expensive and toxic. Many states and cities have very strict environmental laws that stipulate what kind of facility is approved for applying paint. Guidelines for disposal of unused paint and materials vary depending on where you live. It is a good idea to get all of the details before beginning your project. The days of just hanging a sheet in your garage are over.

If you are determined to paint your car in your own garage, then you need to construct a temporary paint booth. Using one dramatically decreases contamination. It should be fitted with the correct lighting, filters, heaters, and downdraft fans to keep dust particles from settling onto the wet surface of your new paint. However, this added side project takes a fair amount of time, money, and effort.

It is difficult but not impossible to get professional-quality paint results at home. But if you have limited or no painting experience you should look for a competent paint shop to paint your car.

Selecting a Professional Shop

It is important to preselect a paint shop before beginning any paint preparation. Art Dorsett, for example, works closely with Mike Tackley of Tackley Auto Body for paintwork.

There are three types of shops that perform paint work. The first is a production shop that specializes in insurance repair. They operate on a thin profit margin and the less time it takes them to complete the work the higher their profit. Be cautious in selecting one of them because they might not take the time required to give a quality finish. The price might be right but the quality probably suffers.

The second type of shop is one that does complete restorations. They usually work on a project from start to finish, rarely agreeing to allow owners to do any pre-paint work. They make their money by charging by the hour and pride themselves on giving their customers a top-quality, finished product.

The third type is an independent shop that performs a variety of body and paintwork. This usually includes crash repair and restoration work.

Many turn out quality work and are sometimes willing to let you do some or all of the pre-paint preparation work.

The condition of the body after the pre-paint preparation has a big impact on final paint results. This is the reason many shops will not paint a car if they did not do the bodywork. If they are unsure of the pre-paint preparation they will probably be unwilling to provide a warranty for their part of the job. If you insist on doing this work yourself, it is critical to preselect a paint shop that is willing to let you prepare the car.

If the shop agrees to this arrangement, it is important to communicate regularly, tell them exactly what you are doing, and ask their advice as you proceed. Be sure to let them know what materials you are using and follow their advice.

Old Paint Removal

Remove all trim and emblems before starting to remove the paint. You may notice in some of the accompanying photos that all of the trim was not removed before starting. These photos were taken for demonstration purposes only.

Razor Blade Method

Using a tool with a flat razor blade is one of the oldest ways to remove the paint from a Corvette's fiberglass body. This chemical-free process can be completed fairly quickly and is the most inexpensive way.

A good place to start is on a long, flat panel, such as a door or a flat spot on a fender. Start slowly and with light pressure. You quickly determine how much pressure is required to scrape the old paint off the panel. You may discover that your car has

Removing paint is a time-consuming and messy process. Several methods are available to accomplish this task and one of the oldest ways is to use a razor blade. It is critical that the blade be kept flat against the body surface to avoid pitting or gouging the fiberglass. Placing a large tarp under the work area to gather all of the small paint fragments is a good idea to minimize the mess.

This close-up shows how to correctly place the razor blade on the surface of the body to remove the old paint. It is easy to see the layers of paint and primer that have been applied to the 1972 Corvette's body. Directly under the paint is the primer; the gray gel coat can be seen underneath the primer.

It took about three hours to remove the paint from the upper fenders and a part of the door. All of the trim is going to be removed before proceeding any further with the paint removal.

many coats of paint, which strip off pretty quickly.

If you slip up and turn the blade a little sideways you risk gouging the body. This requires extra bodywork to fill and sand the gouged area. So try to keep the razor blade flat on the surface at all times.

Chemical Method

Many brands of chemical paint removers are on the market. These chemicals can remove large areas of paint very quickly, but they are very messy. It is much easier to work on small areas at a time. You can minimize the mess on the sides of the car by using tape and paper to catch the paint and solvent as it is removed. Fiberglass is very porous and absorbs the chemicals if not removed quickly. This is another reason it is better to work on a small area at one time; it is easier to clean the area before proceeding to the next location.

When done correctly, the surface does not get nicked or gouged, which can happen when the body is scraped. This method reduces the amount of paint preparation work.

These chemicals are very toxic so remember to wear a long-sleeve shirt, trousers, and gloves to avoid exposing your skin to the chemicals. In addition, always wear goggles or shop glasses.

Most professional body shops prefer the chemical removal method because of the short time it takes to remove all of the paint.

Sanding

Sanding is a lot of work and takes a lot of time to complete. A 150-grit sanding disc is a good place to start but be prepared to move up to a 400-grit if the surface is being scratched. Continue adjusting the grit as you proceed removing the paint. You don't want to use too coarse of a grit because it damages the fiberglass gel coat.

Load up your 16-inch sanding board with paper and start going at it. The time it takes depends on how much paint buildup is on the car.

Prior to painting a fiberglass panel check each one for moisture or contamination with this Tramex moisture encounter tool. Any oil or water that has worked its way into the fiberglass can be detected with this tool. In order to remove the moisture place an ultraviolet light over the area for a minimum of two hours. Recheck the panel to make sure it is dry. Use the ultraviolet light until the moisture is removed.

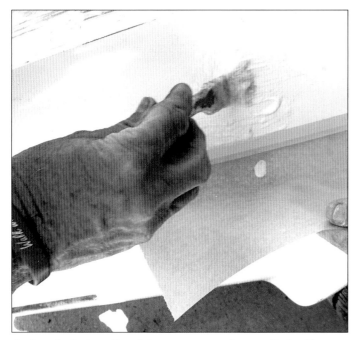

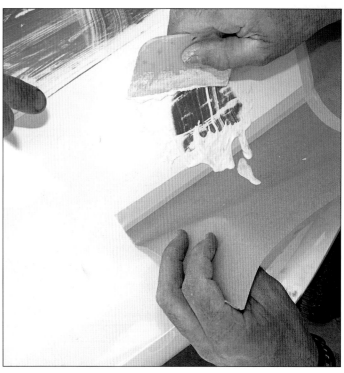

A chemical aircraft paint remover can be applied with an applicator to one area at a time and then allowed to sit for a few minutes until the paint starts bubbling and cracking. The area that is being worked on is masked off to prevent any excess chemicals from dripping onto other parts of the body. Remember to put plenty of paper under your work area. Do not let this chemical sit too long on the surface because it can damage the fiberglass.

Once the paint is bubbling use a plastic spatula to remove the old paint and place it on the paper. It may take several attempts to remove all of the old paint. Once the area is free of paint, discard the paper, remask a new area, and repeat the process. The area at the top of the photo has been cleared of paint; only the gray gel coat remains.

This roof panel from a 1980 Corvette has had its paint removed with chemicals. Light sanding has removed all of the remaining paint that was left behind. A small amount remains around the front of the panel and it will be removed when the trim is detached.

PAINTING

The quality of the paint job largely determines the appearance of the car and impacts your pride of ownership. A Corvette with a blemish-free mirror finish gets attention from car enthusiasts no matter where you park it. This is not to undermine the importance of having your Corvette in sound mechanical condition. But having a sparkling Shark body on top of sound mechanicals makes you want to keep pampering your baby for a long time. If you intend to paint your car at home, be sure you know the costs involved, both time and money.

Before you take your Corvette to a body shop to have it painted, it's a good idea to reconfirm the total price of the job and have a clear understanding of what I call the "scope of work." This includes materials required, how many hours of labor are required, labor rate, schedule for work completion, and total price. You should also have an agreement for the hourly rate for any extra work that is not part of the scope of work.

Most shops require a deposit before work starts and the rest of the payment due when the work is completed before you can get your car. Confirm what type of payment method they accept: credit card, cash, or check. They have the legal right to hold your car until all payment disputes are settled. I cannot emphasize this point enough: Do your homework, get recommendations, and call the better business bureau to see if the shop you selected has had any complaints.

Body shops work on very hectic schedules. Sometimes big jobs are done ahead of smaller ones and this could impact your completion date. It is best to work out your finished date requirements in advance and be sure it's part of your scope of work up front.

Your guarantee should not only include quality of the paint, but also

Tom Otto from Tackley Auto Body is carefully spraying the first coat of paint on Art Dorsett's 1980 Corvette. Tom is applying the paint in a heated downdraft paint booth. Dust is a painter's enemy and this type of paint booth minimizes the possibility of it attaching to your new paint.

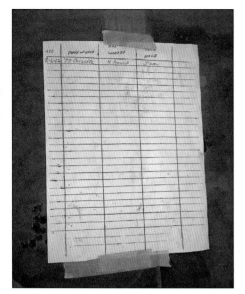

Body shops use some type of form to keep track of the hours they work on an individual job. The form is usually placed somewhere on the car where it is visible to the customer and technician. When the job is completed these forms are used to verify the total hours that it took to complete the work. This helps the body shop management stay within the budget agreed upon with the customer at the beginning of the job.

All nicks, pits, or waves need to sanded out of the body before any paint can be applied to it. Sanding blocks can be refilled with new paper and used with either dry or wet sanding material.

A variety of sandpapers is used to complete a high-quality paint job. The heaviest grit to remove large buildups on the panels is 80. The least abrasive that is used to achieve a mirrorlike final finish is 3,000 wet/dry grit paper.

Large surfaces, such as the door, are a perfect place to use a sanding backing board. Measure your progress by running your hand over the sanded surface to determine if there are any uneven areas.

Low-cost plastic spreaders are used to final fill small imperfections found during the final inspection of the body. These fillers are epoxy based and cure very quickly, so they can be sanded and rechecked before the primer is applied. The spreaders can be used many times over, provided you clean them at the first sign that the material you are spreading is getting hard.

protect against paint bubbling, peeling, blisters, or any other surface blemishes.

Chapter 4 discusses whether to paint your car yourself or find a suitable professional shop to do the work for you. By now you have made that decision and your car is almost ready to be painted. Before going through the painting process let's talk about the painting tools, equipment, and supplies used to correctly paint a car.

Tools and Equipment

Whether you paint your car yourself or have a shop do the work, it's a good idea to be familiar with the various tools of the trade.

- Sanding Block: A small, flexible, rubber sanding block has slots in both ends. The slots allow you to hold the sandpaper in place while you sand your car.
- Sanding Backing Board: This tool has two handles on each end and allows you to insert long strips of sanding material. It helps eliminate the typical washboard surfaces that are common on Corvette fiberglass panels. These boards usually measure 16 to 17 inches and are around 3 inches wide.
- Mixing/Filler Tool: You need a flat piece of material to mix the body filler and a flat spreader to

apply the filler onto the body. Inexpensive plastic spreaders usually cannot be reused once the material hardens and should be thrown away.
- Disposable Paint Masks: Sanding creates a lot of dust and low-cost disposable masks are a good investment to keep your lungs clear during this part of the job.
- Safety Glasses: Anytime you are grinding or sanding with a power unit you need to protect your eyes with safety glasses. One fragment that flies into your eye can cause serious injury.
- Air Compressor: These are used to blow the surface clear of all dust and sanding debris as well

as for operating the paint spray gun. Compressors come in 120- or 220-volt power requirements. The 220-volt is more efficient and is worth the extra initial purchase cost. The best compressors usually have a minimum of 5 hp.

- Spray Gun: Gravity-feed guns have the paint container on top of the spray nozzle and are usually preferred by professional painters. Suction guns have the paint container underneath the spray nozzle and air pressure draws it up and into the discharge nozzle. Gravity-feed guns typically use the entire paint product while suction guns sometimes leave unused paint in the bottom of the container. Gravity guns produce a very uniform spray of paint and they are much easier to clean. They also use lower pressure to apply the paint, which reduces excessive overspray.

- Power Buffer: One of the last steps in completing a quality paint job is buffing the car to

This is a Husky gravity-feed spray gun. The paint container is located on the top of the gun and uses gravity to feed the paint into the spray head.

eliminate scratches or small flaws. A good power buffer simplifies this process. Paint supply companies offer a wide range of buffing wheels and glazes to maximize the final shine on a new paint job.

Supplies

The painting process uses many supplies that can only be used one time. It is important to have an adequate amount of these materials on hand as the job progresses.

- Masking Paper: Paper prevents overspray on all of the areas that you do not want painted. Painting a car uses a lot of paper. The car has to be covered when it is primed and then when it is painted. Buying rolls of masking paper saves you time and aggravation and makes the job much easier.

- Masking Tape: The best width for this type of job is 1 to 2 inches. 3M products work really well. They have good adhesive qualities and do not leave glue residue when they are removed.

- Paper and Tape Stand: These stands hold the paper roll and tape so when you pull off a piece of paper, so you can roll the masking tape onto one side of the paper. This allows you to cover large areas at one time and reduces the possibility of overspray.

- Sandpaper: Preparing your car for paint and painting your car require a large amount of sandpaper. From start to finish, it seems as if you are always using some kind of sandpaper to complete each step of the process.

First, you need need numerous sanding grits for your sanding block and sanding backing board. The least expensive way to buy sandpaper is in rolls. You can buy these in bulk and cut what you need as your job progresses.

The best place to start is to get rolls of 80-, 150-, and 220-grit sandpaper. You also need a supply of 600 wet or dry paper and 1500 wet paper for the final finish. The lower the number, the more abrasive the paper. The 1500 is extremely fine and is good for polishing minor scratches in the surface of the paint before buffing.

- Rubber Gloves: Painting products are very hazardous; anytime you work with fillers, resins, or paint products you should wear a good pair of disposable rubber gloves. Sometimes they cannot be reused so have plenty of spares on hand.

- Lacquer Thinner: You need to have a supply on hand to clean tools as well as the paint gun. it does a great job cleaning but the thinner is toxic, so wear gloves when handling it. Remember to use it in an open area so the fumes disperse quickly. You can buy this product in 5-gallon containers and save money.

- Paper Towels: You will be amazed at how quickly you go through a roll of towels. They are perfect to quickly clean up a mess or to dry your hands or equipment after cleaning.

- Hand Cleaner: Most auto supply stores sell good, industrial hand cleaners in tubs. It is a good idea to have an adequate supply on hand at all times.

- Fiberglass Fillers: These are used during the paint preparation process, but you also need to use them to fill small nicks and bubbles that appear during the priming process. Remember that fiberglass flexes and stretches. Any filler you use should be able to stretch with the car. 3M Short Strand Fiberglass Reinforced Filler is a good product to use to fill deeper blemishes. For general filling and smoothing Evercoat's Plasticworks can take care of small problems.
- Tack Cloth: These sticky little rags are used to clear the painting surface of any fine dust, dirt, or grit that might have been missed during the initial cleaning. They are available in small packs, and it is good to have a small supply on hand.
- Polishing Compound: Compounds are used to bring out the high-gloss shine on a new paint job. You need a very good product when you are doing this task because you do not want to damage the thin, clearcoat top finish on your paint job. 3M makes very good final polishing compounds.
- Scotchbrite Pad: These are available in different grits; red is the most common color to use to clean various trim parts.
- Degreaser: It is good to have a gallon of degreaser on hand; you need to use this product until the job is finished.

Paint and Primer

Here are the types of paint and primer you need to know about:

- Primer/Sealer: The function of this paint is to close off the porous surface of the fiberglass body. A good primer/sealer protects the Corvette body against any adverse impact the new paint might have on the panels. Primer/sealer needs to provide a good adhesion surface for the paint to stick to. Primer/sealers with epoxy meet all of these requirements and are popular with body shops. They should be the type that dries quickly, is thick enough to fill minor defects on the body, and is easily sanded.
- Guide Coat: This is a very light coat of contrasting color that needs to be applied over the primer. This coat shows any imperfections on the body when you use your board to sand the surface. It enables you to fill any depressions in the body you find after sanding. 3M Dry Guide Coat works well for this step.
- Basecoat: This is the part of the paint system that holds the color. A gallon of paint is usually enough to paint an entire Corvette body, especially if you mix one part color and 1-1/2 parts of reducer. Most body shops can mix almost any color you desire. Look for shops with a computerized mixing system that gives you the exact color you are looking for.

  When products such as PPG Deltron are mixed with a fast-drying reducer, they dry very quickly and do not create a lot of overspray or waste. This helps to eliminate drips and sags in the paint.
- Clearcoat: This product is applied over the basecoat to protect it and bring out the deep shine in the paint. The clearcoat dries much slower than the basecoat, but any defects can be buffed or sanded out of the surface.

Painting

At this stage, the bodywork is complete. Closely inspect the surface before proceeding. Any small nick, wave, or dip should be corrected.

Now it is time to begin taping all of the nooks and crannies. Large rolls of paper make this job go quickly, especially if you use a paper and tape stand. The paper protects the unpainted area from overspray. If the color is being changed, it might be a good idea to have the doors removed and paint jambs and doors separately. It is easier to paint these areas with the doors off the car. If you are keeping the same color, these areas need to be protected with tape and paper.

After the taping is complete spray the car with a coat of primer/sealer. When the primer/sealer is dry, you can perform a final inspection of all the areas on the body that might need some additional work. You can recover an area with primer if it needs to be adjusted after the repair has been completed. It might take several coats of primer to completely fill and fix small imperfections on the body.

When the final coat of primer is dry, apply a guide coat to the car's surfaces. After this has been applied, wrap a 6-inch-long stick with 400-grit sandpaper. Use two hands to sand the car in a back-and-forth motion. The guide coat shows you the low and high spots on the surface of the body. Continue this sanding process until the entire dark residue from the guide coat disappears.

Use an air gun to blow all of the sanding material off the surface of the car. When this is complete use a spray bottle filled with water and paper towels to wash the panels to remove any remaining sanding material.

You can now move the car into the paint booth. Use a tack cloth to clean the surface of the car before applying any paint. Many painters use urethane paints because they are durable and meet volatile organic compounds (VOC) rules.

Put on enough basecoat color and clearcoat to allow for color sanding. The clearcoat protects the paint from the sun's UV rays. If it is too thin, it starts turning white and flaking off the car. Color sanding takes some of this clearcoat surface off, so a thicker coating safeguards against sanding through it.

Color Sanding

After the paint is applied, wait for the car to dry before proceeding. Turning up the heat helps. (If you have a shop paint your car they oven bake the car until it is dry.) Then the car needs to be washed. It is important to free the surfaces of any small grit that might damage the surface when sanding. This work should be done in a clean, dry area. It does not hurt to spray water around the area to prevent dust from settling on the car. This is a good time to go over the car with a tack cloth.

Attach a 1,500-grit disc of sandpaper to a variable-speed orbital sander then switch to 2,500. Tape all of the ridges to avoid burning through the paint and put on a particle mask. Never linger in one spot for too long.

Once the car is completely sanded, start wet sanding with 3,000-grit wet/dry sandpaper. Soak this sandpaper in a bucket of water with some dish soap beforehand to soften it.

Wash the car again to remove any stray dirt. When it is dry use a another tack cloth to make sure the surface is clean.

Next, keep water on the surface while you sand it in light strokes. When this task is completed wash and dry the car again.

Attach a wool buffing wheel to the orbital sander. Using the lowest speed spread small amounts of buffing compound onto the car and buff with extreme care.

The final phase is to reinstall the window glass (if removed), clean the unpainted areas, and reinstall the interior and the various trim pieces that were removed from the body during disassembly.

Painting the Body

1 Apply Masking Tape and Paper

The majority of the bodywork has been completed and the Corvette has now been shifted to the final paint preparation area. Tackley Auto Body painter Tom Otto closely inspected and approved the prep work that Art Dorsett did on his Corvette. The seams are smooth and the body gaps are even on all sides.

It is now time to begin putting masking tape and paper on all of the areas that are not to be painted. Paper and tape prevent the difficult-to-remove overspray from falling on the underbody and interior components. Tom has taped and papered the rear window and gas tank filler.

The downdraft, heated paint booth is in the background. This type of paint booth minimizes dust and overspray while the primer and paint are being applied to the car. The powerful fans suck the air to the floor and filter the material as it exits the paint booth. Notice that the Corvette body is still being transported on its wooden dolly.

1 Apply Masking Tape and Paper (continued)

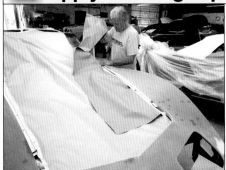

Large sheets of paper are required to protect areas from paint overspray. Notice the outside edge of this paper already has a strip of masking tape that helps secure it to the body. Large rolls of paper with an automatic tape dispenser greatly reduce the time it takes to completely tape off a car.

Paper and tape are applied around any opening that might allow paint to enter and cause overspray. Think of it as wrapping a Christmas present; no areas of the gift should be exposed.

The first year that Corvettes had under-hood windshield wipers was 1973. When the hood has been removed on these models, use paper and tape over the windshield and back to the roof bar. Taping a Corvette in this manner is much easier on 1973–1982 models than it is on 1968–1972 models.

This Corvette has been moved into the paint booth to receive its first coat of primer/sealer. All necessary openings are sealed with tape and paper to avoid getting overspray on unpainted areas. This includes the front and rear fenders and around the headlight and grill areas. This step requires a lot of attention to detail so nothing is missed before the painting begins.

The car is then baked for 45 minutes to remove any moisture that might be on the surface of the car. Once the car has cooled the primer/sealer is applied.

2 Properly Mix Paints

Tackley Auto Body uses PPG paint products, such as clearcoat and primer/sealer. Each of these paints is mixed with epoxy and reducers to harden the paint and thin it enough to be forced through a spray gun. Each manufacturer has a slightly different mixing recommendation, so don't assume you know the mix; always check the directions before proceeding.

Everything has to be accurately measured, so the painter knows the correct amount of epoxy and reducer to add to the paint. Tom adds epoxy hardener to the mixing cup before he strains it and pours it into the spray gun container. This paint gun container holds 1 quart of paint. About 1½ quarts of primer/sealer completely covers a car.

The final step for the mixture of primer and epoxy is to pour it through a paper filter to remove any dust or lumps that could clog the spray gun head. Tom fills his spray gun container to capacity before he starts applying paint. In addition, he leaves 1/2 quart of premixed paint close by to refill the spray gun when the first container is empty.

3 Apply Primer/Sealer

The primer/sealer is applied to the car. This coat of paint fills all of the small imperfections on the surface of the body. The spray gun should be kept around 12 inches above the surface and level with contours of the body. It is sprayed in one long continuous pattern to the end of the panel then moved up 3 inches and sprayed back the other way until the car is completely covered.

After the primer has dried Tom fills and finishes any small imperfections that might appear before the final basecoat/clearcoat paint is applied. A second coat of primer/sealer might have to be applied depending on what is found during the post-primer inspection.

4 Inspect Paint and Spot Sand Imperfections

Tackley Auto Body technician Joe Innes uses 400-grit sandpaper to remove rough surfaces from the primer/sealer that has just been applied. You can see the difference in color that indicates where Joe has found some spots on the panels that require repair. When this sanding is complete, the car is returned to the paint booth to receive a final coat of primer/sealer.

5 Apply Guide Coat

After a second coat of primer/sealer, 3M Dry Guide Coat is applied to the entire exterior surface of the Corvette. The dark color shows all of the surface imperfections that need to be removed before the body is painted with its basecoat/clearcoat final finish.

This is accomplished by using a sponge applicator to apply the dry coat that is part of the 3M Dry Guide Coat product. It is a fine powder that applies easily so the entire surface of the car can be covered very quickly.

6 Sand Guide Coat

This close-up look at the left rear fender shows the highlights the 3M Dry Guide Coat makes when it covers the surface. To remove all of the coating, 400-grit sandpaper is wrapped around a 6-inch stick. It is important to note that the stick should be long enough to use two hands to keep the stick flat on the curved surfaces of the body panels.

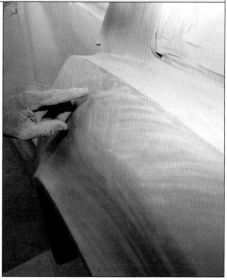

Tom is pointing out a very low spot on the left rear fender. The correct way to sand curved surfaces on the fender is to use a crisscross stroke. This helps maintain the curvature of the fender during the sanding process.

6 Sand Guide Coat
(continued)

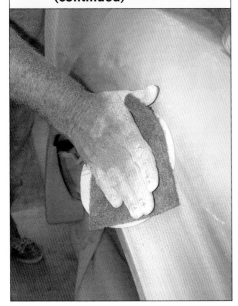

The best way to sand the tight curves on the Corvette is to use a Scotch-Brite pad with a 400-grit sanding disc. Tom is using the palm of his hand and not his fingers because fingers may leave dimples in the surface of the fiberglass that are difficult to remove. All of the 3M Dry Guide Coat has been removed from the top of the left rear fender after the sanding was completed.

7 Clean Body Surface

Tom painted the doorjambs and reinstalled the doors. He is now giving the car a final cleaning with a Scotch-Brite pad and an air hose to remove all of the sanding dust from the body panels. He will recheck to make sure the paper and tape is secure and has not received any damage from rips or moisture. Every area that is not to be painted should be completely covered.

Now it is time to use a spray bottle with water and paper towels to completely clean the body panels. This step usually takes half a day to complete.

8 Reload Spray Gun

Back in the paint room it is time to reload the spray gun with the basecoat color. Tom is filtering the basecoat paint to make sure it is dust and lump free before he heads back to the paint booth to spray the car.

9 Apply New Basecoat

Tom is applying the new basecoat Dark Claret paint. Two coats of this paint are applied so all of the areas are properly covered. The clearcoat needs a good surface to adhere to. Mixing the epoxy into the paint allows it to dry rapidly.

10 Sand and Buff Paint

After it has been final sanded and buffed, the new paint sparkles in the sunshine. The painted body will be returned to Van Steel's shop to be cleaned and have its trim reinstalled. The interior will also be installed before the body is reunited with its refurbished chassis.

FRAME RESTORATION

As discussed in Chapter 1, the C3 Frame design was carried over from the 1963–1967 C2 Corvettes. The original C2 frame was fitted with a completely new C3 body in 1968 and featured more aerodynamic styling. The knife-blade upper front end that housed the headlights in the C2 was replaced with a lower and smoother nose on the C3. This greatly reduced the car's tendency to lift at high speeds and it became a much more stable sports car. At the rear a small spoiler helps to keep the rear planted to the pavement.

This new Shark design proved to be very popular with Corvette owners, and that popularity helped to keep this car in production in various forms for 14 years. The body changes were subtle during its entire production run. Minor styling changes were made to the 1968–1972 models, including door handles, side vents, and exhaust tips. In 1973 an injection-molded urethane bumper cover, new hood, and front fender vents were installed on the Corvette. In 1974, a rear crash bumper was introduced. A large rear window was added in 1978 and new front and rear bumper covers were added in 1980; these remained to the end of production in 1982.

The original C2 frame design was very robust yet inexpensive to produce, and many C2 parts interchanged with the C3. The frame is a boxed-steel design and almost identical from 1968 to 1979. The 1980–1982 Corvettes were fitted with different rear frame rails to accommodate the new aluminum rear axle housing, but the rest of the frame is similar.

To control costs Corvette engineers used many existing front suspension components from the standard GM passenger car line. Up

Corvette frames are like the foundation of a house. Any rust or damage on your existing frame affects structural integrity and safety. This damage needs to repaired before you reinstall the body. Powdercoating before reassembly protects this vital component for many years. This is the perfect time to completely rebuild the steering, front and rear suspension, and the differential.

front, stamped-steel upper and lower control arms, supported by coil springs, were installed. Rubber bushings reduced noise and vibration. A transverse leaf spring rear suspension that uses stamped-steel trailing arms is unique to Corvette. While this front and rear design is much heavier than on newer Corvettes, it has proven to be trouble free.

When restoring a Corvette body and frame, pull the engine and transmission because it opens up a lot of working space and allows you to easily disassemble and inspect the rest of the frame's components.

Inspection

Carefully remove all of the components from the frame and make a parts list. Each removed part should be cleaned and inspected to determine if it is reusable. If it is not, a replacement part should be added to your purchase list. If the old part is reusable it should be bagged, tagged, and stored.

The downside of the boxed design is that it tends to collect water and salt in the inside of the box in critical strength areas. If this is not managed correctly the frame becomes heavily corroded and rusts.

You should closely inspect the frame rails in front of the back wheels because this area typically experiences heavy corrosion. Another spot to carefully inspect is behind the front wheels. This area accumulates a large amount of road moisture and is slow to dry out.

However, some frame corrosion is not catastrophic. If you locate some trouble spots that were not visible during your inspection they can be repaired. This is because almost any part of the C3 frame is available from aftermarket suppliers. It is worthwhile for aftermarket suppliers to keep producing these parts because of the cars' popularity. Suppliers such as Van Steel are equipped with a frame jig that allows them to check the frame's measurements against factory specifications. Rusted parts

can be removed and new replacement sections can be welded back in with no loss of strength.

The C3 frame holds all of the working parts that give the C3 strength and performance. Careful inspection and disassembly of each part helps determine what to replace, refurbish, or reuse. Remember that suspension, steering, and brake assemblies are put under tremendous stress during spirited driving. It's vital for your safety that you replace any worn or damaged parts with new or refurbished parts. It is money well spent and will provide many miles of enjoyable and safe driving.

Engine and Transmission Removal

After all of the fuel lines and electrical connections have been removed start removing the engine, transmission, and driveshaft from the frame. They are connected with two forward motor mounts and the two bolts below the rear of the transmission. The driveshaft is connected with bolts at the differential and a yoke at the front of the driveshaft. Connect a hoist onto the engine prior to unbolting any of these components to prevent damage.

After the engine and transmission have been removed, use a four-point lift or a floor jack to lift the frame and place it on safety stands. This allows access to the parts on the top and bottom of the frame that need to be removed. Once the frame has been securely lifted off the garage floor, remove the wheels. Inspect the suspension for damaged, bent, or broken components prior to removal. This is a good time to take photographs and make notes on what you discover.

The frame has been successfully removed from the body and moved to a suitable work area where disassembly work can begin. At this point all of the car's running gear is intact, including the engine, driveline, wheels/tires, brakes, suspension, and fuel tank. To properly repair and restore the basic frame all of these components must be removed.

All wiring must be securely out of the way before removing the fuel tank from the frame. If a sticker is attached to the tank, use plastic to protect it. These complete stickers tell the story about what was installed onto the car at the factory. If the sticker is peeling off, carefully remove it, place it in a plastic bag, and store it in a safe location.

Cover any opening on the engine, such as carburetor or valve cover openings. Make sure no debris falls into the engine. Attach a chain to the engine block and to an overhead lifting device. Use either a block and tackle or a rolling engine stand. Remove the two engine mount bolts and the two that are beneath the rear of the transmission.

Release the 1968–1979 driveshafts by removing the four 7/16-inch bolts that secure it to the differential. Use an 8-mm 6-point socket to remove the 1980–1981 4-speed driveshafts. On 1980–1981 automatic transmissions, remove driveshafts with a 1/4-inch 12-point socket. Make sure the wrench is fully engaged before turning the bolt to prevent stripping the bolt. Use an 8-mm 6-point socket to remove the 1982 automatic transmission driveshaft.

Hoist the engine/transmission out of the frame. Unbolt and remove the transmission from the engine bellhousing. Mount the engine on an engine stand. Place the transmission on wooden blocks next the engine. The engine stand should be strong and stable enough to transport your engine to an engine overhaul shop if it needs serious rebuilding or freshening.

The engine, transmission, driveshaft, and fuel tank have been safely removed from the frame. It is now time to raise the frame to begin removing the front and rear suspension components. Use a four-point hydraulic lift, safety stands, or an overhead block and tackle. A four-point lift is the easiest because it raises the frame high enough to reach all of the underneath bolts and components.

Starting at the front locate and remove the 9/16-inch upper shock mounting nuts. Locate and remove the 1/2-inch lower front shock mounting bolts on the underside of the front control arms. Remove the two front shocks from their mounting locations and bag and tag them for reinstallation or add them to your parts lists if they cannot be reused.

Use a hydraulic lift or a floor jack to raise the frame off the floor. If the frame is on a lift, secure it to the arms of the lift to help keep it steady. If using a floor jack, secure it with safety stands. Locate and remove the two 1/2-inch bolts that secure the lower shock to the lower control arm.

Front Suspension Removal

The C3 front suspension design is very similar to that of other passenger cars of that era. The upper and lower control arms are stamped steel and are secured to the frame with bolts, brackets, and bushings. A coil spring is located between the upper and lower control arms. A cast-steel steering knuckle is secured to the control arms with ball joints. The knuckle holds the wheel spindle, wheel bearings, brakes, steering, and anti-roll bar fittings.

When disassembling the suspension take great care as the coil spring is compressed and under pressure. You cannot allow the compressed spring to slip because it could cause serious injury.

Front Shocks

The front shocks are located inside the upper and lower control arms in the front suspension. The shocks are secured with three bolts and because of the way the suspension is designed, the opening in the

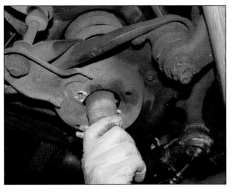

Once the upper and lower shock bolts have been removed carefully pull the shock out of the suspension control arms from below. If it is reusable, tag and bag it for future reassembly or place this part on your order list.

lower control arm limits the size of a replacement shock. Pay particular attention to the size and condition of the shocks during the removal process. Make sure any replacements that you are considering fit into this opening before ordering new ones.

Anti-Roll Bar

Anti-roll bars help prevent the Corvette from leaning too severely during hard corning. Large bars on the front and rear reduce this tendency, but can produce a harsher ride if they are too stiff. Spring rate and shock absorber damping also deter-

The front anti-roll bar is secured with two end links. Remove the two 9/16-inch nuts on the top of each link. Remove the links from the lower control arm and the four 1/2- or 9/16-inch bolts (depending on what year the car is) that secure the bar to the frame. Use an impact wrench or 1/2-inch-drive ratchet to remove the four 9/16-inch bolts (two on each side) from the front frame rails. (These bolts are subjected to corrosion in northern states and can be very stubborn to remove. Treat them with WD-40 or Liquid Wrench to loosen them.) Remove the two lower anti-roll bar links from the lower control arm.

mine your car's ride quality. Think carefully about how you will be using your Corvette. For example, will you use it as a daily driver, weekend

If the bolts are badly corroded, it may be necessary to use a cutoff wheel to remove the anti-roll bar bracket. A torch is not recommended as it might damage the bolt holes. The remaining part of the bolt has to be drilled and taken out with an easy out. Use a liberal amount of lubricant for this.

cruiser, autocrosser, or a road racer at your local racetrack? Your decision impacts how stiff or soft you want your suspension to ride. The base suspension from the factory is the softest; the F41 or FE7 optional suspensions are the firmest.

Small-block Corvettes were equipped with front anti-roll bars if they were not ordered with the optional F41 or FE7 sport suspension packages. Big-block cars featured a rear anti-roll bar. The rear bar improves handling in tight turns and is usually a worthy addition if your car is not equipped with one. Many aftermarket performance companies offer a wide variety of replacement anti-roll bars. A good size to start with for a C3 is a 1-1/8-inch bar in the front and a 3/4-inch bar in the rear. This size is a good compromise between a reasonably compliant ride and precise cornering capabilities.

Smaller front bars increase body roll but produce a smoother ride. However, if you are happy with the way your car handles and it is not equipped with a rear anti-roll bar stick with this setup, but install new rubber bushings.

Steering Hardware

Corvettes built between 1968 and 1975 were equipped with manual or power-assisted steering (N41). Starting in 1976, the base price was increased to include this option as standard equipment. However, 173 Corvettes delivered in 1976 did not have power steering. All 1978–1982 Corvettes were equipped with N41 as part of their standard equipment.

The manual steering system is connected on each front suspension knuckle with a tie rod end. A series of rods are connected and one rod is

This a view of the various rods that make the 1968–1982 system operate. This car is equipped with power steering; the steering-assist valve and hydraulic hoses are connected to a pump in the engine bay.

Newer Corvettes are equipped with a rack-and-pinion steering system that is less complicated than the ones found on C3s.

To remove the cotter key that secures the tie-rod nut to the rear of the steering knuckle, use a pair of pliers to crimp together the cotter key ends. Tap the cotter key out of the nut with a small hammer. The nut is located on the suspension upright. Apply the correct force with a mallet to break the tie rod from the knuckle.

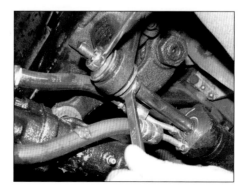

On Corvettes with power steering, the steering box swing arm is attached to the power valve with a 3/4-inch nut. Remove the cotter key prior to removing the nut from the shaft. The shaft usually falls free with a light tap.

Disconnect the power steering hydraulic lines and drain them during the body/frame removal process. The power steering power ram is connected to the frame with a 9/16-inch nut. To remove it, place a 9/16-inch wrench on the outside nut while holding the rod with a 1/2-inch wrench. This prevents the rod from turning while the nut is being loosened.

connected to the steering box swing arm. It is secured with a 3/4-inch nut and held in place with a cotter key. Cars equipped with power steering have an additional hydraulic ram that is connected to the frame for support and needs to be removed from the frame during disassembly. A power valve is connected to the steering swing arm and is also secured with a 3/4-inch nut.

Steering Box

The steering box is located on the left side of the frame rail right behind the upper control arm. This heavy unit is attached to the frame with three bolts. Most of these boxes usually need an overhaul to eliminate play in the steering caused by high mileage or spirited driving.

This is a perfect time to look into buying a refurbished unit. Many specialty shops can rebuild your old unit or exchange it for one that has been refurbished.

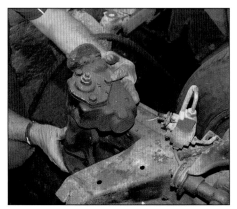

Three 9/16-inch nuts secure the steering box to the frame. Use a 9/16-inch socket with an impact wrench to remove these nuts. After the nuts have been removed, rock the steering box back and forth to release it from the frame. Use caution when removing this component as it is fairly heavy. Get a firm grip on it and be sure your feet are clear during this step.

Brake Calipers

All C3 Corvettes are equipped with four-piston disc brake calipers in the front and rear. A 1/4-inch hose feeds fluid to the calipers, which are held in place with two bolts at each wheel. These calipers left the factory without stainless-steel inserts and were prone to rusting and leaking early in their life. In 1965 an aftermarket vendor developed a process to insert stainless-steel sleeves into each piston cylinder, which pretty much solved this leaking problem. If the brakes are not leaking, they probably have these inserts. Refurbished calipers feature stainless-

steel inserts along with new pistons, seals, and gaskets.

Front Steering Knuckles

Each front suspension upper and lower control arm is connected to a steering knuckle at the top and bottom. This knuckle serves several purposes: braking, steering, and connecting the suspension. These sturdy units rarely need replacing unless they are bent or the spindle is rusted or damaged.

After the knuckles have been removed, carefully inspect them for any flaws. Replacement units are available. Be sure to save all of the bolts and mark them accordingly.

Use an open-end wrench to remove the 1/4-inch brake lines from the front calipers. Have a container or rag ready to collect any brake fluid that might spill out of the line once it is removed from the caliper. Use a ratchet and socket to remove the two 5/8-inch bolts that secure the front brake caliper to the suspension upright. Slide the front brake rotors off their spindles to remove them. This is a good time to remove the front brake rotors. Sometimes these rotors are secured with rivets. If they are, drill the rivets out prior to removal.

Front Suspension Spring Removal

1 Position Frame and Floor Jack

Place a floor jack under the lower control arm. Raise the floor jack. This prevents the coil spring from coming loose during suspension disassembly. Leave about 1 inch of clearance between the jack and the lower control arm. This allows room for the suspension to clear the upper ball joint when the bolt is loosened. Leave the upper ball joint nut on the stud to prevent the spring from exiting its spring cradle.

Double-check to make sure the frame is properly secured.

The next steps are easier if the engine is installed or several helpers are sitting on the frame to add weight.

2 Remove Ball Joint

After removing the cotter pin from the upper ball joint nut, use a 3/4-inch wrench to loosen but not remove the nut from the ball joint. Strike the front suspension steering knuckle with a mallet until it drops onto the 3/4-inch ball joint nut.

Continue to keep the floor jack firmly up against the lower control arm after the knuckle drops down onto the bolt. This prevents the spring from breaking free of the upper ball joint.

Keep the spring in its mounted position until it's time to remove it. A spring that slips during this process can cause serious injury, so exercise the utmost caution. Don't take chances with your safety.

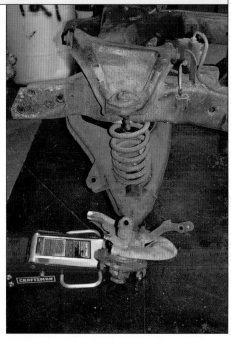

Raise the jack high enough to allow removal of the 3/4-inch ball joint nut. Once the nut has been removed, slowly lower the jack until the steering knuckle is free from the ball joint. Lower the knuckle (shown). Now lower the jack to the fully down position, but do not remove it.

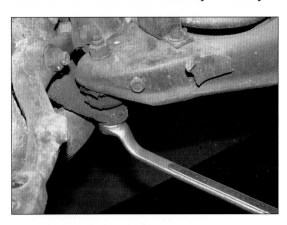

Use a 7/8-inch wrench to remove the lower control arm ball joint nut. Again do not forget to extract the cotter key prior to taking the nut off.

3 Remove Spring

Carefully grab the spring to determine if it is loose in the upper and lower control arm housing. If it is loose enough, remove it (shown). Do not force it if it is not loose. The bottom control arm needs to be lowered. If the control arm is difficult to lower, loosen the two 5/8-inch bolts on the front and rear of the control arm bushings. You do not want this spring under any tension. If it is free remove it from the control arms.

Once the spring is free, use the jack to raise the suspension knuckle back to the top ball joint stud and reattach the 3/4-inch nut, turning it about four turns. Lower the jack. Strike the lower ball joint with a mallet until the upright is free from the lower control arm. Now the top nut can be removed along with the upright. Again, be careful when removing this part as it is a heavy unit.

Control Arm Removal

Upper Control Arm

A floating arm is attached to the upper steel stamped control arm, which uses rubber (factory) or poly (aftermarket) bushings. Two bolts secure the shaft in place. The shaft has two holes so two bolts can be put through them to attach the arm to the frame. Nuts secure the arm to the frame. Place shims between each shaft and frame to align the front suspension. Straight frames usually have one or two shims at each bolt. If you find an excessive number of shims, the frame may be damaged. If you notice a lot of shims on one side of the car, the frame's condition can be verified when it is completely disassembled and put on a frame alignment rack. The correct measurements can be provided by Van Steel or your local body shop.

Repeat this process on the other side of the front suspension. The top of the coil spring is held in place with this unit.

Lower Control Arm

The lower control arm is also made of stamped steel and features a steel shaft supported by rubber or poly bushings. The bushings are screwed into the shaft at each end with bolts holding it together. This arm serves as the resting place for the bottom of the coil spring. It is also used to attach the bottom of the shock absorber.

The anti-roll bar also attaches to the lower control arm. The arm fits into two metal channels under

Use a long pry bar with a tapered end to remove the control arm shaft off the bolts that secure it to the frame. Once the control arm has been removed, tap the two upper control arm bolts out of the frame and tag and bag them for reassembly if they are undamaged.

The upper control arm shaft bolts need to be removed with an 11/16-inch wrench on the inside and a 5/8-inch nut on the tire side of the control arm. Determine how many alignment sleeves are stacked between the control arm shaft and frame. Make a note on how many there are and where they are located. This can help determine if the frame is damaged. If there are too many shims on one side the chassis is probably bent.

Now that the upper control arm has been removed it's time to remove the lower control arm. Loosen the front and back 5/8-inch bushing bolts. This enables the control arm to move up or down. Three bolts secure this control arm to the underside of the frame. Two 5/8-inch bolts are in the front and a 13/16-inch top bolt secured by a 7/8-inch nut is located in the rear. These must all be removed.

Once the bolts have been removed the control arm can be removed from the frame. Make sure that the suspension bolts have been completely removed from the frame before attempting to remove the arm from the frame.

Place sandbags above the differential and make sure the frame is secure before removing the rear transverse spring. You do not want the frame to bounce off the lift or safety stands.

Attach a pair of locking pliers under the rear spring near a left or right shackle bolt. Place a floor jack under the locking pliers and raise the jack until the shackle bolt spins freely. When the shackle bolt spins freely, you have adequately compressed that side of the spring. (In this photo, a small pipe and a floor jack are used). Use a 13/16-inch wrench on the top and remove the 7/8-inch nut on the bottom. Repeat this process on the opposite side. If you're not comfortable performing this procedure on your own, take the car to a professional shop.

Sometimes the shackle bolts and nuts are too badly corroded and cannot be loosened. If all else fails use a torch to quickly burn through the bolt. Or use an angle grinder and a cutting disc to cut off the nuts. Keep a safe distance during this procedure.

Remove the four 13/16-inch bolts securing the rear leaf spring to the frame. Make sure the jack is securely holding the spring, because if it slips while supporting the spring injury could occur. It is a good idea to get a second person to help hold the spring as these four bolts are removed because the spring suddenly falls once the bolts have been removed. Use caution during this step.

the frame below the engine. A small metal plate sits on top of the lower frame at the front flange. The front two bolts on the control arm shaft are bolted to this plate.

Rear Suspension Removal

In 1963, General Motors introduced the first independent rear suspension system on the Corvette, and the design was carried over and fitted to all C3 models. It features two stamped-steel trailing arms that are held in place with a single bolt at the front of the wheel well. The trailing arms house the parking brake, brake rotor, shock absorber mount, and rear spring attachment points. A transverse multi-leaf steel spring is bolted to the differential and connected to each trailing arm with a link. In 1981 automatic Corvettes with standard suspension were equipped with the new fiberglass-reinforced transverse rear spring; it became a standard spring material for the front and rear of all 1984 and later Corvettes.

Rear Leaf Spring

All C3 Corvettes left the factory with three types of rear springs. Two were metal and were offered in nine leaves for standard suspension cars and seven leaves for heavy-duty applications. The third type was a fiberglass-reinforced rear spring that became available in 1981 for cars with automatic transmissions and standard suspensions. The metal springs were bundled together in the middle and bolted to the rear differential with four bolts. These springs are very heavy and can cause serious injury if not handled correctly.

Before removing a spring, check to see if the rear of the car is sagging on one side or the other. This could indicate bad adjustment on the end links, spring weakness, or metal failure. These springs are very strong and rarely fail, but failure is possible so it's best to check them now. Look for cracking in the spring surface, bent leaves, or severe rust that has worked its way through the metal.

Rear Shocks

The rear shocks perform an important function in the operation of the rear suspension. The lower shock mounting is attached at the rear of the trailing arm and the top is bolted to the frame. Both attachment points help control the move-

ment of the rear spring and trailing arm travel.

Tire technology has made giant leaps forward since these cars left the factory. A good set of shocks can help your C3 handle the improved traction capabilities of new tire technology.

Strut Rod Removal

1 Remove Lower Shock Cotter Pin

Use a pliers to flatten and remove the cotter pin from the lower rear shock mount bolt. Use a 15/16-inch socket to remove the nut.

2 Remove Lower Shock Nut

Use a 3/4-inch wrench to remove the nut from the mount. The lower part of the rear shock can be removed from the shock mount.

3 Pry Shock Mount from Trailing Arm

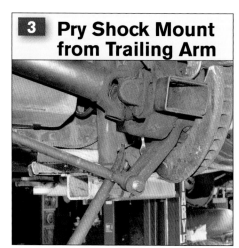

Place a large pry bar between the shock and the strut rod to begin removing the shock mount from the trailing arm assembly. This shock mount needs to be completely removed before the trailing arm can be released.

4 Drive Shock Mount from Trailing Arm

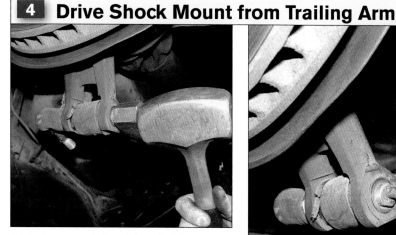

Attach a special nut (available at most Corvette supply stores) to the shock mount stud to prevent damaging the threads on the mount. Once the nut is installed, use a mallet to strike the nut until it is flush with the rear suspension upright.

Once the nut is flush, remove it and place a large center punch onto the middle of the bolt. Strike the bolt with a mallet until the shock mount is completely free from the suspension upright.

5 Pull Trailing Arm from Suspension

Apply upward pressure on the trailing arm to release the strut rod from the suspension. Pull the strut rods straight down to the vertical position to prepare for the next step.

6 Mark Strut Rod Washers and Nuts

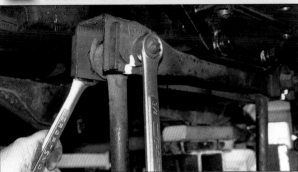

Before removing the strut rods apply a dab of paint to the bracket and the strut rod washers, so the washers and nuts can be returned to the same side during reassembly.

The washers adjust the rear suspension camber settings. Marking them with paint saves the previous settings (if they were correct). Use two 3/4-inch wrenches to remove the strut rod bolts from the bracket.

Half-Shafts

The independent rear suspension on C3 Corvettes is far different than a solid axle rear suspension in a muscle car. The Corvette trailing arms are connected to the rear differential with two axles called half-shafts. A U-joint is attached to each end of the half-shaft. This allows the shaft to move up and down with the suspension movement. (Big-block cars use larger bolts to compensate for the extra torque of those engines. However, the design philosophy is identical.) When removing these units, carefully inspect the universal joints for signs of rust and grinding as you rotate them. They should be completely free of noise and rust. If they have any of these indications replace them.

Use a 5/8-inch socket to secure the outboard trailing arm half-shaft on 1968–1979 cars; they are held in place with French tabs. Soak the bolts with WD-40 or another thread lubricant if they are corroded and frozen. In extreme situations, heat may need to be applied with a propane torch. These tabs must be bent straight prior to removing these bolts. Save this French tab assembly so it can be reused during reassembly.

The 1980–1981 automatic transmission half-shafts are secured to the trailing arm with 1/4-inch 12-point bolts. The 1980–1981 cars with 4-speed transmissions use 8-mm bolts to secure their half-shafts to the trailing arms. Automatic transmission 1982 cars are secured with 8-mm bolts.

Use a 5/8-inch wrench to remove the rear brake caliper bolts. Check to determine if the rear rotors are held in place with rivets. If they are, they must be drilled out prior to rotor removal.

Once the rear caliper has been removed the parking brake cable connector must be released from the U-shaped bracket. The bracket and cable are next to the caliper bolt hole (arrows). When the rotor has been removed, the parking brake assembly is exposed.

Brake Calipers and Rotors

Two large bolts hold each brake caliper in place. Each caliper is purpose-built for the wheel it is attached to, and you should always inspect each one for leaks before removal. You need to completely remove the calipers from the car.

With the caliper still attached, place the end of the brake hose into a plastic bottle. Push each caliper piston flush with the bore to evacuate the old fluid from the caliper. After all of the fluid is removed, seal the plastic container and dispose of it at a recycling center. Brake fluid is caustic so be very careful not to spill any during this process. If you spill it on a painted surface, it may remove the paint.

Most rotors can be removed easily unless they have been riveted. If they are riveted, drill the rivets out prior to attempting to remove them. Remember, the parking brake assembly is located beneath the rear rotor.

Differential

The differential is one of the bulkiest components to remove. Made of heavy cast metal, it is built to withstand all of the abuse and power sent to the rear wheels. It is easiest to remove while it is still attached to part of the frame, but out of the car.

Differential and Driveshaft Removal

1 Remove Nuts

Remove the nuts that secure the half-shafts to the differential. Two attachment methods are used to secure the shaft to the differential. One is a heavy-duty cap on high-horsepower cars. The other uses a U-bolt (shown) on low-horsepower cars. Use a 9/16-inch socket or wrench to remove them.

2 Remove Pinion Mounting Bolt

Use a 5/8-inch wrench on the top and an 11/16-inch socket on the bottom of the front pinion-mounting bolt to remove the bolt. The differential is resting on the frame and once the nut is removed the bolt should be easy to remove.

3 Remove Differential

Place a floor jack under the center of the differential and firmly support it because you don't want it to hit the garage floor and sustain damage. Loosen but do not remove the two 5/8-inch bolts that are under the transverse frame. These two bolts hold the differential in place. Use a long pry bar to work the frame loose from the side rails. Once it is loose, make sure the jack is supporting the frame. Now remove the two 5/8-inch bolts. At this stage, the floor jack is supporting the differential, so be careful.

Slowly lower the jack to release the differential from the frame. Once it has cleared the frame, roll the unit out and store it in a safe location for further disassembly. Keep in mind that the Corvette differential weighs 105 pounds, so it takes some muscle to lift it off the jack.

Rear Trailing Arms

One large bolt holds each of the two rear trailing arms in place. Located in front of the wheel well, this bolt serves as a pivot point for suspension movement and alignment settings. Steel shims are used to adjust the rear toe on the trailing arms, so you should pay particular attention when removing these arms from the frame. Make a note of the amount and thickness of these shims when they are removed.

Trailing Arm Removal

1 Remove Trailing Arm Fasteners

A 5/8-inch bolt holds each rear trailing arm in place. This bolt runs from the inside to the outside of the rear frame in front of the rear wheels. An 11/16-inch nut holds the bolt in place and it is located on the outside of the frame; it's held in place with a cotter pin. Use a pliers and hammer to drive out the cotter pin from the nut before removing the trailing arm bolt. Use a 5/8-inch wrench on the inside and an 11/16-inch wrench on the outside to remove the nut.

2 Remove Trailing Arm Bolt

Once the nut has been removed, strike the bolt with a mallet to drive the bolt through the frame. This exposes the head of the bolt to allow enough room to wedge it out of the frame on the inside. This bolt needs to be completely free of the frame before you can remove the trailing arm.

3 Pry Out Trailing Arm Bolt

Place a notched pry bar on the exposed trailing arm bolt. Rock the pry bar back and forth to work the bolt out of the frame. You may have to place a wrench between the frame and the pry bar to get more leverage to get the bolt completely out of the frame.

4 Separate Trailing Arm from Frame

Once the bolt has been freed, remove the trailing arm from the frame. If the trailing arms are not bent or damaged, suspension companies can restore them. They can repair, sandblast, powdercoat, and install new bearings for minimal cost.

Remaining Frame Parts Removal

The fuel and brake lines need to be completely removed along with the parking brake cable and pulleys. Make sure all bolts have been removed before continuing.

Frame Evaluation

Most Corvette specialty shops price their frame repairs based on how many original parts can be refurbished and the condition of the frame. If the suspension components are in good condition, they can be reconditioned and reused. Parts that cannot be reconditioned must be replaced with new parts. This includes bearings, fuel/brake lines, and rubber bushings.

A shop can usually remove the suspension, sandblast/powdercoat the frame, refurbish parts, and reinstall

Your completely disassembled C3 frame should look like this when you are finished. All brake lines, fuel lines, and securing hardware have been removed. This frame is now ready to be inspected for damage, repaired, and made ready for reinstallation.

Shops use a frame alignment rack to determine if frame measurements are within factory specifications. The rack allows the operator to verify front, rear, top, and length measurements. This is done with dial indicators, levels, and a variety of other frame tools. Any measurement out of spec can be corrected.

These measurements can be made at home without a frame alignment rack. You just need a completely flat floor surface. (Use a level to confirm that the floor is flat.) Place the frame on four scissor jacks. Use a tape measure to make sure the frame is straight. You can then take your frame to a shop for straightening.

the refurbished parts in about three weeks. If you do the work yourself, your frame can be repaired, sand/bead blasted and powdercoated in a much shorter time at a greatly reduced cost.

Common problem areas on C3 frames include the underside of the front crossmember. Damage occurs in this area when contact is made with a curb or a manhole cover. Rust often develops after it is damaged.

Rust is also a problem on frames that come from colder areas with salt-laden roads. It is often found where the main frame connects to the rails that support the rear suspension. Rust around the body bolt mounts is common, particularly on those located under the windshield post. Also carefully check the two rear mounts behind the rear wheels as they receive a lot of moisture. Almost any damaged frame

can be repaired thanks to the large availability of new old stock (NOS) frame parts.

Straighten Damaged Frame Sections

Once the frame has been disassembled, inspect for damage and trueness. A steel brush is used to locate and clean off the serial number. This is a good way to find out if the serial number or VIN matches the VIN plate on the body. If it doesn't match, the frame is not original. This means it is not a numbers-matching car and cannot be resold as one.

Closely inspect the lower control arm mounts that are welded to the rear of the front crossmember under

the engine. These are prone to breaking welds and must be repaired. A straight, aluminum, boxed bar cut to 26-3/8 inches is used to determine if the front frame cradle is bent. Again this is a common problem and can be corrected on a frame alignment rack.

As I mentioned earlier, the front subframe on a C3 Corvette can bottom out on curbs, manhole covers, and other road anomalies and incur damage. The damaged subframe section can be removed and the surrounding metal repaired. A new replacement section can be installed once the old part is removed and the surrounding area is ground smooth. After a new section is installed and the weld marks are ground down, the repair becomes invisible.

The rear frame rails were replaced on this chassis. The frame rail section was welded to an insert and lined up on the frame alignment rack to verify it meets factory specifications. A professional shop should perform this work so the frame rail maintains its integrity. If the weld should crack or the frame rail fail while in use, it could cause a serious or catastrophic accident. Therefore, do not perform this repair at home.

Another common frame area to closely inspect is the front lower control arm brackets. These brackets are welded to the frame and are prone to breaking; they must be repaired prior to reinstallation. It is very difficult to properly align the car with these damaged brackets. You should not see any cracks around the welds that secure these brackets to the lower frame.

This view shows how a smaller frame section was used to support the new rail that is being installed. Both sides were completely welded (top to bottom) to provide the correct frame strength. The finished welds were ground down to provide a seamless repair.

This is what the frame rail repair looks like on the bottom of the frame. When this work is completed it will have a factory appearance and have fully regained its original strength.

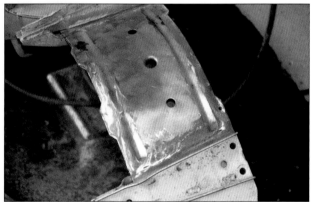

The lowest part of the C3 frame is the cradle under the engine. This part often receives damage from manhole covers and road debris. If the damage is extensive a Corvette restoration shop can completely cut the damaged section out and replace it with an NOS part. Once again, a professional shop should perform this repair.

All frames are placed on a frame alignment rack before they are powdercoated. The correct measurements can be found at your local body shop or by calling Van Steel to determine if the frame meets factory specifications.

Rust Repair

Rust is the common enemy of steel parts on C3 Corvette frames. Water usually collects near the wheels and over time the frame rusts. Each rusted section can be replaced by welding a new NOS section into place. All welding should be done on the frame alignment rack to verify the frame alignment is correct. New sections are reinforced with smaller steel box inserts, tack welded together into place, and then stitch welded to ensure the structure is strong. This returns the frame to its original design strength. After installation the welds are ground down and the surface is prepared for bead blasting and painting.

Paint or Powdercoating Preparation

There are two methods for stripping the finish off the frame: media blasting and acid dipping. You must pick one before the frame is painted or powdercoated.

Bead blasting removes all the frame's surface rust and some off the rust inside the frame rails.

Media blasting removes all rust and scaly paint on the outside off the frame. Tree bark is the media of choice because it does not pit the metal. The finished product looks as if it were covered with primer, but it is not. The bead blasting process only cleans the outside surfaces of the metal. Finished bead-blasted

Once the frame measurements have been verified or corrected and all rust damage is repaired the frame is ready to be cleaned. (Walnut shells, soda, or tree bark are acceptable media for this task.) The media strips and cleans the surface, like the ones shown in the photo. Or you can acid dip the frame, which is a more thorough and less time-consuming process. The decision as to which process to use should be based on the condition of the frame. After the frame is sandblasted or acid dipped, it should be pressure washed to remove all dirt and grease from the surfaces.

frames should be acid washed and oven dried before they are painted or powdercoated.

Heavily rusted frames or those that have had new sections welded into place should be acid dipped. Usually acid dipping is double the cost of bead blasting, but is a very advanced method for completely cleaning metal, such as a corroded Corvette frame. Most acid dipping shops use new products that are biodegradable. Few shops perform this work so you may have to do a little research to find one nearby. If one is not close you can ship your frame to them.

The correct process does not remove any metal, only corrosion, grease, and dirt. Because the acid is a liquid it covers all the inside and outside parts of the frame. When the acid dipping process is complete shops wash the frame with water to dissolve the acid. When the frame is returned, handle it with gloves to prevent body oils from rusting the exposed metal on the frame. If you decide to paint the frame or powdercoat it, find a shop that acid washes and bakes out the moisture before applying paint.

Powdercoating is my choice to protect the frame because it uses an electrical charge that applies a powder to cover all exposed metal. It is less prone to chip and peel and has proven to be very durable.

Powdercoating shops offer a wide variety of colors. When the powdercoating process is done, the frame has a high gloss or satin appearance. If you want an NCRS finish on the frame it should be lightly sanded

Acid Processes

Don't get confused by the terms acid washing and acid dipping. They are two different processes. The dipping immerses the entire frame in a solution to strip off rust and any contaminants. The washing is done to a frame that hangs on a rack and does not fully immerse it into a solution. After the frame is acid washed, a powdercoating shop puts it into an oven for 30 minutes at 400 degrees F to remove all of the remaining acid and moisture. ∎

When the washing process is complete, the parts should be put into an oven and baked for 10 minutes at 400 degrees F to eliminate all moisture. This is how the parts appear after they have been cleaned and baked in the oven.

A DPS Powder Coating technician applied black powdercoat material to two C3 frames. The powder is electrically charged and the frame is grounded, which enables material to cling to the metal. The powder is shot so that it completely covers both the inside and outside of the frame.

and sprayed with the correct NCRS satin black paint to replicate the original finish.

Once a color is selected, the powdercoating shop uses high-pressure washers to remove any particles left over from cleaning. The pressure washer is inserted into the box sections of the frame to remove any dirt or grease that may have been missed.

Once the washing is complete the frame is put into an oven for 10 minutes and baked at 400 degrees F until all of the moisture is removed.

Next, the frame is horizontally mounted on a rolling rack, and pushed into a spray booth. The operator inserts a vibrating tube into a large box of powder. Air hoses push the powder into a gun located in the spray booth. The operator applies the powder to the grounded frame with an electrically charged spray gun. The operator ensures that the powder is blown into all crevices on the frame.

Once the appropriate amount of powder has been applied, the rack is rolled into a high-temperature (400 degrees F) oven and baked for

10 minutes. After the baking is complete the frame is removed from the oven and placed into a cooldown area. After the frame cools it is carefully inspected to ensure it has no blemishes.

The finished frame is returned to the frame alignment rack to make sure no damage occurred during the cleaning and powdercoating process. Once it passes inspection it is ready for the owner to pick it up and begin the rebuilding process.

After the frame has been removed from the powdercoating process and is cool enough to touch it is time to load it and make its journey home. This frame has been inspected and a semigloss black finish added.

Once the frame is completely covered with the powder, it is rolled into an oven. This powdercoating rack at DPS holds two C3 frames are baked at 400 degrees F for 10 minutes. This causes the powder to adhere to all of the frame's metal surfaces.

SUSPENSION AND DIFFERENTIAL REASSEMBLY

At this stage, the frame has been inspected, repaired, and finished. All of the light rust damage has been repaired. Any accident damage or rust that has eaten through the frame has been cut out. New parts have been welded into place by a professional Corvette repair shop. This is the perfect time to install refurbished or rebuilt components.

Place the frame in a low-traffic and well-lit area so it can be safely reassembled. Placing it on a large piece of non-shag gray (or any light color) carpet makes it easier to locate dropped parts. The carpet stops parts from bouncing under a table or into a small crevice. Place the frame on four safety stands that are sturdy and protected with pieces of cardboard.

Set up several large tables so assembly parts can be laid out in their correct order. This saves a lot of time during the reassembly process when trying to locate the next part to install onto the frame.

Front Suspension

The front suspension is the perfect place to start reassembling

the foundation of your C3. Simply reverse the disassembly procedure discussed in Chapter 6.

Tubular upper and lower aftermarket control arms are available from Corvette suppliers such as Van Steel. These parts reduce the unsprung weight of your front suspension and are just as strong as the stamped-steel factory parts. However,

if you are just going to use your car for cruising and not racing the factory parts work very well.

Component Evaluation

This is a good time to refurbish or replace the steel control arms. Several well-known Corvette specialty shops offer like-new components at a competitive price that includes

A C3 Corvette's differential is the centerpiece of the car's rear suspension. The differential is solidly mounted to the frame and is connected to the engine with a driveshaft. The transverse leaf spring bolts to the differential and is connected to the rear suspension trailing arms. All of these components should be evaluated, inspected, and repaired or replaced as necessary.

---

a warranty. Each part is cleaned, inspected for cracks, aligned, and powdercoated. New ball joints with rubber or polyurethane bushings are included in the rebuild process. These control arms come ready for installation. In my opinion, this is money well spent.

However, if this is not in your budget, at a minimum you need to replace the ball joints and the rubber bushings.

This is also a good time to steam clean the parts and repaint or powdercoat before reinstallation.

Now that the frame has been returned to your work area, reconfirm your factory frame measurements. To take the desired measurements, refer to the top right photo on page 87. The frame is light enough for two people to carry it to your work area for assembly.

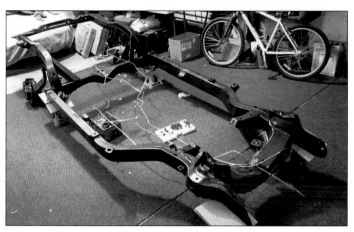

This frame has been carefully placed on four safety stands and four large pieces of cardboard to protect the frame from any scratches. The large gray carpet remnant makes the reassembly process more comfortable and dropped parts are more easily found. Start gathering various bits and pieces, such as small bolts and brake and fuel lines, and place them in your work area.

Van Steel uses this square piece of aluminum cut to the proper specification to measure the distance between the two upper control arm brackets. The correct measurement is 26-3/8 inches. This is an important area to reinspect before you start installing your parts because the crosspiece that runs under the engine is prone to bending. Any mismeasurement makes it difficult to align the chassis correctly. The two rear lower control arm attachments must also be securely welded to the frame.

Your completed front suspension should look like this unit, which is installed on a 1980 Corvette. The anti-roll bar has not been installed and is the only missing part in this photo. The upper and lower control arms secure the coil spring. The new shock runs up the middle of the spring and is attached to the upper frame and the lower control arm. This car received a new steering knuckle, wheel bearings, and brake rotor.

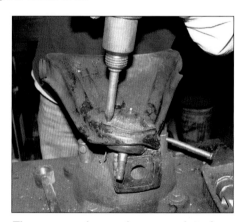

The suspension undergoes a lot of stress, and this is the perfect time to rebuild or refurbish these parts before they are reinstalled. Many Corvette part suppliers sell complete suspension components that have been refurbished. They start the process by disassembling the old parts. The ball joint rivet heads are ground down flush and then chiseled out of the upper control arm with an air chisel.

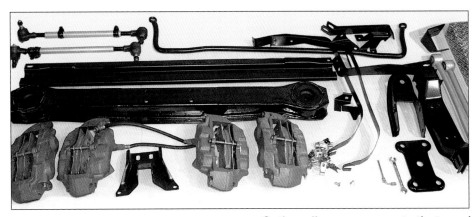

After the bushings, ball joint, and steel shaft have been removed from the control arm, the shop inspects for cracks or other damage. If it meets specifications, it is shot peened to remove all accumulated grime and paint. This process is the best for identifying any cracks. The parts are then sent to the powdercoating shop to have their surfaces covered and protected. Shown here are a front lower control arm (front) and a rear trailing arm (back). Send as many parts as possible to the powdercoating shop in order to get the most for your money.

Gather all necessary parts that need to be installed onto the frame. Large tables are an excellent place to organize these pieces. This helps keep critical parts within easy reach.

Organize and inventory your parts before starting the assembly process. Lay out the critical components of your front suspension assembly as shown. This includes the upper and lower control arms, steering knuckle with brake rotor, installed wheel bearings, and coil spring. The dust caps are used to cover and protect the front wheel bearings.

Upper Control Arms

The upper control arms are used to adjust the car's front suspension caster and camber settings. This is done with thin shims inserted between the frame and the control arm's steel shaft. Do not tighten the two bolts that secure the upper control arm's rubber or poly bushings until the car is ready to be driven. The suspension must have time to settle on the springs before these bolts are tightened. This is a very important step to remember.

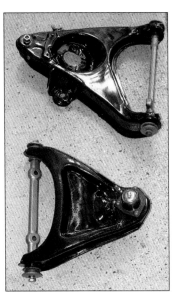

Two 3/8-24 x 7/8-inch bolts secure the steel shafts that are included on the refurbished upper control arms. The upper control arm bushings are now fitted with new rubber units. The lower control arm has also received new ball joints and new bushings. Both are now ready to be installed into the frame.

After the powdercoating has been applied to the control arm, it is returned to the assembly area. A new ball joint is installed and the steel shaft receives new rubber or poly bushings. A piece of wood or a half piece of pipe is placed on the inside of the control arm to keep the arm from bending while the bushings are being pressed into the control arm.

1 Install Bolts

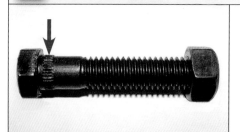

Two 7/16-13 x 2¼-inch bolts secure the upper control arm to the frame. Each bolt has a wedge near the head (arrow) that prevents it from moving once the suspension has been mounted.

Place a long flat bar onto the head of each bolt and hit the bar with enough force to push the head flush against the frame. Don't be afraid to hit the heads forcibly because they are designed for this procedure. Once the bolts have been secured, install the upper control arm bracket.

2 Install Upper Control Arm Bracket

Slide the control arm steel bracket through the two bolts and thread on the 11/16-inch nuts. Do not tighten the nuts yet. The upper control arm rubber bushing bolts should remain loose until the project has been completed. When installing the control arm, don't forget to replace the factory alignment shims (two in the rear and one in the front). Tighten the 11/16-inch locking nuts to 50 ft-lbs.

Lower Control Arms

As with the top control arm, the lower ball joint is bolted to the steering knuckle with one nut. The anti-roll bar end is attached to the lower control arm with a link. A large rubber bumper is attached to the lower control arm. This bumper is designed to hit the lower frame rail if the suspension is fully compressed; this helps avoid damaging any suspension components if a bump is taken too hard. This simple but effective design is very robust and gives long, trouble-free service when maintained properly.

1 Install Bolts

The lower control arm includes a steel shaft and is attached with two 7/16-20 x 1¾-inch bolts at each end of the arm. The shaft is fitted with rubber bushings. Use a 5/8-inch wrench to snug these bolts. Use the same procedure on these bolts as discussed in step 2 above. By leaving them just snug, the arm is able to move up and down freely during the next steps.

2 Install Bolt Screw into Retainer

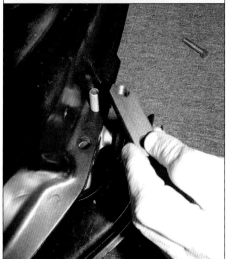

A small retainer at the front of the lower frame holds both front lower control arm bolts in place. The bolts screw into this retainer and you must take extra care not to strip the threads when you secure the steel shaft to the frame. Torque the two front bolts to 70 ft-lbs with a 5/8-inch socket.

3 Install Nut on Control Arm

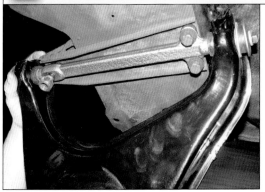

A 9/16x18x2⁵⁄₃₂-inch bolt secures the rear lower control arm to the frame. This bolt has a 13/16-inch head. Insert it through the control arm steel shaft from the top. Attach a nut to the bottom of the bolt using a 7/8-inch socket on the nut and a 13/16-inch wrench on the bolt head and torque it to 100 ft-lbs.

4 Install Control Arms

The upper and lower control arms should look like this once they have been installed. Do not tighten the upper and lower control arm bushing bolts yet. These arms need to be moved up and down during the spring and steering knuckle installation. They will be tightened and torqued when the completed car is sitting on its wheels and ready to drive around the block.

Spring

The 1968–1982 Corvettes use a steel coil spring in the front suspension. The weight and type of engine (small- or big-block) largely determines the spring rate of the particular car. The standard front coil spring is rated at 474 pounds. Cars equipped with a big-block require a firmer spring as does the F-41 sports suspension option. Be sure to select the correct front spring for your particular model and/or application.

Optional equipment, such as air conditioning, also impacts the spring rates that are recommended by the factory. Original-equipment spring rates usually give the best ride if your

The spring should look like this when installed in its correct position. Notice how the end of the coil spring rests in the lower control arm. If it is not properly seated use a pipe wrench to rotate the spring into the correct position.

Place a floor jack under the lower control arm so it rests on the jack. Push the spring up into the upper control arm spring well in the frame. Use a long pry bar or long screwdriver to push the lower part of the spring into the lower spring well. You can also kick it with your shoe to push it into its deep well.

Rotate the spring until the end rests against the lower control arm spring well dimple. Make sure the spring is properly seated in the control arm so it does not slip. Once the spring is securely in both wells, slowly raise the jack to prevent the spring from popping out of the upper and lower spring wells.

only intent is cruising with your restored Corvette. However, if you are going to aggressively drive your Corvette or use it for autocross competition, install a front spring with a higher spring rate.

Remember to buy springs in pairs because each manufacturer has slightly different production methods that affect spring rate and height. The lower control arm has a deep well that supports the bottom of the front suspension coil spring. The control arm has a dimple stamped into it and the end of the bottom coil must rest next to this dimple.

The installation procedure is the same for all front coil springs. It is not difficult but care must be taken to avoid injury to yourself or others.

Steering Knuckle Spindle

The steering knuckle spindle plays a crucial role in front suspen-sion dynamics. It connects the upper and lower control arms via two ball joints. In addition it houses the front wheel bearings, brake rotors, cali-pers, and brake lines. The front steer-ing system connects to the spindle on each side of the car to provide steering to the front wheels. This part takes a lot of stress and should be closely inspected to ensure that it is in excellent condition before installation.

Steering Knuckle Installation

1 Install Knuckle Wheel Bearing Assembly

Install the spindle dust shield gasket onto the spindle. Push the gasket to the back of the spindle. Grease and pack the inner and outer bearings with wheel bearing grease. Push the inner seal onto the spindle assembly. Install the outer bearing and follow that with a flat washer. The flat washer has a notch that matches the one on the spindle to prevent it from turning.

Install the nut and tighten it until the hub barely turns. Loosen it one-quarter turn and install the cotter key. Recheck the adjustment after putting 100 miles on the car.

2 Attach Spindle to Front Suspension

Insert the lower ball joint stud into the opening on the steering knuckle. Use a 1/2-inch-drive torque wrench with a 7/8-inch nut and torque it to 75 ft-lbs.

Be sure the cotter key hole lines up. If it doesn't, adjust the nut until the opening is located. Install a cotter key through the opening and bend back the two wires to prevent the nut from coming loose. Clip off the excess ends with a pair of cutting pliers.

3 Install Steering Knuckle

If you have someone stand on the upper control arm during this procedure, installing the steer-ing knuckle is easier because the suspension is being compressed from above and below.

Slowly raise the jack, while the upper knuckle ball joint opening is placed into the top control arm ball joint stud. Observe the coil spring and make sure it stays securely in its upper and lower wells. It must not slip because it can cause injury if it does.

Once the knuckle has been pushed into the ball joint stud, secure it with a 3/4-inch nut and torque to 45 ft-lbs. Once this nut is secure, your helper can exit his or her perch on the frame.

If the cotter key hole doesn't line up, adjust the nut until the hole is located. Install a cotter key through the hole and bend the two wires back to prevent the nut from coming loose (as you did on the lower ball joint). Clip off any excess wire with a pair of cutting pliers.

Slowly lower the jack to see if the upper and lower control arms securely hold the coil spring in place. Once the spring has been secured, remove the jack. Use two 11/16–16 x 7/8-inch bolts to attach the front caliper bracket and dust shield to the knuckle. Torque these bolts to 70 ft-lbs with a 5/8-inch socket.

4 Inspect Steering Knuckle

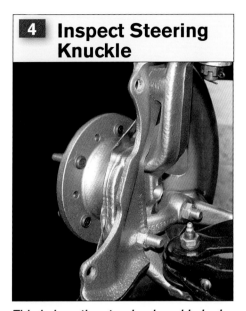

This is how the steering knuckle looks when it is properly secured to the upper and lower control arms.

5 Install Dust Shield

Install the wheel bearing dust cap along with the caliper bracket and dust shield.

Bump Stop

The bump stop is a triangle of rubber mounted to a metal bracket. This bracket is attached to the lower control arm on each side of the front suspension. The bump stop protects

Once the spring has been correctly installed, install the lower control arm bump stop. Use two 1/2-inch bolts and two 1/2-inch nuts to secure the rubber bump stop to the lower control arm. Torque these bolts to 35 ft-lbs. These bump stops play a very important role in protecting the suspension in case you hit an unexpected bump too fast and the suspension bottoms out. These rubber bushing are strong enough to absorb the impact under most conditions.

a severe bump or hole in the road. These are fairly inexpensive and it is a good idea to install fresh bump stops when putting the front suspension together.

Shock Absorbers

The shock absorber is inserted from the bottom of the lower control arm and secured with two bolts in the front suspension. It uses rubber

bushings and washers to minimize noise in the car. They are attached to the frame between the upper control arms with one bolt.

As a general rule, shock absorbers do not have a long life. Depending on your driving style and the type of shock installed, expect to get 15,000 to 30,000 miles on a new set. Original-spec shocks have a service life that's at the lower range of this estimate, while premium aftermarket shocks last at the upper range.

Aftermarket suppliers offer a wide range of C3 Corvette shock absorbers. Some even include multi-step adjustments to dial in the ride you want. For autocross or track day events, set the shocks on the firmest setting as this provides the best handling. Just be sure to dial them down after you are finished playing or your fillings might fall out.

Shocks lose their effectiveness slowly, so keep this mileage in mind when you are budgeting for maintenance.

Steering Box

The steering box contains worm gears that turn the Pitman

Install the lower washer and rubber bushing onto the shock shaft. Feed the shock through the bottom of the lower control arm and insert the top of the shaft into the opening on the frame. Push a rubber bushing onto the upper shock strut until it seats against the frame. Add a washer and use a socket and ratchet to tighten the 9/16-inch nut onto the shaft.

Secure the lower shock with two 1/2-inch bolts and torque to 35 ft-lbs. You may have to use a small wrench on the upper shaft to prevent it from turning as you tighten the 9/16-inch nut. Tighten the nut when the rubber has been slightly compressed on the shock shaft. Do not overtighten. Repeat this process on the other side.

Three bolts fasten the steering box to the left side of the frame. Use a torque wrench to secure the box with 9/16-inch bolts and torque to 30 ft-lbs.

This cutaway of a C3 steering box shows the inner workings of this critical part. The large block moves up and down the shaft as the steering wheel is turned. The block is attached to the Pitman arm gear that turns the steering system when it moves back and forth.

Third-generation Corvettes use a series of rods attached to the steering box and the suspension steering knuckles to turn the wheels. Power-assisted versions feature a hydraulic pump that is driven off the engine, and it pushes fluid into a ram that greatly reduces the steering effort.

The ram (shown) is attached to the relay rod. Notice where the relay rod is attached to the passenger-side idler arm sleeve. The tie rod screws into the sleeve and connects to the steering knuckle. The relay rod also connects to the idler arm (far right). The idler arm provides support to the steering system and is connected to the passenger side of the frame.

The ram mounts to the relay rod (right) and connects to a bracket on the frame on the driver's side. Two hydraulic hoses connect to the ram and provide fluid pressure to make the unit operate.

The relay rod connects to the steering box Pitman arm (lower left). This is a manual steering application, which is why power steering components are not seen in this photo.

arm, which is attached to the bottom of the unit. At the top of the box, an adjuster is used to tighten worn gears.

Steering is a vital function for the car's safe operation and a worn or failing steering box needs to be replaced. If your box has high mileage and exhibits free play, it should be exchanged for a refurbished unit with new gears and original equipment adjustments. Refurbished units are fairly inexpensive and return a Corvette's steering to its original responsive feel.

Steering Linkage

The 1968–1982 Corvette steering linkage was first used in the 1963 Stingray. The recirculating ball unit is attached to an arm connected to a relay rod. The relay rod connects

The completed steering system looks like this unit underneath a 1972 Corvette. Notice that it is equipped with power steering. All of the power steering hydraulic hoses are installed.

Two U-shaped brackets that fit over two rubber bushings secure the anti-roll bar to the frame. Four 1/2-inch or 9/16-inch bolts, depending on the year the car was built, fasten the brackets to the frame.

The bolts that you bagged and tagged when you removed this unit should be the correct size. Torque them to 30 ft-lbs.

Connect the anti-roll bar to the lower control arm via an end link on each side of the front suspension. Two 9/16-inch nuts secure the links. Hand tighten until the bushings are slightly compressed. You might have to wait until the weight of the engine compresses the springs enough to install the links, or have some friends sit on the frame to help make the connection.

The trailing arm in this 1969 convertible is being removed so it can be overhauled by Van Steel.

to tie rods on both ends, and those are attached to the steering knuckles. This is how toe-out and toe-in are adjusted on the front suspension. It is a little complex but works very well when adjusted correctly.

A belt drives the power steering pump. The pump is connected to the power valve and the power steering cylinder. The fluid pressure reduces the effort it takes to turn the steering wheel. The seals tend to leak if they sit or have high mileage. Low fluid greatly increases the pressure it takes to turn the wheel and quickly burns out the power steering pump if oil is not added. This should be part of your routine maintenance check under the car.

Anti-Roll Bar

Standard non-performance Corvettes are fitted with a front anti-roll bar that is designed to provide a smooth ride. They are usually 3/4 to 1 inch in circumference. Cars that are equipped with FTL and big blocks are fitted with larger front bars and rear anti-roll bars to help balance the handling.

The aftermarket offers anti-roll bars for both front and rear suspension that are larger and stiffer than the stock anti-roll bars. The larger the bars, the more taut the ride. However, cornering speed is greatly increased with bigger units.

Rear Suspension

The C3 rear suspension was an engineering breakthrough when introduced in 1963 on the C2. The design was so successful that it was carried over for the entire C3 production run with only minor changes. The most important change occurred in 1981 when the factory installed a composite rear leaf spring. These springs were installed on Corvettes built at the new Bowling Green assembly plant. They provided a better ride and reduced the unsprung weight of the rear suspension.

With the C3 rear suspension design, the differential is mounted to the center of the frame and two half-shafts connect to the rear wheels. Two trailing arms are bolted to the frame on each side and held up with a transverse steel spring (1968-1980). The trailing arms house the parking brake, brake calipers, and rotors. The rear shock absorbers are attached to the trailing arms at the bottom and to the frame at the top.

This system greatly improved handling and ride and that is why it was installed on all C3 Corvettes.

Trailing Arms

C3 rear trailing arms are made from boxed steel and welded for strength. One bolt holds these arms in place. Add or remove shims to adjust the toe-in or toe-out of the rear suspension.

When you disassembled the frame, you paid particular attention to how many shims were installed before removing them. Reinstall the suspension with the same number of shims to return it to its previous setting. Even if you use the same shims in the same location, always take your completed Corvette to an alignment shop. A professional can put the correct suspension settings back into your car.

The arms are robust but the bearings are prone to failure. Refurbished trailing arms include new bearings as part of the price. If you are refurbishing these trailing arms yourself it is wise to include new bearings. To reassemble the trailing arms, simply reverse the disassembly procedure discussed in Chapter 6.

Trailing Arm Installation

1 Remove Trailing Arm Assembly

Remove the parking brake hardware (reverse the procedure that starts in Step 3). Use a 9/16-inch wrench to remove the four nuts that are located underneath the parking brake hardware. Insert a pickle fork between the trailing arm and the bearing support legs. Use a hammer to strike the pickle fork to knock the trailing arm away from the bearing support. (Van Steel uses a special fixture to press the spindle out of the bearing support.)

Remove the races and seals and clean the trailing arm in a parts washer to remove the grease and grit.

Shot peen the rear trailing arm until all the paint and grime have been removed. Then insert the arms into a special jig to verify that they are straight. If they pass the inspection, send them to the powdercoating shop so their surfaces can be powdercoated to prevent deterioration.

2 Reassemble Trailing Arm

Reassemble the powdercoated arms. Add the right rear bearing support to the unit. (The front trailing arm bushings have already been installed here.)

3 Rebuild Parking Brake Assembly

Install and adjust the parking brake assembly prior to mounting the rear brake rotor. It is easier to install the lower adjuster and the spring first on the workbench. Lift them and spread the shoes to mount them on the upper pivot bolt. Install the side pins with a spring cup and then install the upper spring.

Final adjustment is complete when the brakes and new parking brake cables have been installed in the car. Verify that each bolt has been properly installed and torqued to specifications by marking them with White-Out.

4 Install Brake Rotors

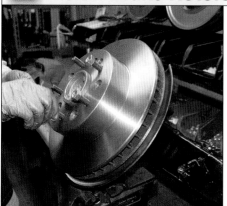

Install the rear brake rotor over the hub and check it for runout to verify that the rotor and bearings are within factory tolerances. Tolerances of .005 or less are the runout target.

Any out-of-spec measurements cause an annoying vibration that can be felt throughout the vehicle. It is critical to catch any imperfections on the workbench and not on the car. If your rotors are new and out of spec, return them to the vendor for a refund. You need to have properly functioning brakes with no thumping or pulsating from out-of-spec rotors.

6 Install Trailing Arms

Install the trailing arm into the slot in the frame. Insert the trailing arm bolt through the trailing arm. Lift the trailing arm from the rear and place a 1 x 1-inch piece of wood into the same place that the shims go. This puts the trailing arm in the correct ride height position and makes putting the half-shafts and strut rods into the car much easier. The shims will be installed later; do not put them in now. Also do not tighten the trailing arm. This will be one of the last bolts to tighten.

5 Verify Trueness of Trailing Arm

Place a dial indicator over the rotor to to verify rotor trueness. Secure and tighten all lug nuts. The rotor is now ready to be installed. Notice that these rotors have been matched to the spindle for trueness with White-Out. It is not necessary to return the same unit to your car. It is much quicker to exchange your old trailing arm for a refurbished one.

Differential

The differentials are basically all the same inside, but you find some minor changes during an overhaul. The outer case material changed to aluminum in 1980 to reduce the weight of the rear suspension. Subtle changes were made to the rear frame to accommodate this new differential. This new design can be found in all 1980–1982 Corvettes.

Many Corvette suppliers offer bearing and clutch pack kits that make an overhaul procedure much easier. The kits include all of the necessary parts.

When taking a differential apart, be sure to mark the left- and right-side pieces. It also helps to place a piece of colored tape on each side of the bench to keep the left- and right-side parts separated. Laying them out on your workbench in the proper order will help you identify the correct placement of these parts during reassembly.

Teardown

When draining the oil from the differential, check for a burning odor, which indicates overheating of the gears and case. Also check the oil for any metal fragments, which tell you a gear tooth might be chipped or broken.

This cutaway of a C3 differential reveals the components to inspect when the rear case cover is removed. Teeth marks on the Posi-Traction case indicate that the bearings are worn and the pinion gear is hitting the case.

Worn or Broken Gears

After the oil has been drained, remove the back cover on the differential. Slowly rotate the gears to check for any obvious signs of one gear rubbing on another.

Loose Gears

Move the gears back and forth to check for looseness and play from side to side. If you find this problem replacing the bearings and shims should correct the issue.

If your original differential is not making noise and does not show any evidence of abnormal wear, reinstall the old shims. Your objective here is to install fresh bearings, seals, clutch packs, and races to replace any worn parts in the differential.

A J tool from General Motors is required to accomplish this task. Use an adjustable micrometer to verify the thickness of any shim before installing it. This photo shows a typical pinion bearing with a crush sleeve between the inner and outer bearing. Note that a shim (.028 in this case) is below the inner bearing and the driveshaft yoke has been attached to the outer part of the pinion bearing.

Install Pinion Seal and Driveshaft Yoke

1 Lubricate Pinion Seal

Apply silicone lubricant before installing the seal gear into the housing. Use engine assembly lube to perform this task. This is a good preventive maintenance procedure to makes sure the parts are not dry.

2 Install Pinion Seal

It is important to make sure that this seal is correctly seated into the top of the differential housing. Use a large piece of pipe or something that is the same diameter as the seal. Make sure it sits evenly on the lip of the housing then use a hammer to gently tap the seal into place. Be careful; the seal is easily damaged.

3 Establish Seal Clearance

The thickest shim in your clutch pack (.045 inch) is used to ensure that the bottom part of the seal does not bottom out, which causes leakage. Carefully continue to tap the seal in place while moving the shim around to ensure that the gap is the same all around.

4 Install Driveshaft Yoke

Install the washer. Use a liberal application of silicone on the washer (shown) to make sure there are no differential oil leaks. Then install the nut and tighten until you get the proper drag on the nut (18 to 22 inch-pounds) on new gears. On used gears it is 15 to 17 inch-pounds.

5 Seat Driveshaft on Pinion Shaft

Place a solid bar such as a damaged pin (shown) on the driveshaft yoke. (You can also use a large punch or another piece of solid metal.) Tap it several times with a mallet or hammer to make sure it is seated properly on the pinion shaft.

6 Measure Pinion Resistance

Confirm the drag or load on the pinion by using an inch-pound torque wrench. About 18-inch pounds is common for this step. Do not overtighten this nut because the bearing could seize.

Posi-Traction Clutch Pack

The Posi-Traction unit has small clutches that are stacked on each side of the springs; they are held in place with these springs. They perform an important function. If one wheel loses traction the clutches engage and lock both wheels to provide added traction. Worn Posi-Traction clutches often chatter at low speeds when making a sharp turn. New clutches usually cure this problem.

This illustration shows some but not all of the major parts in a Posi-Traction unit.

1. Posi case
2. Pinion shaft
3. Pinion lock screw and washer
4. Pinion gears
5. Pinion thrust washers
6. Side bearings
7. Clutch pack guide
8. Clutch discs
9. Clutch plates
10. Yoke

Assemble Differential

1 Stack Clutch Pack

Lubricate all of the clutch discs thoroughly on both sides with GM Posi-Traction additive. Don't forget to do this; it's important.

First start stacking a side gear with a clutch disc that has two tabs or ears on it. Five of these discs have tabs. This tab piece goes onto the side gear first, and then every other disc added to the stack does not have tabs. Four discs without tabs are on each side. The final piece is a shim that determines the side yoke measurement. The best place to start is with the shim that came out when it was disassembled. The endplay on the side yoke should be .005 to .010 inch.

2 Install Clutch Pack in Housing

After the clutches and side gears are installed, insert a thrust washer on each side of the unit. Rotate the Posi clutch pack unit (shown on a jig in step 4) until you have enough room to insert the washer.

3 Measure Endplay of Side Yokes

You are looking for a clearance measurement of .005 to .010 inch. If it is not within this range, the assembly needs to be removed and a different-size shim installed. Repeat this process until you get the correct measurement.

4 Install Spring Plates

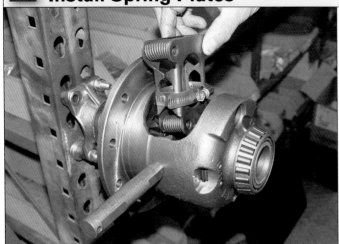

Assemble the spring plate and put it into a vise. Secure it with a hose clamp around the center and then tighten the clamp enough to compress the spring plate so you can slip it through the window (shown).

Once the spring is in the proper position, loosen and remove the hose clamp. The springs push against the clutches with more force as the car's speed increases. They lock the clutches and provide power to both wheels. Recheck the side yoke endplay. If there is excessive play, add shims to eliminate it.

5 Break In Limited-Slip Differential

Van Steel constructed this tool to spin the Posi-Traction unit on a jig that is mounted to a post. They spin it fifty times to the left and 50 times to the right. Then it's removed from the jig and turned around to repeat this process in the opposite direction.

This helps break in the limited-slip differential before it is put into service. The clutch plate stack should set in and therefore be ready for service once the differential is installed in the car.

6 Install Ring Gear

Install the ring gear onto the Posi unit with new Grade 8 bolts and lock washers. Use a locking adhesive on the threads and torque each one to 60 ft-lbs. Cross tighten them as you do to secure a tire using the star method.

7 Install Side Bearings

Use a mallet to carefully tap the side bearings into the case. Make sure that they are completely seated. Check the side plate end play again.

8 Install Differential into Housing

Place the limited-slip unit in the differential housing. Cautiously tap the side shims into the case to avoid damaging the cast-iron shims. (If you are using steel shims, this is not a problem.)

If you use the original ring-and-pinion gear that was removed the fit does not require much adjustment. Torque the side caps to 60 ft-lbs.

Backlash occurs when you take your foot off the throttle; you hear a clunking noise coming from the rear of the car. Adjusting the backlash is the best way to eliminate gear noise.

After the shims have been installed, attach a dial indicator to the differential housing to check the gear backlash. Put the dial indicator on zero; rock the ring gear back and forth to determine how much play it has while the pinion gear remains stationary. The measurement should be .006 to .008 inch.

Add or remove shims that were installed in step 8 on page 105, depending on how far the measurement is from the desired specification.

Yellow or white dye (or marking compound) is usually found in a differential kit. Apply some dye according to the kit instructions.

To check the gear pattern, hold the yoke with one hand and turn the ring gear back and forth with the other hand and a 9/16-inch wench on the ring gear bolt. This marks the gears with the dye and shows your gear pattern.

Gear Mesh Pattern

If using a differential rebuilding kit, it includes a dye to help determine the gear mesh pattern. You use shims to make it match the desired pattern.

Frame Member

The completed differential now needs to be attached to the frame crossmember. It is best to sit the differential onto a jack and then install the frame member.

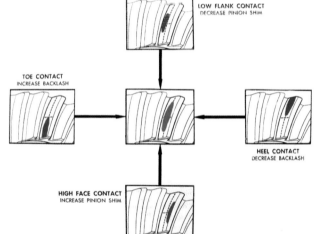

The ideal contact pattern (centered on the teeth) is the drawing in the middle. If your backlash is too large or too small you can shift the shims from one side to the other. If you take two shims out of one side, for example, you must place the same number onto the other side. (Photo Courtesy Van Steel)

The easiest way to prepare the differential for installation is to place it onto a floor jack. Attach the frame crosspiece to the differential with two 7/16-18 x 1⅛-inch bolts and 7/16-inch lock washers.

This differential has been assembled and is ready for installation.

Half-Shafts

Half-shafts connect the differential to the rear wheels. They are fitted with universal joints so they move through the arc of the suspension's travel as it encounters changes in the road surface. Big-block cars use a different attaching method than

Raise the differential and cross frame with the floor jack until you can secure it to the frame with two 5/8-inch bolts. Torque the bolts to 70 ft-lbs.

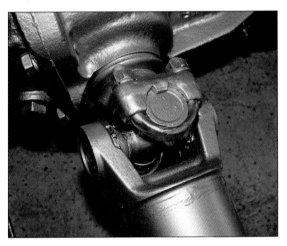

Small-blocks from 1968 to 1979 use two U-bolts on each side to attach the shaft to the differential, which are secured with 9/16-inch nuts. Tighten the nuts evenly on both sides and make sure the lock washers are crushed. Once they are snug, go one-quarter turn more with a wrench. Be careful to not over tighten them, as it damages the roller bearings.

small-blocks. Make sure you have the correct bolts.

Rear Suspension Strut Rods and Shock Absorbers

You can adjust the strut rods to change the rear suspension camber setting on your Corvette. The rods mount under the differential and connect to the trailing arms on the same bracket as the lower shock mount. If you marked these parts during disassembly, re-torque the bolts to the same location. This is a good procedure to complete before taking the car to the alignment shop.

Rear Spring

Two people may be required to reinstall the rear steel spring. Four bolts in the middle secure it. Each outer end of the spring is connected to the rear of the trailing arm with a link. This spring is under a lot of tension and might require the use of sandbags to be placed on the frame to help attach these end links.

Big-block half shafts from 1968 to 1974 use 9/16 x 14 x 3³¹⁄₆₄-inch bolts and heavy-duty caps. Once they are snug, go one quarter of a turn more with your wrench. Be careful to not over tighten them, as it will damage the roller bearings. The 1980–1982 automatics use 12-mm x 1.75 x 10.9 x 35-mm bolts and 1980–1981 4-speeds use 12-mm x 1.75 x 10.9 x 80-mm bolts. Tighten the nuts evenly on both sides. Once they are snug go one quarter of a turn more. Be careful not to overtighten, as it will damage the roller bearings.

Four 9/16-inch bolts fasten the half-shaft to the trailing arm bearing. Install a French lock that serves as a washer. These bolts should be torqued to 30 ft-lbs and the tabs on the French locks need to be bent (shown). This prevents them from loosening and backing out.

Odds and Ends

Congratulations! The major mechanical components have now been correctly installed into your refurbished frame. It also has the front and rear suspension and the differential. This is the perfect time to install the gas tank between the back frame rails.

The strut rods attach to the differential bracket with an adjustable camber bolt with two reducing washers inside the bushing on the differential side only.

The other side connects to the bearing support leg and the shock mount is pushed through the legs and the strut rod. This configuration is why the small piece of wood was placed in the trailing arm to keep the ride height closer to factory specs. It is much easier to install the strut rod with the trailing arm in this position. Four bolts with 9/16-inch heads fasten both strut rods. Torque them to 35 ft-lbs.

Notice here that the shock absorbers have been mounted and the half-shafts are bolted to the trailing arms and differential. The rear transverse leaf spring and spring bolts have not been installed. Remove the wood when this is complete.

This job is easier if someone is helping. Rest the spring on a floor jack and raise it to the differential to attach it with the steel plate and four 13/16-inch bolts. Torque these bolts to 100 ft-lbs. Make sure the guide pin on the spring aligns with the guide hole in the differential.

With the center of the spring secure, install the spring end links. To start, place a pair of locking pliers on one end of the leaf spring. Get some friends to sit on the frame as you perform the next part. Drop the end link into the opening at the rear of the trailing arm. Place a floor jack under the spring and slowly lift the spring until you are able to attach a nut to the bottom of the end link bolt. Once the bolt is attached with the nut and washer, slowly lower the jack. Your friends can now exit the frame.

Use a 13/16-inch socket on the top and a 7/8-inch wrench on the bottom to tighten the bolt. Insert a cotter key in the provided hole. Repeat this step on the opposite side.

The frame has now been completed and rolled outside for a final inspection. We mounted tires to make this job easier.

The upper shock bolts (5/8- and 11/16-inch nuts) were torqued 60 ft-lbs. The 3/4-inch lower nut was torqued to 40 ft-lbs. The 3/4-inch inner camber bolt was torqued to 70 ft-lbs. The 15/16-inch shock mount nut was torqued to 75 ft-lbs.

Also install the gas tank at this time.

BRAKE SYSTEM INSTALLATION

Four-wheel disc brakes were introduced to the Corvette lineup in 1965. The caliper is fixed to the suspension and split into two sections. Each caliper section holds two floating pistons that push against two brake pads in the front and rear of the car. This GM caliper is a constant-contact design, which means the pistons, brake pads, and caliper are always in contact with each other.

Each brake piston has a return spring beneath it so it stays in contact with the brake pads. Flexible hydraulic lip seals on each piston slide along the side of the caliper bore to keep the fluid contained in the system. If the brake rotor has excessive runout, it can cause the piston seals to flex and allow air into the brake system.

Rotor runout should be carefully monitored and should not exceed .005, so brake system integrity is maintained. Another point to keep in mind is that excessive rotor run-out creates noisy, squeaky brakes. This is caused by the brake pad backing plate moving from side to side and rubbing against the caliper housing and retaining pin.

In 1967 General Motors introduced a second piston design, which was used until the end of the 1982 production year. This cast-aluminum and anodized brake piston is a one-piece construction and less prone to admitting air into the braking system.

Two types of brake pads were delivered from the factory. An organic pad was the most common and it was riveted to a steel backing plate and held in place with a single center pin.

The other type of brake pad was designed for competition use and was part of the J-56 competition brake package. This brake pad was a made of a special semimetallic mixture that was bonded to the backing plate. This was later changed to a design

Corvettes produced from 1968 to 1982 were factory equipped with four-wheel disc brakes. Each brake caliper is fitted with four pistons for excellent brake performance. The parking brake assembly is housed inside the rear wheel rotor with small brake shoes. A center handle inside the car activates the brake shoes when it is pulled up. Early cars may or may not be equipped with power brakes. Power brakes became standard in all Corvettes starting in 1977.

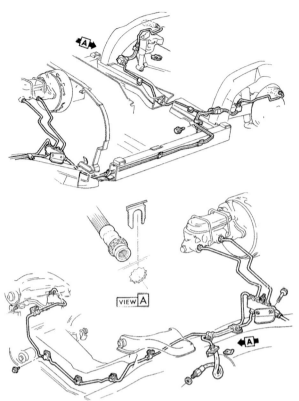

This diagram illustrates the correct routing of the entire braking system. Fluid is routed from the master cylinder into a brass junction connector on the front driver's side of the frame. Individual lines are connected to this connector and routed to each wheel, which has its own brass fitting. The junction connectors serve as a place to connect the rubber brake lines that are routed to each caliper. The lines are secured onto the frame rails with clips and bolts. (Photo Courtesy Mid-America Motorworks)

that had the pad material molded through the backing plate for better endurance. These pads were held in place with two pins. The rear and the front brake pads used the same friction material and were held in place with a single retaining pin.

Brake calipers manufactured from 1965 to 1971 were cast from ductile iron. The material was strong and had the ability to flex without breaking. In 1972 the caliper material was changed to gray iron, which was not as strong and durable as the ductile iron units. When any moisture entered the braking system, both types of calipers were prone to rusting.

The rusting caused the brakes to leak. Today, aftermarket suppliers offer refurbished C3 calipers with stainless-steel inserts to eliminate this issue.

These brakes were fitted to all 1965-1982 Corvettes. That is a lot of cars equipped with this brake design. If your calipers leak, getting a new set of refurbished calipers is an effective way to solve this problem.

Brake Lines

Stainless-steel brake lines serve a critical safety function on your Corvette. When you press your foot on the brake pedal you expect your car to stop swiftly and safely. If your brake lines are damaged or rusty and are leaking fluid somewhere in the system you could have a catastrophic brake failure. To avoid this problem, replace all of your existing brake lines with new units. Aftermarket vendors offer pre-bent brake lines to fit any C3.

There are four flexible brake lines on every C3 Corvette braking system. Two are connected from the hard lines to the calipers in the front and two are connected over the trailing arm bushings in the rear. Original equipment hoses are constructed with an internal rubber line surrounded by woven fiber filler that is covered with a protective rubber jacket. This design has proven itself through many years of successful service. It's designed to handle high pressure and continuous flexing without failure. It is a good idea to install the lines while the frame is free of suspension and brake components. Take your time and make sure every fitting is secure and the brake line clamps keep the lines from hitting any part of the frame or suspension. Once you have completed this task it is time to move on to the fuel lines.

1 Install Proportioning Valve

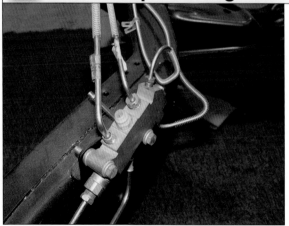

Bolt the brass proportioning valve to the frame under the master cylinder. All brake lines are routed through this valve.

The system is split for safety reasons. The front and rear brakes work independently of each other so two assemblies continue to function if the other two stop working.

2 Install Brass Rear Junction

The brass junction near the driver-side rear wheel delivers fluid to the passenger-side rear brake and has a fitting to connect the driver-side rear brake hose to it. This junction eliminates the need for two brake lines to be routed to the rear of the car for fluid delivery.

3 Install Rubber Brake Line

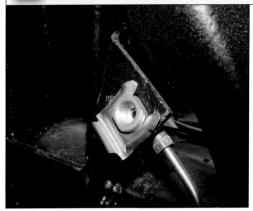

This is one side of the rear brass brake fluid junction. The rubber brake line is attached to the junction and then routed to the caliper. Screw the brake line into the fitting and make sure it is tight (not just snug) and push the clip into place.

Fuel Lines

During the C3 evolution from 1968 to 1982 the fuel system underwent subtle changes to address growing environmental concerns. Gasoline vapors were deemed to be hazardous to the environment, and manufacturers were directed to eliminate them. Corvette engineers added a charcoal filter to absorb these vapors, which first appeared in the 1970 model year.

A line runs from the tank on the driver's side of frame to the canister that is located near the engine. Two fuel lines run from the fuel tank to the fuel pump on the passenger's side. The larger line feeds the engine and the smaller line returns unburned fuel to the tank. The single fuel vapor

The charcoal canister gas line on this 1980 Corvette shares space with the brake line that runs along the driver-side inside part of the frame. The coiled wire on the brake line minimizes any rubbing between the two lines to avoid wearing through the brake line. These canisters were added to some Corvettes in 1970 to improve emissions control.

Two fuel lines are routed along the passenger's side of the frame. The large one is the fuel line and the small one is the return line that sends fuel back to the tank. Both are connected to the fuel pump. This is the correct way to attach these critical lines to the frame to avoid any rubbing that could cause them to break. They are secured with 1/2-inch self-tapping bolts.

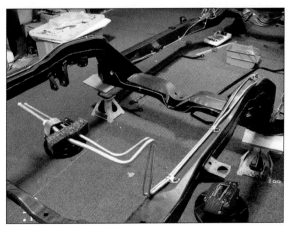

This photo shows how the two fuel lines are routed to the gas tank at the passenger-side rear of the car. The vapor line can be seen in the background attached to the frame rail on the opposite side of the car.

line shares space with the brake line on the driver's side of the frame. The two fuel and return lines are attached to the passenger's side of the frame.

Follow the same guidelines as when installing the brake line to ensure no lines vibrate against the frame or become kinked in any way. A fuel line rupture could ruin all of your hard work.

Brakes

All Corvettes produced from 1965 to 1982 came from the factory with four-wheel disc brakes. Power assist (J50) was an option from 1968 to 1976, but from 1977 to 1982, it was standard equipment.

The J56 special heavy-duty brake package was mandatory when ordering Corvettes with the L88 engine option. This robust braking system was only produced in 1968 and 1969, and few cars were so equipped. The cast-iron calipers featured four pistons and were quite effective at stopping a C3 Corvette. Non-powered brakes require a pretty heavy foot to stop the car. Power brakes greatly reduce braking effort and are a worthy option. If your car does not have power brakes, Corvette aftermarket suppliers offer upgrade kits that allow you to convert your car to this much-needed upgrade. The overall braking system design is simple, easy to install, and easy to maintain.

Many aftermarket suppliers offer refurbished C3 brake calipers with stainless-steel inserts. Your old calipers need to be exchanged for these new units; they will be refurbished and resold to another customer. The stainless-steel inserts extend the service life of your braking system, but I strongly advise you to flush the brake fluid every year, particularly if

Corvette introduced the four-piston brake caliper as standard equipment in 1965. Owners could order drum brakes (option J-61) for a savings of $64.50. A total of 316 buyers chose this option.

The basic design remained the same all the way to the 1982 model year. The weakness in this system was the use of cast-iron brake cylinders. Over time moisture accumulates in the cylinders and rusts the bores. The rust tears the rubber seals and the brakes start to leak.

The aftermarket designed a solution to this problem. Stainless-steel sleeves were inserted into the bores—no more rust.

Here the two pistons on the right are equipped with lip seals, which were original equipment. The pistons on the left feature upgraded O-ring seals, which improved sealing.

When buying refurbished calipers check to make sure they are fitted with stainless-steel sleeves.

you only drive the car on the weekends. Moisture accumulation is a big enemy of C3 brakes. Annual flushing of the brake system slows this process and helps ensure proper and safe operation of the brake system. It's very cheap insurance.

Front Brakes

Vendors offer a complete front brake set with all of the necessary components. You can also assemble the parts on your own and save some money.

The front brakes are attached to the suspension steering knuckle and secured with two bolts. The front brake calipers are only fitted with one brake fluid bleeder valve. This makes purging the braking system of air a simple process. Do not bleed your brakes until you are close to completing the body/frame installation (see Chapter 12).

1 ## Inspect Front Brake Kit

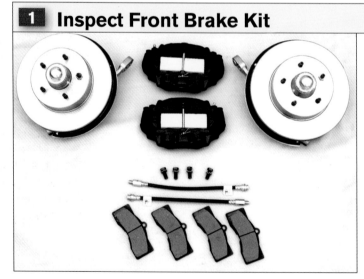

This is a complete front brake package that includes calipers, rotors, front wheel bearings, brake pads, new bolts, and brake hoses.

2 Install Front Brake Pads

Before the brake pad is inserted into the caliper, make sure all of the pistons in the caliper are fully retracted into their bores. You might need to use a putty knife or a flat piece of metal and a screwdriver to push the pistons down into the calipers bores so they are fully retracted. The two brake pads are held in place with one large pin that goes through the caliper and the two brake pads. Once the pads have been secured in place, insert the pin and a cotter key on one end to prevent the pin from backing out. The optional J56 special heavy-duty brake package was fitted to 267 Corvettes in 1968 and 115 in 1969. They were recommended for road racing only. Each caliper was fitted with two pins to hold the pads in place during competition events. The standard single-pin caliper system is a very effective way to stop your Corvette.

This is a refurbished rear 1968 to 1982 brake caliper. It includes stainless-steel sleeves and upgraded pistons and gaskets. Notice that each rear caliper has two bleeder screws that must be cleared of air when the system is being flushed. (The front calipers have one bleeder valve.)

3 Install Cotter Key

Use a needle-nose pliers to correctly bend the cotter key after the pad and caliper have been installed onto the rotor. Installing it this way prevents the pin from causing a rattle, and it does not turn or bind.

4 Install Rotors

Slip the front brake rotors over the lug nut studs on each front steering knuckle and secure them with lug nuts to prevent them from shifting when installing the brake calipers.

5 Attach Brake Hose

Use an open-end wrench to insert a brass washer (front only) between the brake fitting and the caliper. Before mounting the caliper to the front suspension install the brake pads and make sure the brake pistons are fully retracted into the caliper.

Push on the pads until they are seated against the inside surface of the caliper. It helps to loosen the bleeder screw before doing this step because you won't be working against the hydraulic brake pressure that may be behind the pistons.

6 Position Brake Caliper

The brake pistons should be fully retracted in the calipers and the brake pads placed in the caliper. Then the caliper should slip easily over the rotor. Line up the mounting holes on the calipers with the mounting bracket and secure them.

7 Secure Brake Caliper

Two 7/16 x 1⅛-inch bolts secure each caliper. This is a special bolt size and length. If the bolts are too long they hit the rotor. These bolts are fitted with a 5/8-inch head and need to be torqued to 70 ft-lbs to minimize them working loose during spirited driving.

8 Install Brake Hoses

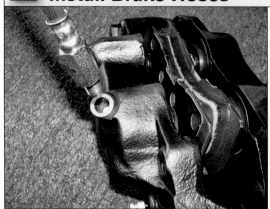

Attach a flexible brake line to each caliper to force fluid into the pistons. If you're going to complete an original restoration, use OEM-type hoses even though they expand, crack, and deteriorate over time. Brake performance also deteriorates over time with these hoses.

Many owners opt to install steel-braided brake lines because they maintain hydraulic pressure more consistently and don't stretch and expand like rubber hoses. These lines undergo a lot of stress, and it is always a good idea to install fresh ones when the brake system is rebuilt. These lines should be tightened to 30 ft-lbs to make sure they are tight and leak free.

9 Install Caliper onto Rotor

All four pistons must be all of the way inside the caliper bores before attempting to install the caliper onto the rotor. Slide the retaining pin into the caliper and install the cotter pin. Use a 5/8-inch socket to secure the caliper to the caliper mounting bracket. Torque to 70 ft-lbs.

10 Inspect Caliper and Rotor

This is the completed front brake caliper and rotor that is attached to the front suspension. Once the rear brakes are installed, mount wheels to make it easier to move the frame around your work area.

Rear Parking Brake Assembly

Third-generation Corvettes used a unique parking brake system. It includes a 6-inch-diameter, mechanically actuated drum brake located inside each rear brake rotor. The parking brake handle is located on the center console.

When the handle is pulled to engage the parking brake, it is connected to a spring-loaded cable under the center of the car. Four small brake shoes (two on each side per wheel) expand against the inside of a small drum inside the brake rotor to set the brake.

This parking brake design is very similar to the design of the standard drum brakes on 1963 and 1964 Corvettes. A screwdriver is used to loosen or tighten the pinwheel adjusters for the shoes and adjust the brake shoe travel.

Rebuilding one of these units takes a little patience but they last a long time when the job is done correctly.

All 1968–1982 Corvettes use this parking brake assembly. It consists of two brake shoes that are fitted inside the rear brake rotor; the brake shoes push against a small drum inside the rotor. When the parking brake is applied, the shoes lock onto the inside of the brake rotor. Springs located on the top and bottom of the shoes hold them together. The brake adjuster slips between the two shoes (at bottom here).

1 Install Bolts on Caliper Bracket

2 Install Rear Hub Bearing Support

Four bolts hold the caliper mounting bracket and the rear bearing support in place. Install these bolts on the inside of the control arm and press them into place.

Slide the rear bearing support over the four bolts that were pressed into the trailing arm. Make sure the support is fully seated onto the trailing arm.

3 Install Caliper Mounting Bracket

Place the caliper mounting bracket over the four studs that show through the rear bearing support.

Use a wrench to torque down the four 9/16-inch nuts that secure the rear bearing support and the caliper mounting bracket. Torque these nuts to 40 ft-lbs.

4 Install Backing Plate

The backing plate has two pins, which hold the brake shoes in place. Hold these pins against the underside of the backing plate with tape. Otherwise, the pins could drop while you are trying to secure the brake shoes.

5 Mount Pivot Block

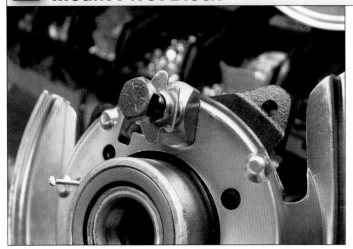

A bolt with a 3/4-inch head holds the pivot block in place. The top of the brake shoes rests on the pivot block, which keeps them from turning inside the drum.

Use an open-end wrench to hold the pivot block in place while tightening the bolt. Torque this bolt to 60 ft-lbs. Use a torque wrench if you don't have an impact gun.

Use a pair of pliers to bend the locking tabs onto the head of the nut to prevent it from loosening.

6 Install Parking Brake Lever

Insert the parking brake lever into the upper slot on the backing plate. The parking brake levers are stamped "left" and "right." Make sure to use the correct one for the side you are working on.

Turn the parking brake lever 90 degrees to the right to seat it correctly onto the backing plate. The parking brake cable attaches to this unit to tighten the shoes onto the rear rotor. Attach the cable to the arm as in step 2 on page 120 when the arm is installed into the car.

7 Install Brake Shoes

Slide the previously assembled brake shoes under the pivot arm and feed the pins through the holes in the brake shoes.

A spring and a cupped washer hold the brake shoes in place. Place the washer and spring over the pin and turn the washer 90 degrees to lock it into place.

Place one hooked end of the upper spring into one hole in the shoe. Use a spring hook tool or a slotted screwdriver to stretch the spring far enough to insert the other hooked end into the other hole.

Once the spring has been seated into both holes in the shoe, place a screwdriver behind the spring and push it outward. Make sure the spring is secure and correctly seated in its holes.

8 Install Brake Rotor

Using a hydraulic press, press the axle spindle into the rear bearing support. If you don't own a hydraulic press, take the spindle and bearing support to a professional shop to have the rear axle spindle pressed on.

Here a technician is holding a second axle spindle to show what it looks like unmounted. You need a hydraulic press to insert this part correctly into the bearing support.

Slide the rear brake rotor over the wheel studs. The rotor should slide over the assembly easily unless the brake shoes are out of adjustment. Secure the rotor with two lug nuts.

9 Measure Runout on Rotor

Check the runout on the rotor with a dial indicator. Zero is the ideal reading, but up to .005 is acceptable. Sometimes you can turn the rotor on the axle spindle to improve the readings. Do not put washers between the axle spindle and rotor to correct excessive runout. This quick fix is not a long-term solution to a runout problem.

10 Install Parking Brake Shoes

It is possible to install new parking brake shoes with the axle spindle in place. Stretch out the shoes, slide them under the axle spindle, and snug them up against the pivot block.

11 Install Spring and Washer

Carefully pry the shoe away from the axle spindle to provide enough room to install the spring and washer. Repeat this process for the other side. The other end of the spring can be installed after these washers are secure.

Trailing Arms

The restored parking brake assemblies have been installed onto the refurbished trailing arm. You are now ready to install the complete units with their new rotors onto the frame.

One bolt secures the trailing arms in the front and another bolt fastens both axle shafts in the rear. The rear transverse spring attaches to both sides of the rear trailing arm, and a shock absorber dampens the suspension on each side. The rear brake calipers are attached to the trailing arm with two bolts with 5/8-inch heads that should be torqued to 70 ft-lbs.

Bleeding the Braking System

Every time the brake system is opened, it must be purged of air that has entered into the system. If air is not evacuated from the system, you have a spongy brake pedal. It is more desirable to bleed the longest line first. The normal sequence is: driver-side rear inner, driver-side rear outer, passenger-side rear inner, passenger-side rear outer, driver-side front and passenger-side front. This method purges the air out of the system. Use a clear container so you can watch the flow of bubbles diminish as the fluid is drained from the system.

This trailing arm kit includes calipers, brake hoses, brake pads, brake lines, and new caliper bolts. Reuse the original trailing arm bolt that you removed from the trailing arms. (If you misplaced it they are available from various vendors.)

Install the trailing arm into the frame by reversing the removal procedure outlined in Chapter 6.

Parking Brake Cable

A single lever on the center console actuates the parking brake cable. The cable is routed through the body to a single roller that is mounted to the center of the frame behind the transmission. The other end of the cable has a bracket attached to it that connects to a spring-mounted equalizer mounted on the frame in front of the differential. The cable is routed through a bracket and it holds two parking brake cables that connect to the rear calipers. These two cables are held in place with two brackets that are mounted to each trailing arm. The cables connect to the parking brake lever that operates each parking brake.

1 Install Cable

This is how a completed parking brake cable system looks after it is installed. A piece of string holds the end of the cable that is threaded through the nylon roller. When the body of the car is attached, this end is fed through the floor to the parking brake handle inside the car.

2 Install Catch Ball

A small catch ball is attached to the end of the parking brake cable. Thread the cable under the parking brake lever on the inside of the brake rotor. Notice the parking brake lever is stamped with "LS" for left side.

3 Install Brake Cable Return Spring

The end of the cable has a coil spring to help return the brake lever to the closed position. This spring needs to be secured under the nylon clip on the rear trailing arm.

4 Anchor Parking Brake Cable

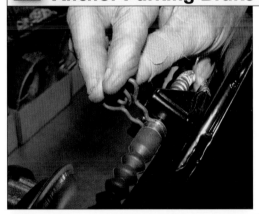

Slide the cable bracket into its clip that is also on the rear trailing arm. Secure the bracket with a spring clip (shown).

Completed Rear Brakes and Suspension

The rear brake assemblies are now successfully mounted onto the rear trailing arms and suspension. The frame is ready to have its engine and driveshaft installed prior to installing the refurbished body onto the completed frame.

Here is what the completed rear trailing arm assembly looks like. The rear brake calipers are mounted to the rotors and the brake hoses are connected to the brake lines. The parking brake cable is secured to the trailing arm with a clip. The calipers are attached to the trailing arm with two 5/8-inch headed bolts that are torqued to 70 ft-lbs.

ENGINE REBUILD OR REPLACEMENT

Third-generation Corvettes came with many different engine outputs, from mild to wild. Depending on your budget and power needs there are many ways to reach your goal. You can choose to rebuild the engine yourself, find a reputable machine shop to do the work for you, or purchase a crate motor to install.

This chapter looks at various engine rebuilding methods to help complete your restoration but it does not provide a complete step-by-step guide for how to rebuild your engine. If that's what you need, three good CarTech books are *How to Rebuild the Small-Block Chevrolet* by Larry Atherton and Larry Schreib, *How to Rebuild the Big-Block Chevrolet* by Tony Huntimer, and *Chevrolet Small-Block Parts Interchange Manual* by Ed Staffel.

Here, you get some engine development background and an overview of how owner Ed Scoppa removed, overhauled, and reinstalled his 350-ci small-block into his 1969 Corvette.

Development History

The heart and reputation of any Corvette sits beneath its fiberglass hood. Zora Arkus-Duntov and his team extracted maximum performance out of production-line engines. This included developing and adding multiple carburetors, fuel injection, and high-performance camshafts to improve Corvette performance. Corvette sales were growing as more people became aware of the cars' impressive performance.

Early Corvette Racing History

In 1957 Arkus-Duntov introduced an all-out race car called the SS at the 1957 12 Hours of Sebring endurance race. Because of its rapid development, it did not fare very well. Unfortunately shortly after the race, GM executives established a new policy that all divisions were to terminate all racing agreements and activities. Arkus-Duntov was stunned but decided to stay with Corvette. Ford, Chrysler and General

Your engine is a vital part of your Corvette. Crate engines are fairly inexpensive compared to rebuilding an original engine. However, if your car is equipped with rare options, it might be money well spent to do a quality rebuild on your existing engine to keep it numbers-matching.

Motors also signed this agreement in 1957 but Ford and Chrysler chose to ignore it. This forced Arkus-Duntov to improve Corvette performance with no executive support, a risky position in any corporation.

Fortunately a few key executives supported Arkus-Duntov's performance-improvement efforts. He found innovative ways to get around this executive order by developing off-road special performance parts for the Corvette. He and his staff also used their vacation time to attend racing events to provide private teams with engineering support. Meanwhile, Ford actively supported racing, manufacturing engines for the fearsome Cobra. The 3,300-pound Corvette was no match for the lightweight 2,000-pound Cobra. To compete with the Cobra, Arkus-Duntov's team secretly developed a 2,000-pound Corvette in late 1962. His intention was to offer these special Corvettes to private racing teams. Unfortunately GM executives caught wind of his idea and put a lid on it. The five lightweights that were built became known as Grand Sports and were spirited out the back door to private race teams.

Undaunted, Arkus-Duntov heard of a new Chevy big-block 427-ci engine that was being developed for trucks. He had that engine stuffed into a couple of standard Stingrays. They showed up at Daytona and captured the pole position. While the press called the engine the "mystery motor," General Motors named it the Mark IV. More important, Arkus-Duntov knew this was the engine Corvettes needed to beat the Cobras.

The mystery motor was put into the first production Corvette in 1965. It had 396 ci and was rated at 425 hp. This was also the first year Corvettes were equipped with four-wheel disc brakes.

In 1966 the engine was enlarged to 427 ci and a prototype racing version engine debuted at the 1966 24 Hours of Daytona. Long-time Corvette racer Roger Penske owned the car. Corvette engineer Gib Hufstader tended to the engine. The Corvette won the GT class and repeated this performance at the 12 Hours of Sebring.

In 1967 one of Corvette's new engine options was called L88. It was strictly for off-road use only and quickly became the car to beat on the sports car racing circuits. The biggest problem with this engine being installed into the C2 body was the car's terrible aerodynamics. The wing-like nose caused the car to pull the front off the ground at high speeds. For the most part, this problem was solved with the introduction of the C3 Corvette in 1968. All of Arkus-Duntov's and his engineering team's hard work finally paid off with the C3 Corvette. The car was still overweight, but the impressive torque and horsepower of the underrated L88 made up for the weight. Rated at 430 hp, it was well known among racers that a stock L88 engine produced between 540 to 550 hp on the dyno. Success on the racetracks helped promote sales in the showroom.

Dawn of the C3

As a third-generation Corvette owner it is important to know that not all Corvettes in this generation were created equal. The 1968-1972 Corvettes with the L79, L88, ZR1, ZR2, or L89 were high-performance cars built in very limited numbers. Because of this, they are sold at ultra-high prices compared to a standard street Corvette.

This is what makes owning one of these cars so much fun. You can buy a daily driver that has the DNA of a winning international sports racing car at a reasonable price. General Motors provided owners with a variety of engine choices during the 1968–1982 production run.

The Flint engine plant built the small-blocks and the Tonawanda plant built the big-blocks.

In 1969, the Corvette was offered with the greatest number of engine options, which was eight. In 1982, the final year of C3 production, customers had only one choice.

The 1972 fuel crisis and strong environmental pressure forced Corvette engineers to scuttle performance for the rest of the decade and concentrate on fuel mileage and emissions output. Air pumps, catalytic converters, and electronic engine controls were all introduced during the later days of C3 production. In 1968 and 1969, the Corvette reached its peak horsepower at 435; the lowest was 165 hp in 1975.

The fabled L88 was a full-purpose racing engine; only 80 were installed in Corvettes in 1968 and 116 in 1969. Chief Engineer Zora Arkus-Duntov and his team built this engine package for one purpose: to beat the Ford Cobras. This engine went on to win numerous sports car championships and, therefore, Corvette collectors covet it.

In 1971, General Motors decided to lower compression ratios on all of its engines so lower-octane fuel could be used. As a result, horsepower and torque ratings plummeted. One example of the impact of this decision was on the base 300-hp Corvette engine. The lower compression resulted in a loss of 30 hp on that engine in 1971.

In 1972, horsepower output measurements changed from gross to net. A gross number was the engine's horsepower without any accessories. A net output was horsepower with all of the accessories hooked up. Using the same 300-hp engine as an example, the rating dropped from 270 hp gross to 255 hp net. In spite of these changes Corvettes still performed better than the majority of American cars at the time.

The third-generation Corvette readily accepts any engine option that was available from 1968 to 1982, and it accepts LS and many other crate engines. This engine-swapping flexibility allows you to pick your performance level to fit your driving requirements and budget. If you want a nice cruiser that is quiet and provides adequate performance, stick to the lower-horsepower choice. If you want an all-out street bruiser, pick an L88.

Engine Rebuilding Overview

Ed Scoppa purchased his Corvette with the intention of fully restoring it in his spare time. He chose to have his existing engine rebuilt, rather than installing a Chevrolet Performance crate motor. Scoppa retained the original block and heads in his Corvette, so he made a lot of notes before he began removing the engine. This included taking photos of the engine and writing down the locations of pulleys, hoses, and any other items to help in the reinstallation. He also documented the colors and finishes of major engine components. Once his documentation was complete he removed the Corvette's body.

The frame components could now be easily removed in his garage for restoration. The engine was unbolted and removed with a block and tackle that he built in his garage. Once the engine was free, he placed it on a steel frame so it could be transported to the engine-building shop. Scoppa wanted his 300-hp engine

1968–1982 Engine Block Casting Numbers

All casting numbers are located on the top driver-side surface at the rear of the block.

Year	Casting Number	Cubic Inches	Horsepower
1968	3914660	327	300 (early, unverified)
	3914678	327	300, 350
	3916321	427	390, 400, 430, 435 (early)
	3935439	427	390, 400, 430, 435 (late)
1969	3932386	350	300, 350 (early)
	3932388	350	Unverified
	3956618	350	300, 350 (mid)
	3970010	350	300, 350 (late)
	3935439	427	390, 400, 430, 435 (early)
	3955270	427	390, 400, 430, 435 (early)
	3963512	427	390, 400, 430, 435 (late)
	3946052	427	430 ZL1 (aluminum)
1970-1971	3970010	350	300, 350, 370 (1970); 270, 330 (1971)
	3963512	454	390 (1970); 365, 425 (1971)
1972	3970010	350	200, 255
	3970014	350	200, 255
	3999289	454	270
1973-1974	3970010	350	190 (1973); 195 (1974), 250
	3970014	350	Uncertain
	3999289	454	270
1975-1977	3970010	350	165, 205 (1975)
		350	180, 210 (1976–1977)
1978	3970010	350	175, 185, 220
	376450	350	Uncertain
	460703	350	Uncertain
1979	3970010	350	195, 225
	3970010	350	190, 230
	14010207	350	190, 230
	4715111	305	180 California
1980	14016379	350	Uncertain
1981-1982	14010207	350	190 (1981), 200 (1982)

to produce more horsepower, so he decided to upgrade it to 350 hp with a new cam and headwork.

After a lot of research and phone calls, Scoppa selected Southern Style Racing Engines in Pinellas Park, Florida, to rebuild his engine. Owner George Pils has extensive experience in rebuilding Chevrolet engines for street and race applications. His shop is equipped with high-tech machinery to complete any required rebuilding procedure. His engines have brought owners championships in NASCAR, sports car, and drag racing events.

If you do not have the equipment or skill set for rebuilding an engine, shop around your area for a high-quality machine shop to do this work for you.

Disassembly

Southern Style Racing technicians carefully disassembled the engine. Every part was cleaned and inspected to determine if the part could be reused or had to be replaced.

Serial Numbers

Refer to the sidebar "Serial Numbers" on page 147 to determine the year your engine block was produced. Each block also has the VIN stamped into it and serves as a handy cross-reference to see if it is the original engine block.

Fuel and Spark Systems

The electrical system ignites the fuel that powers your Corvette engine. The fuel is delivered to the carburetor via a fuel pump and the electrical system does the rest. Here is a brief overview of the fuel and spark systems.

Fuel Pump

Five different fuel pumps were installed into various C3 Corvettes. Each one was built for a specific engine application. It is very important to use the correct fuel pump for your engine, as the flow output for each one is different.

Here is a breakdown of the five different Corvette fuel pumps for the various engines that they fit:

1968–1969	427
1968–1969	327/350
1970–1972	LT1
1970–1974	454
1970–1981	350
1982	fuel tank electric pump

Corvettes were fitted with mechanical fuel pumps from 1968 to 1981. The pumps were located on the lower front passenger side of the engine. The pump brought fuel from the tank in the back of the car and sent it to the carburetor. A return line sent the unused fuel back to the tank. Stainless-steel lines were used to transport the fuel; rubber hoses are not recommended.

For 1982, Corvettes used an electric fuel pump that was located inside the fuel tank. This was the first year this system was installed into a Corvette.

Carburetor

Corvettes were fitted with a variety of carburetors. Three individual Holley 2-barrels were fitted to 400-hp engines in 1968, and to 400- and 435-hp 427-ci engines in 1969.

The 4-barrel Rochester Quadrajet was fitted to all other engine options in different variations until the end of production in 1981.

In 1982, General Motors introduced the ill-fated Cross-Fire fuel injection system. It used two throttle bodies to measure the fuel for the engine and produced 200 hp.

Spark Control

The factory installed a breaker-point ignition system on most 1968–1974 Corvettes to control spark. The exception to this rule was cars equipped with the K66 transistorized ignition option (called the High-Energy Ignition, or HEI). This option was only available for 1968 and 1969 high-performance Corvettes. A total of 11,159 1968 and 1969 Corvettes were delivered with this innovative spark system. It was a very successful application in L88-equipped Corvettes.

The HEI system was modified and became standard in all Corvettes produced from 1975 to 1981. It eliminated the need for points and produced a hotter spark for better emissions control.

Computer Command Control was introduced into Corvettes in 1981. The computer controls various functions inside the engine with a series of sensors that measure fuel, spark, temperature, and other functions of the engine. This system was also installed into 1982 Corvettes.

General Motors identifies its engines with numbers on the block. This is an early 1974 engine built on December 27, 1973. This number can be found above the bellhousing on the top driver's side of the block.

Cylinder Honing

The cylinders in a block tends to wear after extensive use and can cause low compression and oil leaks.

Cylinders can also wear unevenly as they age.

Measure your cylinder block with a micrometer. If it needs an overbore, take it to a qualified machine shop. Having a shop run a rotary hone up and down the bores is the best way to correct this condition. To accomplish this a large plate is tightly bolted on top of the block with holes for each cylinder. This plate mimics a head being bolted onto the block, and it stretches the block back into its original shape. A three-headed hone is inserted into each cylinder; it turns at 155 rpm until the cylinder is bored to its desired opening.

If you can perform this job at home use a ball cylinder hone. Attach it to a hand drill that can be run up and down the cylinder bores. Make sure you use a lubricant.

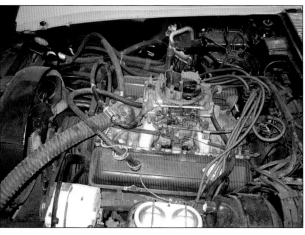

The best place to start documenting your project before disassembling the engine is to inspect what factory parts still remain on the car. For example, this 1969 Corvette has a factory-installed 300-hp 350-ci engine. It still retains its original factory fan shroud and fan. The A/C evaporator is still on the firewall, but the compressor has been removed. The engine retains its original factory orange paint. The power brake booster is another clue to what this car was originally fitted with when it left the St. Louis Assembly Plant.

All of these clues help you return your car to factory specifications if that is your goal. If you located a tank sticker when you removed the body this is even a better document to determine your Corvette's original specifications. (Photo Courtesy Ed Scoppa)

After the body is removed from the frame, use an engine hoist to lift the engine out of the chassis. While the engine is free and clear, take the time to check serial numbers and document all factory-installed items. This includes headers, bolts, brackets, transmission, etc. (Photo Courtesy Ed Scoppa)

Southern Style owner George Pils recommended bumping this engine's output from 300 to 350 hp. It was accomplished by opening up the heads to accept 2.02 intake valves and installing a 350/350 Corvette factory camshaft. The cylinder bores were honed .030 to correct any imperfections that might have occurred over time in each cylinder. The block was also decked to make sure the heads and block were a perfect fit.

The engine was completely dismantled and every part carefully cleaned, including the block, heads, and manifold before starting any machine work.

1 Install Torque Plate

These cylinders didn't suffer major damage or wear so only a hone was necessary to clean them. A torque plate is attached to the top of one side of the engine before the honing process begins. The three hones are attached to the rotary bar that is hanging above the block. As the hones are lowered into the cylinder bore the plate keeps the block square during the honing process. The plate also acts as a guide to help maintain the correct clearances.

2 Use Cylinder Hone

The hone turns at a very low speed as it is inserted into the cylinder wall. It continues to turn until the desired bore is reached. This process is repeated on all eight cylinders. In this case, the engine was bored .030 inch over its stock specification.

3 Inspect Hone Job

This is what a finished honing process should look like. The torque plate will be removed before the block is taken to the decking machine.

Decking the Block

After the cylinders have been honed to the correct measurements, the block is secured to the decking machine. A large disc is run back and forth over the top of the block to remove any uneven surfaces. Machine shops attempt to remove only the smallest amount of material from the block that is required to make the surface even.

You may lose the VIN during this process but it is the best way to get a quality engine rebuild. You can always restamp your block if needed.

This block has been secured to a flat plate on the surface grinder. The deck on top of the block is ground flat to eliminate any imperfections that can occur over the life of the engine. This ensures a tight seal when the heads are placed back onto the completed block.

A resurfacing wheel with a carbide insert works well on cast-iron heads and blocks because these machines spin very slowly. For example, a resurfacer with an 11-inch wheel turns at 140 rpm.

The block has been successfully decked; it will provide a tight seal between the head and block when the rebuilding process is complete. This tight seal provides ideal cylinder pressure, which maximizes performance. An engine with a leaking head gasket is an unhealthy engine.

Rebuilding the Block

Before the reassembly process begins the block is checked for cracking and all internal surfaces resurfaced. Ed decided to install all new components into the block including crank, pistons, rods, bolts, etc., to give his engine long-lasting durability.

1 Resurface Interior Parts

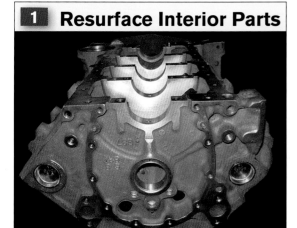

All interior parts of the block have been resurfaced to prepare it for the rebuilding process. Notice that new freeze plugs have been installed in the front of the block. This is the kind of attention to detail to look for when selecting a quality machine shop to rebuild your pride and joy.

2 Organize Engine Parts for Assembly

Here are some of the critical components that need to be installed into the block during the rebuilding. They include the pistons, rings, rods, rod pins, bolts, and crankshaft. In addition, rod and crankshaft bearings and caps are needed to complete the lower-end rebuild.

3 Torque Main Bearing Caps

The crankshaft, main bearings, and main seals are the first parts to be installed. The block is assembled on a rotary engine stand so the pistons, rods, and rings can be inserted into the top of the block. The rotary stand allows the block to be turned over so the rod bearing caps and bolts can be attached to the crankshaft. Southern Style Racing Engines rechecks the torque on each main bearing bolt after the rods are installed.

4 Install Camshaft

The cam bearings need to be properly lubricated. After the camshaft is in the block, the timing gears and timing chain are next to be installed. The timing chain connects the crankshaft and the cam on the front of the engine. Then the oil-pickup tube is installed on the oil pump. Finally, everything is double-checked for correct sealing and tightness.

Head Work

The heads were cleaned and milled to ensure proper matching surfaces between the block and the heads. The valve bores were increased to accept the larger intake and exhaust valves that operate more efficiently with the 350-hp GM factory camshaft.

1 Install Larger Valves

The heads have been bead blasted and the valve seats have been opened to allow the installation of the larger valve set that includes 2.02-inch intake x 1.60-inch exhaust. These larger valves were part of the high-performance 350-ci/350-hp option. The heads have been slightly shaved to make sure they fit tightly on the refurbished block.

2 Install Valve Retainers

The intake and exhaust valve springs are held in place with caps and retainers. Use a spring compression tool to insert the valve into the head from the underside. Install the rubber seal over the valve stem and then add the spring. Insert the tool and squeeze the spring. Add the retainer, remove the compression tool, and let the spring rest against the retainer.

Engine Reassembly

The engine block has been rebuilt and both heads are ready to be reinstalled onto the engine. Any worn mechanical parts and critical internal engine parts have been replaced with new ones.

All engine fasteners must maintain their torque specification or an engine failure can result. For example, a broken head bolt can cause a gasket leak that could be terminal to the engine. Used bolts lose their clamping force over time; they have been stretched and are prone to breaking when they are reused. It is money well spent to use new parts.

A pin in the block holds the head gasket in place, so the technician can install the rebuilt head onto the short block. Each head is secured with 34 bolts.

Finally, the pushrods and rocker arms are installed to complete this part of the rebuild.

Engine Testing

Most quality machine shops, such as Southern Style Racing Engines, have their own dyno to test and verify their work. After the engine was assembled, it was run on the dyno to check water temperatures and gasket seal. The engine passed all the tests and was ready for delivery.

Southern Style Racing ran the completed engine on its dyno with a 2-barrel carburetor to make sure the engine had the correct oil pressure and maintained its water temperature, and the gaskets were leak free.

Engine Delivery

Once the dyno testing was complete, all engine openings were sealed to ensure no contaminants could get into the engine. Inexpensive GM value covers were added to avoid damaging the original Corvette valve covers. The block was wrapped in plastic and mounted onto Ed's portable stand so he could easily transport it.

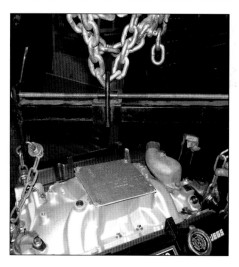

An engine lift was attached to the block with bolts as shown. The adjustable crank keeps the engine balanced as the accessories are added to the engine. Notice the blue tape used to seal all the openings.

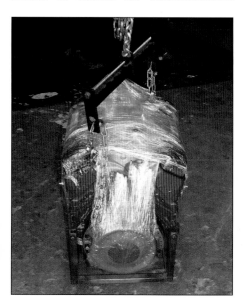

The engine was lifted out of the delivery truck with a forklift and Ed's Harbor Freight engine lift was attached to two places on the manifold. The lift is equipped with a crank so the engine can be kept even as it is being lifted. This is an inexpensive and handy device to have on hand for this part of the installation.

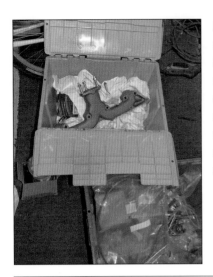

Remember all those storage bins you filled with bags of removed parts? Now is the time to start unpacking and organizing them.

This wooden pallet was used to store the transmission, bellhousing, and exhaust pipes. It made it easy to move them around the work area with a dolly.

Engine Accessories

After the engine has been completely assembled, the engine accessories can be installed. Drivetrain components are included in this group, such as the clutch, pressure plate, throw-out bearing, shifting fork, bellhousing, transmission, engine mounts, and anything else that does not interfere with the engine installation.

1 Install Clutch and Pressure Plate

The clutch and pressure plate have been installed behind the flywheel.

Several 9/16-inch bolts attach the bellhousing to the block. Make sure to install the gasket and torque the bolts to 30 ft-lbs.

2 Install Bellhousing

On the inside of the bellhousing, position the clutch fork and place the throw-out bearing prior to mounting the unit onto the back of the engine.

3 Mate Transmission to Engine

After the bell-housing has been secured, it is time to install the transmission. You can complete this part yourself with a jack, or have a friend assist you.

Once the transmission is snug against the bellhousing, install the four bolts to hold it in place. Use a 3/4-inch socket to tighten them to the housing. Then torque the bolts to 70 ft-lbs. These bolts take a lot of stress so make sure they are properly torqued before proceeding to the next step.

This is a view of how the transmission looks after it has been successfully mounted to the engine.

Engine Installation

To install the engine, you need a block and tackle attached to an overhead beam, A-frame, or sturdy engine hoist. (If you happen to have a forklift to lift the engine over the refurbished frame so it can be lowered onto its mounts, use it!)

The two front engine mounts are bolted to the front of the frame. The transmission serves as the rear engine mount. It rests on a bracket that is attached to the frame where the exhaust pipes go through the center of the frame. The exhaust hangers attach to this transmission mount.

Many times, mating the transmission to the engine provides better balance to the engine/transmission assembly, so it's easier to maneuver it into the engine bay and transmission tunnel. Using an engine hoist or a cherry picker to install the engine is a delicate and sometimes time-consuming process as you make small adjustments to get the engine properly positioned.

Some owners do not perform a frame-off restoration and therefore the fenders, bumper, and front body-work are installed on the car as the engine is lowered into the engine bay. If this is the case, I strongly recommended getting at least one person to help because you need one to lower it and steady the engine while another person guides it into position.

After the engine is installed add the headers, engine brackets, pulleys, belts, and wiring.

Some items, such as the fan, should not be installed until the body is dropped onto the frame.

1 Install Engine on Hoist

Once the engine has been rebuilt, it's time to install it into its rightful home: the chassis. Two motor mounts and one transmission mount hold the engine and transmission in place. It's a personal decision whether to separately install the engine and transmission or install the engine and transmission as a complete unit. Some choose to install these components separately, but in this case, they were installed as a unit onto the bare chassis. As a unit, it's easier to balance and maneuver the engine/transmission on the motor mounts and the transmission support.

The same applies when installing the engine/transmission into the car with the body installed on the frame. Bolt the lift plate or lift tabs to the intake and make sure the bolts are properly torqued. Then run the chains through the lift tabs and secure the chains with the properly sized bolts and washers. Make sure the engine is secured to the chains and hoist. You don't want the engine to come crashing to the floor, causing great destruction and injury.

2 Attach Motor Mounts

Attach the two motor mounts to the block with three bolts each. Use a 9/16-inch socket to secure them and torque them to 30 ft-lbs.

3 Install Motor Mount Bolts

Make sure the engine is secure and in the correct position while running the bolts through the motor mounts. This helps maintain alignment and makes installing the engine easier. Once the engine is lowered into the frame, hold it in place with a large punch to make sure it does not slip while installing the bolt on the opposite side of the engine. Use an 11/16-inch wrench on the bolt head and install a 5/8-inch nut.

Two people should participate in the engine installation procedure. One person should be in front of the engine steadying the engine and lowering it into the engine bay. The other person should be close to the lower end of the engine, making sure that the engine's motor mounts align with the chassis motor mounts.

You often have to lower and move the engine into position at the same time. You do this slowly and methodically, sometimes an inch at a time. Be patient and make sure the engine is stable. A swinging engine can easily cause massive damage to the refurbished frame or to the firewall if the body has already been installed.

4 Bolt Up Transmission

The transmission is secured to this bracket, which is mounted onto the frame with two bolts. Tighten them with a 9/16-inch socket and torque them to 30 ft-lbs. Be sure the transmission mounting pads align with the mounting holes on the frame.

5 Install Remaining Accessories

The engine has now been secured to the frame and the only remaining work to complete the process is to install the carburetor, pulleys, hoses, etc.

6 Adjust Belts

Once the complete engine has been installed, make the final adjustments to the belts. Tighten the belts as snug as possible and then grasp the center of the belt between the two pulleys. Twist the belt from horizontal to vertical. If you can turn it completely over. Check the belts again when the car has been driven for several days. (Photo Courtesy Ed Scoppa)

A Portfolio of Completed Engines

As I mentioned at the beginning of this chapter, C3 engines came in many different configurations available from mild to wild. At the top of the heap were the L88 and rare ZL-1 aluminum big-block engines.

These engines were not designed for everyday street driving. They were cranky at low speeds and prone to overheating if not enough air was getting through the radiator.

General Motors and Corvette engineers transitioned to small-blocks for a variety of reasons, including overall vehicle cost, cus-tomer acceptance, fuel efficiency, vehicle weight, and handling prowess. The small-block was also chosen because it produced less heat than a big-block and was easier to cool. It also left enough room to pack the engine bay with new equipment.

A big-block engine completely fills a Corvette engine bay. This 1969 Corvette is a good example of a tight engine compartment. It is equipped with a high-performance L88 racing engine. The car has no heater, air conditioner, or power steering accessories and the compartment still looks fully packed.

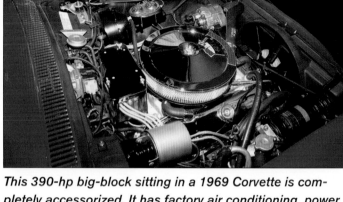

This 390-hp big-block sitting in a 1969 Corvette is completely accessorized. It has factory air conditioning, power brakes, and power steering. The large item on the lower right is the vacuum can to operate the windshield wiper door. The only thing missing on this engine is the air pump, which typically sits next to the air conditioner compressor. These engines produce an enormous amount of heat and there is very little room for it to escape.

In 1971 the engine ratings fell when General Motors required all brands to lower their compression ratios to accept lower-octane (91) fuel. This 1972 small-block was rated at 255 hp, down from 270 in 1971 due to the new engine output measuring system. Net output included all of the auxiliary equipment.

Note that this engine has been slightly modified from stock and has long-tube headers but no smog pump.

This small-block is installed into a 1974 convertible, which features a ram air hood induction system. This is why the air cleaner is ducted the way it is. It also has its air pump installed for emissions control. Small-block engine compartments are packed with hoses and wiring.

This 220-hp L82 engine was the last remnant of the Corvette high-performance engine lineup. It started life as the 350-hp/350-ci (L46 option) in 1969 and is shown here in a 1978 Anniversary Edition Corvette (L82 option).

This completely stock, 11,000-mile 1982 Corvette is equipped with a 200-hp Cross-Fire injected engine. Notice how close the air pump sits to the air conditioner compressor. There is very little room to work inside this engine compartment.

Crate Engines

Some owners decide not to rebuild their engines themselves or have a machine shop perform the work. Instead, they install a Chevy Performance, Lingenfelter, Mast Motorsports, or other crate motor. Any of them is a good value for the money if numbers-matching parts are not a concern.

Small-blocks come in a variety of sizes to fit most applications. One of the most popular engines in this lineup is the economy performance engine. This 350/290 delivers 290 hp at 5,100 rpm and 326 ft-lbs of torque at 3,750 rpm. The engine is delivered in a wooden crate and is ready to run after adding an intake manifold, carburetor, ignition system, starter, balancer, and water pump.

You can purchase the ZZ383 performance engine. This engine is fitted with aluminum performance heads that sit on top of a 383-ci small-block. This engine produces 425 hp and 449 ft-lbs of torque. The heads have 2.00/1.55 valves and specially designed chambers that draw in lots of air and fuel.

Many crate engine suppliers provide a limited warranty.

An LS engine is also a popular option for C3 owners who are not concerned about retaining original equipment.

If NCRS awards are not a concern, Chevrolet Performance sells ready-to-run crate engines. They come complete with a factory warranty and are delivered in a crate.

This crate engine is ready to accept the transmission and any accessories that were removed from the old engine. This view is from the rear of the engine.

TRANSMISSION

During third-generation Corvette production, a variety of transmissions were offered. They include 3-speed manual, 4-speed manual, 3-speed automatic, and 4-speed automatic.

In 1968, the base price of a Corvette included a 3-speed Saginaw manual transmission. The options for that year included a Muncie 4-speed wide- or close-ratio manual transmission and an M40 automatic transmission. If an automatic was ordered, small-blocks were fitted with the T-350 and big-blocks came with the T-400.

The 3-speed manual was also included in the base price of a 1969 Corvette, but was replaced with a wide-ratio 4-speed in 1970. At the end of C3 production in 1982 only a 4-speed automatic transmission was available.

Much as engine choices were reduced during the C3 production cycle, transmission choices were slowly eliminated to help meet stricter emissions and fuel mileage requirements.

Manual Transmissions

During production the C3s were equipped with several manual transmissions. This included 3-speeds, 4-speed wide-ratio, and 4-speed close-ratio. They were built by Saginaw, Muncie, and BorgWarner. The only year a manual transmission was unavailable from the factory was 1982.

Saginaw 3-Speed

One of the more unusual transmissions fitted to C3 Corvettes was the Saginaw manual 3-speed transmission (2.85 first, 1.68 second, and 1.00:1 third). They were part of the standard equipment base price for all 1968 and 1969 Corvettes. The 3-speed was installed behind the standard 300-hp 327-ci engine in

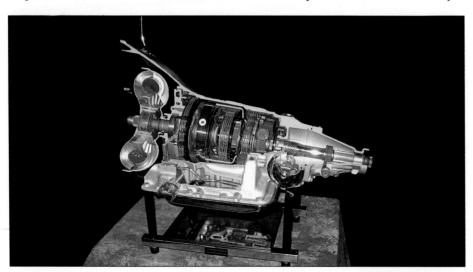

Third-generation Corvettes were fitted with a variety of transmission options. These included a 3-speed manual, close- or wide-ratio manual 4-speeds, or two automatic transmissions, depending on the buyer's preference. Rebuilding an automatic transmission requires a lot of skill and patience. Many aftermarket suppliers offer rebuilt units on an exchange basis and usually include a warranty. (Photo Courtesy Cutaway Creations)

This is the location of the date code stamped on the case of a Muncie transmission.

This is the interpretation of this code: P is for Muncie, 0 is for 1970, B is for February, and 02 is for the second day day, and C is for M22.

The Muncie 4-speed was optional for all 1968–1974 Corvettes. It was available in wide (M-20) and close ratio (M-21 and M-22). Muncie production ended in 1974 when it was replaced with units built by Warner.

Here are the major components of a well-worn wide-ratio Muncie 4-speed transmission. It was originally installed in a 1965 Corvette. The basic design of this transmission remained the same from 1963 to 1974. The P code is stamped on the front lip of the case for identification purposes. This transmission will be completely overhauled and rebuilt with new gears, bearings, shafts, and shifter by Circle Products.

1968 and the 300-hp 350-ci engines in 1969. Dealers used this basic equipment package to offer customers rock-bottom Corvette pricing. In 1968 a total of 326 3-speed Corvettes were built; in 1969 the number fell to 252 for this rare shifter.

Muncie 4-Speed Manual

Muncie 4-speeds were available for all Corvettes from 1968 to 1974. They carried the option codes of M20, M21, and M22. These manual transmissions were optional or standard for all of these model year Corvettes. Muncies can be distinguished from other manual transmissions because their reverse lever is mounted in the extension housing instead of the side cover. The main difference between the Muncie and the BorgWarner is that the Muncie has a seven-bolt side cover and the BorgWarner has nine bolts.

The Muncie M20 was a wide-ratio 4-speed (2.56 first, 1.91 second, 1.48 third, and 1.00:1 fourth) manual transmission. This was the most widely produced transmission installed into early C3s. It was optional in 1968 (10,760 delivered) and 1969 (16,507 delivered). The M20 became standard in 1970 and started being phased out during the 1974 production cycle. It was replaced by the BorgWarner M20 wide-ratio 4-speed.

The Muncie M21 was first offered as an option in 1968 and fitted with close-ratio gearing (2.20 first, 1.64 second, 1.28 third, and 1.00:1 fourth). The M21 close-ratio was available until the end of the 1974 production cycle, and then the BorgWarner close-ratio 4-speed replaced it.

The M22 is a strong and reliable gearbox. Produced in low volume

Serial Number Alpha Codes

Here is a list of available transmissions for third-generation Corvettes. Each type includes an alpha code in its serial number that indicates its manufacturer and type.

Year	Serial Number Alpha Code	Application
1968	S	Saginaw 3-speed (standard in the base 327 Corvette)
	P	Muncie 4-speed Corvette 327 and 427 engines
	K	Turbo Hydra-Matic 400, Corvette 327 engines
	L	Turbo Hydra-Matic 400, Corvette 427 engines
1969	S	Saginaw 3-speed (standard in the base 350 Corvette)
	A	Muncie 4-speed M20 wide-range (2.52:1 1st gear)
	B	Muncie 4-speed M21 close-range (2.20:1 1st gear)
	C	Muncie 4-speed M22 close-range (2.20:1 1st gear) Rock Crusher
	K	Turbo Hydra-Matic 400, 350-ci Corvette engines
	L	Turbo Hydra-Matic 400, 390- & 400-hp Corvette engines
	Y	Turbo Hydra-Matic 400, Corvette 430- & 435-hp engines
1970	P	Muncie 4-speed, heavy-duty aluminum case
	A	Muncie 4-speed M20 wide-range (2.52:1 1st gear)
	B	Muncie 4-speed M21 close-range (2.20:1 1st gear)
	C	Muncie 4-speed M22 close-range (2.20:1 1st gear) Rock Crusher
	K	Turbo Hydra-Matic 400, 350-ci engines
	S	Turbo Hydra-Matic 400, 454-ci engines
	Y	Turbo Hydra-Matic 400, 454-ci engines
1971	P	Muncie 4-speed, heavy-duty aluminum case
	A	Muncie 4-speed M20 wide-range (2.52:1 1st gear)
	B	Muncie 4-speed M21 close-range (2.20:1 1st gear)
	C	Muncie 4-speed M22 close-range (2.20:1 1st gear) Rock Crusher
	K	Turbo Hydra-Matic 400, 350-ci engines
	S	Turbo Hydra-Matic 400, 454-ci engines
	Y	Turbo Hydra-Matic 400, 454-ci LS6 engine
1972	P	Muncie 4-speed, heavy-duty aluminum case
	A	Muncie 4-speed M20 wide-range (2.52:1 1st gear)
	B	Muncie 4-speed M21 close-range (2.20:1 1st gear)
	C	Muncie 4-speed M22 close-range (2.20:1 1st gear) Rock Crusher
	K	Turbo Hydra-Matic 400, 350-ci engines
	S	Turbo Hydra-Matic 400, 454-ci engines
1973	P	Muncie 4-speed, heavy-duty aluminum case
	A	Muncie 4-speed M20 wide-range (2.52:1 1st gear)
	B	Muncie 4-speed M21 close-range (2.20:1 1st gear)
	CK	Turbo Hydra-Matic 400, 350-ci L48 engine
	Y	Turbo Hydra-Matic 400, 350-ci L82 engine
	CS	Turbo Hydra-Matic 400, 454-ci engine

Year	Serial Number Alpha Code	Application
1974	P	Muncie 4-speed, heavy-duty aluminum case
	A	Muncie 4-speed M20 wide-range (2.52:1 1st gear)
	B	Muncie 4-speed M21 close-range (2.20:1 1st gear)
	W	BorgWarner 4-speed, heavy-duty aluminum case
	CK	Turbo Hydra-Matic 400, 350-ci L48 engine
	CZ	Turbo Hydra-Matic 400, 350-ci L82 engine
	CS	Turbo Hydra-Matic 400, 454-ci engine
1975	W	BorgWarner 4-speed, heavy-duty aluminum case
	CK	Turbo Hydra-Matic 400 with L48 engine
	CZ	Turbo Hydra-Matic 400 with L82 engine
1976	W	BorgWarner 4-speed, heavy-duty aluminum case
	AM, XH	Turbo Hydra-Matic 350 with L48 engine
	CZ	Turbo Hydra-Matic 400 with L82 engine
1977	W	BorgWarner 4-speed, heavy-duty aluminum case
	AM	Turbo Hydra-Matic 350 with L48 engine
	CB	Turbo Hydra-Matic 400 with L82 engine
1978	S6	BorgWarner 4-speed, aluminum case, wide-ratio (2.85:1 1st gear)
	ZU	BorgWarner 4-speed, aluminum case, wide-ratio (2.64:1 1st gear)
	ZW	BorgWarner 4-speed, aluminum case, close-ratio (2.43:1 1st gear)
	5WB	Turbo Hydra-Matic 350
	5TL	Turbo Hydra-Matic 350
1979	UH	BorgWarner 4-speed, aluminum case, wide-ratio (2.64:1 1st gear)
	UK	BorgWarner 4-speed, aluminum case, close-ratio (2.43:1 1st gear)
	TB	Turbo Hydra-Matic 350
	WB	Turbo Hydra-Matic 350
1980	ZJ	BorgWarner 4-speed, aluminum case, wide-ratio (2.88:1 1st gear)
	JC	Turbo Hydra-Matic 350, with 305 California engine
	TW	Turbo Hydra-Matic 350, with 350 engine
1981	CC	BorgWarner 4-speed, aluminum case, wide-ratio (2.88:1 1st gear)
	8JD	Turbo Hydra-Matic 350
1982	YA	Turbo Hydra-Matic 700-R4, 4-speed automatic with overdrive

Here, a Muncie transmission is being installed into the back of a 327-ci engine and will be secured with four 3/4-inch bolts that need to be torqued to 70 ft-lbs. One person can do this task but it is much easier when a second person is lending a hand.

This display simulating a Corvette on the St. Louis assembly line is at the National Corvette Museum in Bowling Green, Kentucky. The Muncie M20 wide-ratio 4-speed has been installed behind a 190-hp, 350-ci engine in this 1973 Corvette. (Note the shifter, shifting levers, and the reverse lockout cable.) The transmission is attached to the frame with two bolts on a bracket that bolts to the frame and to the transmission extension. The exhaust is also mounted onto this bracket.

This completely refurbished Muncie is ready to be installed into a 1968 Corvette. The shifter has been installed prior to the transmission being attached to the 327-ci engine. The transmission is equipped with new gears, bearings, and synchronizers.

from 1968 to 1971, the M22 earned the nickname "Rock Crusher" because its straight-cut gears made a distinctive noise while driving. It was designed for maximum performance and could usually be found installed behind L88s and other high-torque big-block engines. Only 336 were installed at the factory. It was very popular with road racers and came with the same gear ratios that were installed into the M21 close-ratio transmission.

BorgWarner

The BorgWarner ST-10 4-speed featured an aluminum case and was phased into Corvette production in early 1974. By 1975, it replaced the Muncie completely. Called the Super T-10, it was offered as a close-ratio (M21) with a 2.43 first, 1.61 second, 1.23 third, and 1.00:1 fourth. The M20 wide-ratio version had 2.64 first, 1.75 second, 1.34 third, and 1.00:1 fourth.

In 1979, the 4-speed option code was changed to MM4, and it was available in both close- and wide-ratio versions.

In 1980 and 1981, only the wide-ratio 4-speed MM4 was available and its ratios were 2.88 first, 1.91 second, 1.33 third, and 1.00:1 fourth. This transmission had wider gear spacing to help increase fuel economy.

The last year the optional L82 engine was available with a 4-speed was 1979. During its last year of production in 1980 the L82 engine was only available with an automatic transmission.

BorgWarner transmissions for Corvettes have a 26-spline input shaft and a 32-spline TH400 output shaft. The 1982 output shaft on the TH350 used a 27-spline output shaft and had a 1-inch countershaft diameter. With the correct bellhousing that matches

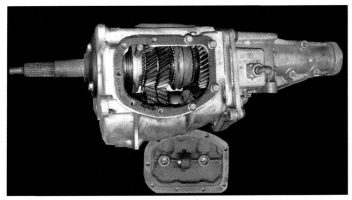

The BorgWarner Super T-10 4-speed manual transmission was first introduced during Corvette production in 1974. In 1975 it became the only manual transmission available for Corvettes. The side cover requires nine bolts to secure it to the case.

Here, one of the shifting forks has been inserted into the gears in the front of the transmission. The W (indicating Warner as the manufacturer) is stamped at the rear of this case.

Many common problems with this transmission, such as gear clashing and high shift effort, are probably due to improper shift linkage adjustment. If the shifter is loose it could be due to worn grommets in the shift linkage or loose shift levers. These are very robust transmissions and it's always a good idea to check the linkage condition and make adjustments before digging into the transmission.

each transmission's bolt pattern they are compatible with GM 327, 350, 427, and 454 Corvette engines.

Troubleshooting Muncie and BorgWarner 4-speeds

If you're having difficulty shifting the 4-speed in your C3, first check to determine whether your engine and transmission mounts are loose.

Raise the car safely in the air and set it on safety stands. Then place a floor jack under the transmission while putting a piece of scrap wood between the jack pad and the transmission. Slowly lift the jack while observing if the engine or transmission moves up or down. Any movement indicates the motor and transmission mounts are loose; you need to tighten all of these bolts. If any of these mounts are separated replace the defective mount.

Next, check the clutch pedal travel. Run the engine at idle with the transmission in neutral and the clutch engaged. Let the clutch out, wait about 10 seconds, engage the clutch, and put the transmission in reverse. A grinding noise indicates the clutch is out of adjustment or some other clutch problem. The shifting forks and synchronizers are prone to wear in these units. This causes gear rattle, difficulty engaging a gear without grinding, and the tendency for the gear to pop out of its position. Faulty clutch and shifter adjustment also impact shifting smoothness.

Transmission Production Codes

The production codes are located on the particular gearbox cases. The nine-digit code breaks down like this: The first digit represents the division. The second is the last digit of the model year. The third represents the assembly plant. The last six digits should match the last six digits of your VIN (identifying the source car). If the numbers don't match, your transmission has been changed; however, even an original engine may have had parts swapped for repair work during its lengthy service.

Saginaw 3-Speed
Built from 1968 to 1969. Production number can be found on the machined surface on the driver's side of the case.

Muncie 4-Speed
Built from 1968 to 1974. Production number is on the passenger's side of the case ahead of the transmission extension.

BorgWarner 4-Speed
Built from 1974 to 1981. Production number is on the top driver's side of the case.

Always check the fluid level in these transmissions, as low fluid also causes erratic shifting. Shifting rods that are out of adjustment is also a common reason that a transmission is hard to shift.

Aftermarket Overdrive Transmissions

If you are planning on doing a lot of highway cruising in your restored Corvette now might be the right time to consider installing a 5-speed manual transmission, such as the Tremec TKO.

One of the GM Turbo Hydra-Matics is also a good choice. In 1968, Corvette's automatics underwent a major redesign. The new M40 Turbo Hydra-Matic was introduced in two versions: the TH350 and the TH400. Both carried the same option code. The factory installed the correct transmission type based on the type of engine ordered. The former 2-speed Powerglide was discontinued in favor of this 3-speed unit.

Tremec TKO

American Powertrain offers its Tremec TKO 5-speed with a .064:1 fifth gear. The ProFit system for the C3 makes installation much easier if your car is already equipped with a manual transmission. You can use the existing bellhousing and clutch with this conversion if they are in good working condition, which saves money.

This conversion requires a new driveshaft, which comes with the ProFit system. The new transmission is longer than the GM 4-speed so a shorter driveshaft is required to align with the rear differential housing. This conversion provides a huge increase in fuel efficiency.

A C3 with a final axle ratio of 3.55:1 turns about 3,000 rpm with the original 4-speed at 70 mph. After the Tremec is installed, the engine operates at 1,900 rpm when traveling 70 mph. This adds life to your engine and greatly improves your fuel mileage. You will also notice how much quieter the car is during cruising.

The TH350 was an immediate improvement over the very slow-shifting 2-speed Powerglide automatic it replaced. Only 2,324 were ordered in 1967, compared to 5,063 in 1968. This transmission was installed into all small-block Corvettes until 1981. It was also used in a wide variety of other GM products, including passenger cars and trucks. It can be easily modified and is a favorite among drag racers because of its performance and rugged construction.

This 350 has been refurbished by Gear Star Transmission Company and modified to handle engine output up to 500 hp/450 ft-lbs of torque. (Photo Courtesy Gear Star)

This cutaway shows a clear view of the torque converter and the various clutches that are installed onto the input shaft of an M40. Automatic transmission fluid (ATF) is pumped through the unit to provide lubrication and pressure to the unit. The ATF enables the valve body to shift the transmission into the correct gear.

Clean fluid and filters help extend the transmission's life and provide positive shifting. Frequent heavy-duty use calls for frequent transmission fluid and oil changes. This keeps the transmission shifting as designed and extends its life. (Photo Courtesy Cutaway Creations)

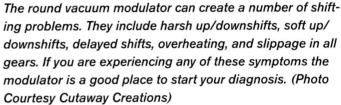

The round vacuum modulator can create a number of shifting problems. They include harsh up/downshifts, soft up/downshifts, delayed shifts, overheating, and slippage in all gears. If you are experiencing any of these symptoms the modulator is a good place to start your diagnosis. (Photo Courtesy Cutaway Creations)

The TH400 was introduced in 1968. In its first year of production it was only available for 390- and 400-hp 427-ci engines. The engineers were not certain it would stand up behind the 430- and 435-hp engines. After extensive testing in 1968 to strengthen it, the transmission became available in 1969 for all big-block engines including the L88.

Each transmission has an identification tag on the passenger's side that includes its type and build date. This particular TH400 came from a Pontiac, so the bellhousing has two mounts on the top, which is different than for a Corvette.

TH350

The TH350 automatic transmission is designed for small-block Chevy and Corvette applications. It weighs 120 pounds and is 21.75 inches long. Its case is cast aluminum and features a 2.52 first, 1.52 second, and 1.00 third. It has a distinctive oil pan that is recessed on the right rear side of the case.

This popular transmission has a good reputation for strength and durability. It can be affordably rebuilt with better components. For example, shifter kits can provide quicker, firmer shifts with less slippage and reduced clutch heat.

You can also change the torque converter to improve your transmission's horsepower capabilities. Aftermarket transmission rebuilders can provide options on how much your TH350 can handle. Gear Star offers three power-output stages for refurbished TH350 transmissions, ranging from 400 hp/400 ft-lbs of torque to 500 hp/450 ft-lbs of torque to 700 hp/550 ft-lbs of torque.

TH400

The TH400 automatic transmission is designed for Corvette big-blocks with engines rated up to 400 hp. It tips the scales at 135 pounds and features

---

TECH TIP

TH400 Changes

The following is a list of changes Gear Star made to the TH400 transmission during overhauls.

- 12- or 13-inch converter
- Master overhaul kit with high-energy friction and steel plates
- High-flow filter
- New kickdown solenoid
- Adjustable modulator
- Transgo shift kit
- New front band
- New BorgWarner low-reverse band
- New Torrington bearings

- Bushing kit
- Thrust washer kit
- New low-reverse spring and roller
- High-capacity, direct-clutch drum
- Heavy-duty, forward-clutch hub
- High-volume, high-flow pump assembly with new gears
- New transmission pan
- New speedometer gear
- Hayden transmission cooler

---

a cast-aluminum case with a 2.48 first, 1.48 second, and 1.00:1 third. In 1969 a heavy-duty version of the Turbo 400 became available for the L71 (435 hp), L88 (430 hp), and L89 (L71 with aluminum heads). A Y code in the serial number identifies them.

This transmission continues to be a favorite with drag racers because it is so strong and reliable. Aftermarket suppliers offer refurbished 400 transmissions with three power options: 450 hp/425 ft-lbs of torque, 600 hp/550 ft-lbs of torque, and 1,200 hp/1,000 ft-lbs of torque.

Transmission Inspection and Testing

1 Disassemble Transmission

This TH400 has been completely disassembled by transmission rebuilder Gear Star. Each part is inspected and replaced if it shows any wear or damage. The torque converter can be seen at the left, and the valve body is also on the left. The case that is sitting on the right will be completely disassembled and cleaned of all its grit and grime in a high-pressure washer then pressure tested for any cracks prior to being rebuilt.

2 Clean Case and Parts

Once all of the parts have been removed from a TH400, Gear Star puts the case into this cleaning basket. The basket spins and hot steam cleans all surfaces until they are completely free of all contaminants. The case is then tested to make sure it has no defects before it is overhauled.

3 Check for Wear or Damage

Any component, such as this forward clutch drum, that shows wear or damage will be replaced. The extra horsepower capability that is built into these refurbished transmissions requires the parts to be capable of handling this extra stress.

The intermediate steel (left) and intermediate friction (right) clutches both show wear and will be replaced. Clutches like these can be found in 350 and 400 transmissions and are very prone to wearing as the miles pile on. It is good practice to replace any parts that show wear.

4 Choose Torque Converter

The stock GM TH400 torque converter is on the right. The smaller, higher-pressure Gear Star torque converter is on the left. These smaller converters are designed to hold more pressure and can handle engines that produce up to 1,200 hp.

5 Choose Bellhousing

Internally both of these refurbished transmissions are built to the same horsepower specifications. The unit on the left is a Corvette TH400 and the one on the right can be used in a Buick, Oldsmobile, or Pontiac. The giveaway is the different mounting outline on the bellhousing.

6 Perform Dyno Test

Here, a hydraulic crane is used to lift and install a TH400 transmission onto the dyno. Without fluid they weigh 135 pounds. Dyno testing is a great way to confirm the transmission's capabilities under stress.

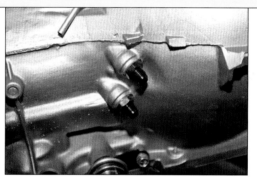

Gear Star has installed new hydraulic fluid fittings on this transmission. During the dyno test the transmission is filled with the correct amount of fluid to check the mechanical workings of the transmission. The top connector sends fluid to the radiator to be cooled. The bottom connector receives fluid from the radiator that has been cooled. This pumping action is important to the health of these transmissions. Because these units produce a tremendous amount of heat, a good cooling system is vital.

A pair of locking pliers is attached to the transmission shifter to allow the dyno operator to shift the test unit into every gear including reverse. If any abnormalities are discovered the unit is sent back to the shop to correct them.

All of the hydraulic lines have been installed. The dyno test checks shifting, pump pressure, transmission temperature, and gear slippage. A printout of the unit's performance is reviewed by the engineers for any potential issues before shipping.

This is what a completely refurbished Gear Star TH400 looks like when all of the work has been completed. Each completed transmission is tested on the transmission dyno to ensure it meets the owner's performance requirements. (Photo Courtesy Gear Star)

TH700R4

In 1982 a new Turbo Hydra-Matic 700R4 was standard equipment on Corvettes. It was the only transmission available and featured a fourth gear overdrive to help improve fuel economy. It featured a 3.06 first, 1.62 second, 1.00 third, and .70:1 fourth. The TH700R4 was strong enough for the 200-hp Cross-Fire 350 engine, but it could not support the higher horsepower levels as did previous automatics installed in earlier Corvettes.

Troubleshooting TH350/TH400/TH700R4

The first step in the troubleshooting process is to check the fluid level.

If it is correct check the downshift cable adjustment. Look for any loose or broken vacuum lines and correct as necessary.

Check the manual linkage to make sure it properly engages the transmission into the correct gear.

Inspect the vacuum modulator, which can cause the following: harsh up/downshifts, delayed shifts, and slippage in low, drive, or reverse. If any of these conditions occur remove the modulator vacuum line and

probe it with a pipe cleaner to see if fluid is present. If it is, replace the modulator.

Inspect the torque converter, which is a mechanical and fluid coupling that connects the transmission to the engine. It serves the same purpose as a clutch pedal in a manual transmission. When the speed increases, the converter spins and multiplies the torque inside the unit. It is important to understand that a one-way or sprag clutch is used in a torque converter. When the converter spins, it spins faster than the engine turns. When the converter slows as the engine speed decreases, it must "catch" or stop so the engine can drive it again. This sprag clutch design lets this happen. It allows the converter to race in one direction only and catches against the clutch in the opposite direction.

A defective sprag clutch won't allow your Corvette to go into low or reverse gear. If your transmission is full of clean fluid and is slow going into gear (or not at all), the problem could be the converter.

To check for a bad converter, the transmission must be removed. The converter has engagement tabs and a spline. Use a couple of long screwdrivers and wedge one of them into the spline to hold it stationary. Try to turn the tab with the other screwdriver. It

should freely spin in one direction and hold firmly in the other. If it doesn't, the converter is faulty.

If the transmission does not move at all, also look at the pump pressure. This is rarely the problem because most pumps are very reliable, but a quick check is a good idea. The following is not a precise test because a pressure gauge should be installed, but it gives you the needed information.

Loosen a transmission cooling line (most are at the radiator) and start the engine. Wrap a rag around the fitting and place it into a container to prevent fluid from going everywhere. A sound pump sprays fluid under a fairly high pressure. If you don't see a gusher of fluid, you

Turbo Hydra-Matic Production Number Locations

Turbo Hydra-Matic 350
1976-1981
The number is located on the passenger side of the transmission oil pan.

Turbo Hydra-Matic 400
1968-1977
The number is attached to the transmission case above the passenger side of the oil pan.

Turbo Hydra-Matic 700R4
1982
The number is located on the passenger side of the oil pan rail. ∎

have a pump problem. Be very careful when performing this procedure, and only run the engine a few seconds to prevent running the transmission dry.

Before condemning the pump, though, remove the service pan and check the transmission filter. A plugged or dirty filter can cause low-pressure problems.

If you decide to investigate further into your transmission I recommend *How to Rebuild and Modify GM Turbo 400 Transmissions* by Cliff Ruggles.

Serial Numbers

Saginaw 3-Speed, Muncie 4-Speed

The 3- and 4-speed serial numbers for 1968–1969 Corvette transmissions all begin with a letter. Next is the last digit of the model year, then two digits designating the day (01 through 31) it was built. The final digit is the gear ratio.

BorgWarner 4-Speed

This transmission serial number begins with a W, followed by the month and day, then the last digit of the calendar year.

Turbo Hydra-Matic 350

This serial number contains the manufacturing location (B for Parma, Y for Toledo, or J for GM Canada), a single digit for the model year (6 for 1976, for example), a letter representing the month (see chart, right), and a number for the day produced (01 through 31), and a letter for the workshift (D for day or N for night).

Turbo Hydra-Matic 400

The number is stamped on the tag on the front passenger side of the transmission. It begins with the last two digits of the vehicle model year then the model and engine type code from the chart to the right. It ends with three digits that represent the calendar days of the year for the build date (which begins when the model-year production started and continues until the end of the model production year).

Turbo Hydra-Matic 700R4

The 1982 transmission stamping begins with a 9 for the model year, followed by the vehicle code YA, then a three-digit build date, ending with a D or N for build workshift.

Calendar Month Codes
(Muncie & Turbo Hydra-Matic)

A	January	K	July
B	February	M	August
C	March	P	September
D	April	R	October
E	May	S	November
H	June	T	December

Calendar Month Codes
(Warner)

A	January	G	July
B	February	H	August
C	March	J	September
D	April	K	October
E	May	L	November
F	June	M	December

WIRING AND INTERIOR INSTALLATION

If you're performing a complete restoration and have followed the book to this point, your Corvette is in the final stages of its journey. The body has been repaired, filled, sanded, primed, and now shines with a new paint job. Your rebuilt engine has been reunited with your refurbished frame.

Before reuniting the body with the frame, install the interior back into the completed body. Or, you can wait until the body has been mounted onto the frame. The advantage of waiting is to reduce the weight of the body when it is lowered onto the frame. It is your choice.

The first thing to do is clean the body and interior and lay out the new carpet on the floor to relax the folds from being stored in a box. I decided to install the interior into the car first because it fit into my schedule better but you can do this in any order.

Wiring

Depending on your situation, reconnect your existing wiring harnesses or replace any damaged or worn ones with new harnesses.

The third-generation Corvette was produced over a span of 14 years. During this time, the country underwent a social shift with a better awareness of emissions and a dramatic rise in gasoline prices. Corvette engineers were forced to squeeze more efficiency out of engines and transmissions to improve mileage. Horsepower declined from a high of 435 to a low of 165 in 1975. It finally stabilized at 200 during the C3's last year of production in 1982. Meanwhile, Corvette customers demanded

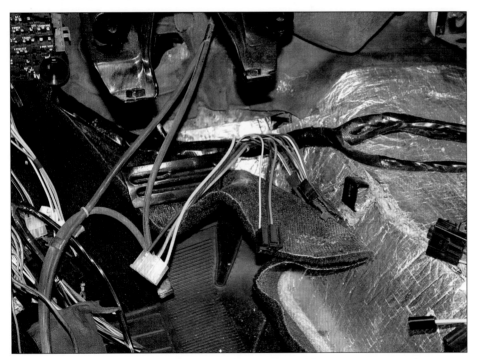

Corvettes, like many cars, are filled with complex wiring to operate various accessories. It is best to reinstall all of the wiring before you reinstall the interior. Many wires are hidden under the carpet so it is best to complete and test your electrical components before reinstalling the interior.

to have more comfort and convenience features added to the optional equipment lists. By 1981, the number of electronic engine controls continued to increase and the engine was controlled by an onboard computer.

The demand for additional optional equipment and electronic engine controls greatly added to the later C3 wiring complexity. As a result, the wiring harnesses had to include plugs for optional equipment whether it was installed in the car or not.

As you begin reconnecting your wiring harness, you may find it has unused connectors. This depends on the year of production and the factory-installed optional equipment

on the car. This is why, in Chapter 3, I recommended that you tag each electrical connecter as it was unplugged. Whether you reuse your old wiring or replace it, this makes your rewiring job much easier and more straightforward.

Before installing new carpet, route all of your wires inside the cabin and back to the rear of the car. A GM Factory Assembly Manual for your year car is very valuable for reconnecting the wiring, and it is much more detailed than a GM Shop Manual. Assembly Manuals are available from restoration parts suppliers and are well worth the money to have on hand.

The connectors and sockets usually fit into one item that requires a power feed. Installation is much easier as long as you marked your connectors when you removed them from the car.

It is best to lay the wires into the interior and route them under the dash, under the center console, and along the sides of the door frames. Once the body has been reunited with the frame and everything is hooked up, you are able to test the operation of your electrical system.

As long as everything was plugged in correctly, each item should work as designed.

Wiring Harness Installation

1 Inspect New Harness

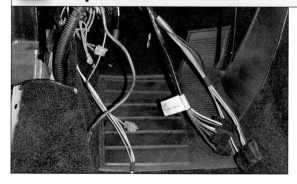

Third-generation Corvette wiring harnesses are available in four major sections: dash, engine, forward lamp, and rear lamp. Depending on the condition of your existing harnesses you can replace any section that is worn or faulty with a new harness and plug it into the rest of your existing system.

This new dash harness was purchased from Lectric Limited, which specializes in producing factory replacement wiring harnesses. It is being installed into a 1972 Corvette and will be plugged into the other original wiring sections.

2 Install Rear Wiring Harness

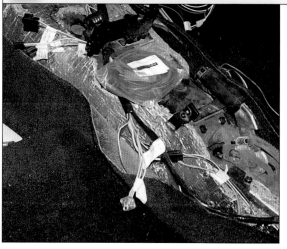

The rear wiring harness was carefully marked with tape at each connector when it was removed. This makes reinstallation much simpler and enables the connectors to plug into their proper locations quickly. Tug on each connector to make sure it is secure. Make sure the wires and connectors are safely out of the way of any screws that may be installed later.

3 Install Lamp Socket and Switch

The passenger courtesy lamp socket and door light switch install into the passenger's side of the dash before the panels are installed. It is much simpler to complete this task with the dash removed from the car.

4 Attach Gauge Cluster Wires

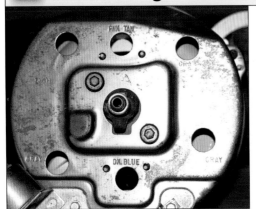

The color of the wires that go on the back of this cluster are stamped into the back of the housing (gray, light blue, etc.). Install new bulbs while you're at it. The tachometer drive connector attaches to the center opening on the back of this cluster. This connector is spring loaded and snaps into place when it is in the correct position.

5 Plug in Headlight Switch

After the headlight switch is installed, locate the headlight connector and plug it into the switch. Again it is much easier to perform this task with the dash panel removed from the car.

Electrical Troubleshooting

You may find that you didn't secure a connector tightly enough or a bulb is burned out when you put power to the system. You can correct these missteps with some simple troubleshooting. A handheld voltmeter with probes can help you tell if a connector is getting its required voltage. This helps you trace that circuit back to its source to determine if it is connected correctly. Before you begin troubleshooting, gather a few handy tools. First select an assortment of automotive fuses that fit your Corvette's fuse panel. You also need a self-powered test light; it looks like a small screwdriver that glows when it is inserted into a wire connector. Also get a test light with a bulb on one end and two probes on the other side; it verifies whether the circuit is getting voltage. An inexpensive voltmeter is a must before you proceed. A small, strong flashlight helps you see wires and connectors that are located in tight places. Be sure to have a wiring diagram for your year Corvette on hand. To round out the list, you need a spray can of electrical contact cleaner, contact grease, a small screwdriver, and a good set of eyes.

A typical circuit inside a car is composed of a battery, conductors (wires), fuse, switch, load, and ground. Typically only four things can cause a circuit not to work: an open circuit, short circuit, high resistance, or an accessory that is defective.

Open Circuit

An open circuit is created when no power is flowing from the power source (battery). This can be caused by:

- Blown fuse or circuit breaker
- Broken wire or broken connector
- Open switch or faulty bulb
- High resistance from a shorted wire or accessory

To find an open circuit carefully inspect for kinked or broken wires. Also look for a wire with damaged insulation that might be touching a metal part. Corroded connectors or terminals cause high resistance and blow fuses. Blown fuses and popped circuit breakers are an indication of an open circuit. Their job is to protect a circuit from overloading, which causes heat that eventually melts the insulation on the wire and causes failure.

A blown fuse is an indicator that a problem exists within the circuit, and the fuse is there to protect it. If the fuse didn't blow, a fire or thermal event is possible.

Your troubleshooting should begin by tracing the faulty circuit from the fuse to the electrical device it powers. Your electrical system has two fusible links that interrupt power from the battery if it detects an unusual surge. These links are usually located above the starter solenoid. Be sure to check these if power is not getting into the cabin.

Short Circuit

When a circuit receives more power than it was designed to handle, a short circuit blows the fuse that protects it almost immediately. Do not replace one fuse with a larger fuse (say, 10-amp with a 15-amp fuse) to get the faulty circuit powered up. This can cause a fire.

Depending on the type of short you are encountering (wire-to-wire or wire-to-metal), you may get odd symptoms. You could turn on a headlight switch and the windshield wipers might start working instead.

Damage or wear from a wire being pinched by clamps or pushed against a piece of sheet metal usually causes short circuits. A connector poking through the wire or a wire routed over a piece of sharp metal that eventually wears through the wiring insulation could also cause it. It is important to locate the fault quickly to minimize any further damage to the electrical system.

Also, circuits can become shorted by an internal problem in the device it is powering, such as a radio or power window switch. Always look for damaged or frayed wires or a burning smell that is emitting from an accessory.

High Resistance

This is caused when a circuit is exposed to a higher load than it was designed to handle. It occurs when a connector is loose, corroded, or not secured to the power terminal correctly. A circuit that has high resistance can dim light bulbs and cause other circuits to run slower. If a ground becomes loose or corroded, it can create high resistance on that circuit. The problem could become so acute that none of the accessories on that circuit function.

Damaged Accessories

A discolored light or a fan making a loud or unusual noise indicates a potential failure. Make sure it is getting the correct amount of voltage and the connector is tight. The repair might be a simple matter of replacing the lamp or switch or fan motor to get everything functioning normally again.

Isolating the Problem

Here's a simple example to isolate a problem. Let's say a taillight is not working. The first thing to try is to replace the bulb. If it works, problem solved.

But what if none of the taillights are working? If you have checked the bulb's fuse and the connectors and still nothing, now is the time to look at the power source to find the problem.

With most electrical problems, just use logical deductive reasoning, and then be thorough and methodical as you inspect, measure, test, and verify the equipment. After all, the best tool is the gray matter between your ears.

Interior

Corvette interiors also evolved during the C3's long production run. From 1968 to 1976 vinyl interior was standard and a leather interior package was optional. In 1968 and 1969 the leather upgrade only included the seats. This option was expanded in 1970 with the addition of cut-pile carpeting, wood grain accents, and carpet trim on the door panels. In 1977 leather seating became standard and the upgrade was included in the base price of the car.

In 1978 the seats received a major upgrade when a pace car was ordered. The pace car interior included redesigned clamshell seats that folded flat on the passenger's side. The new seats featured bolsters that provided more support for the passenger and driver. They were an instant hit and became standard in all Corvettes from 1979 to 1982.

1968–1977 Dash Installation

The dash panels in 1968–1977 Corvettes are different than those in 1978–1982 Corvettes. These earlier cars feature a three-panel dash system that includes the driver-side console, center stack, and storage pockets in front of the passenger. The top of the dash is a separate piece held in place with screws and a series of clips that attach to the lower windshield frame.

If you have misplaced or damaged interior screws, you can order a complete screw package from any aftermarket Corvette warehouse. If your screw holes are enlarged, do not use a bigger screw; instead purchase drywall plastic plugs (like the ones used to hang photos on the wall) from any hardware store. They come in a variety of sizes. Insert them into the enlarged hole to fix the problem. You can use them on any interior reassembly.

The instrument cluster consists of a large tachometer and speedometer. They are enclosed in a metal frame that attaches to the dash panel. The driver-side dash panel also includes a headlight switch on the left and manual headlight door and headlight-override switches under the steering column. This panel includes the ignition switch on 1968 Corvettes.

It is best to assemble and install this side of the dash first. Remember to plug in all of the connectors for the tach and speedometer cables before screwing the unit into the dash frame. The center stack holds all of the critical engine instruments as well as a clock. All of the correct wires should be attached to this stack before mounting it into the dash frame with screws.

At this time, you should install the radio because the passenger's side of the dash is still open, so you can reach around and connect the radio wiring and antenna.

This is now a good time to install the top dash panel pad. Carefully slide the clips into the windshield frame and lower it onto the driver-side console and center stack. Secure it with Phillips screws that you stored during disassembly.

Complete the dash installation by mounting the passenger-side dash cover.

Dash Pad Installation

1 Install Instrument Cluster

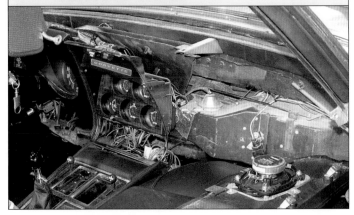

The instrument cluster that includes the tachometer and speedometer is installed onto the driver-side dash panel first. Next plug in the bulbs, wires, and tach, and attach the speedometer cables.

Secure the dash panel into the instrument panel frame; it's much easier to complete this procedure with the steering column removed. All of the wires should be in place before the dash panel is installed. Use a Phillips screwdriver to install the two screws that hold the driver-side panel in place, which is near the steering column.

2 Connect Instrument Console Wires

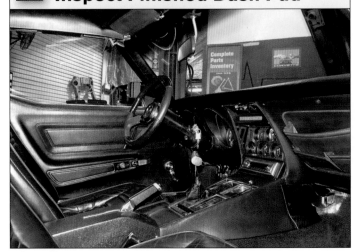

Plug in the color-coded center console instrument cluster wires (your previous tagging should make this task straight-forward). Once the power connectors are plugged into the cluster install the unit into the center opening of the dash.

This is a good time to install the radio because you can reach behind it and hook up the power and antenna connections. The dash pad with the two factory speakers is seen in the foreground of the photo.

3 Install Dash Pad

Once the center cluster is secured, lock the top dash pad into place against the windshield. The top dash is held in place with a bolt that is attached underneath the pad to a bracket on the passenger's side. Use a 5/16-inch socket to tighten it. Steel clips and screws hold this panel in place. Finally, the right side of the dash with the map pockets is installed and screwed into place.

4 Inspect Finished Dash Pad

The completed dash should look like this. The non-factory radio sticks out from the dash, but offers the owner a larger choice of entertainment options.

1978–1982 Interior Installation

Except for the dash panel, the entire interior on our 1980 Van Steel subject car was removed. This included the steering wheel and steering column. The original interior was not damaged or torn but was soiled in some places and the original color was starting to fade after many years of being exposed to the Florida sun. Corvette America provided all necessary new interior parts.

The installation procedure is really just a reversal of the removal process in Chapter 3. Start by installing the center and instrument cluster. It is much easier to perform this task with the steering wheel out of the car. If some of the original engine compartment wires are frayed, you need to install a new harness. (The wiring in this car was left intact with the exception of the engine wiring, which was replaced with a new harness from Lectric Limited.)

Next, return the steering wheel and column to the interior and attach its wiring. The wiring connectors plug into the side of the steering column and each one is different so you cannot install the wrong one. The steering wheel is held in place at the firewall and under the dash.

The various plastic trim panels that surround the windshield and the overhead passenger compartment are next on the list.

Then install the carpets in the driver and passenger compartments. These are preformed pieces and fairly simple to install. They are held in place with the doorsill and a center cover that attaches to each side of the console. The large carpet piece that fits behind the seats and into the cargo compartment should be installed next. The vertical piece in the rear attaches to a rod beneath the window that holds it in place.

The rear carpet is much easier to install in 1978–1982 models because of the large rear windows. They allow room to crawl into the back to secure everything.

When the carpet is in place install the two rear speakers if your car is equipped with this option.

Finally, install items such as the cargo compartment cover, seat belts, seats, and door panels.

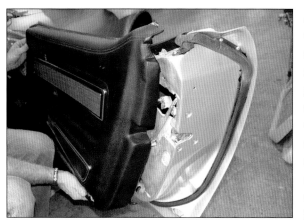

All Corvette door panels clip into the top of the door and are held in place with Phillips screws. The door pull is attached with two screws and the window crank is held in place with a wire clip. The small door lock button that is located behind the door handle is also held in place with a wire clip. The door handle is held in place with a screw. (If you have power windows you do not have a window crank.)

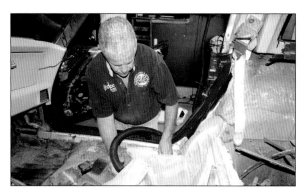

Anything that was stored inside the car must be removed and cataloged correctly so it can be returned to its correct place. Clean all interior surfaces with a vacuum, rags, cleaner and an air hose. Any overspray or dust must be cleaned off these surfaces before attempting to install the interior.

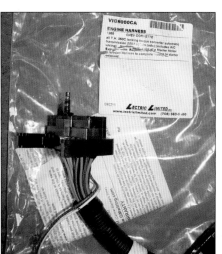

This Lectric Limited harness is a complete plug-and-play unit. It does not require any modification prior to installation. The dash harness bolts onto the firewall on the inside of the car with two screws. The engine harness plugs into the dash wiring harness and is held in place with a single screw from the engine compartment to the dash connector.

Harnesses can be purchased in sections or complete units. It all depends on the condition of your existing wiring system.

Interior Component Installation

1 Install Steering Column

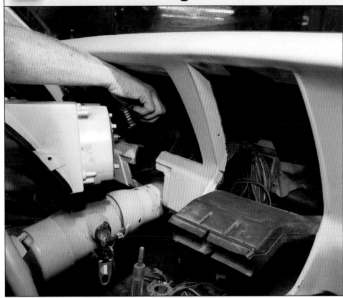

Return the steering column to the interior but do not secure it until the driver's instrument cluster is installed. Connect the speedometer cable onto the back of the cluster, which is held in place with a snap clip. The speedometer cable can be secured by pushing on the bottom of the clip to lock it into place. Plug the power cable into the back of the cluster and then attach it to the dash with Phillips screws.

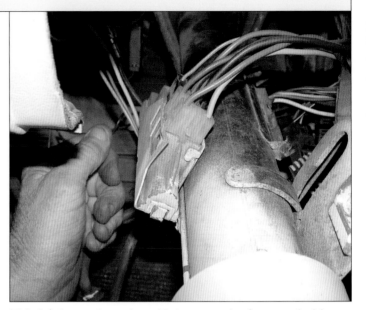

This job is much easier with two people. One can hold the column in place while the second person attaches the wiring and nuts. Two 9/16-inch nuts under the dash and two 1/2-inch nuts on the firewall hold the column place. First install the two 1/2-inch nuts on the firewall studs. The steering column should be low enough so that the wires can be plugged into the side of the column. Each bundle of wires must be matched with the plug on the column.

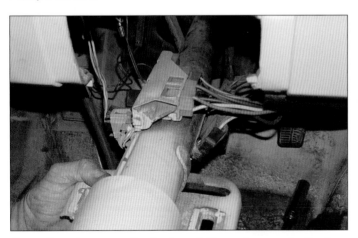

Once the wires are attached push the column onto the two studs under the dash panel. Secure it with two 9/16-inch nuts and tighten them to 30 ft-lbs.

Tighten the two 1/2-inch nuts that are on the inside firewall above the brake pedal. Use a long extension to torque them to 25 ft-lbs. Reinstall the lower cover after hooking up the headlight-override vacuum switch.

2 Install Upper Trim Panel

The upper panel trim is attached with Phillips screws and bolts. The center trim piece (shown) is held in place with the overhead light holder. Two 7/16-inch bolts hold this light socket in place. Continue installing the upper roof and windshield trim with Phillips screws.

3 Install Front of Console

The front of the console is secured with two 1/4-inch nuts and must be attached when reinstalling the cover. It is helpful to locate these nuts with a mirror before attempting to tighten them.

4 Inspect New Seat Covers

Art Dorsett ordered a complete new Doeskin 1980 duplicate GM factory interior from Corvette America that matches his original factory-installed leather. The set includes new driver- and passenger-side leather-covered seat cushions, door panels, carpet, and armrests. The interior will look factory fresh when it is completed.

5 Inspect New Carpet

Remove both passenger- and driver-side carpets from their boxes to lay flat on the floor. (They will be held in place with the lower door trim cover.) Do the same with the rear cargo carpet. It is best to leave them in this position for a while to enable them to regain their shape.

6 Install Front Carpet

The replacement carpet sections are pre-formed and fit into the car with only minor trimming. The driver-side carpet is held in place with the side door trim plate and the center console carpeted cover (not yet installed when this photo was taken).

7 Install Rear Carpet

The rear cargo compartment carpet comes in one molded piece. The front of the cargo compartment is covered with a form-fitted piece of carpet that fits behind the seats and console cover.

Carefully push the carpet into place and secure the rear of the carpet at the back of the rear luggage compartment cover. The back of the cargo compartment is held in place with a U-shaped retainer that must be clipped onto a rod that runs across the top, underneath the rear luggage cover. Once it is clipped on one end it is easy to slide it onto the rod.

On 1968–1977 Corvettes the rear carpet is five separate pieces, driver/passenger-side, fenderwells, rear bulkhead, cargo area, and the piece behind the rear seats. They must be installed as individual pieces. The back piece is glued onto the rear bulkhead.

The original carpet on the 1978–1982 Corvettes was not glued and may need to sit for a while to return to its factory shape.

8 Install Cargo Compartments

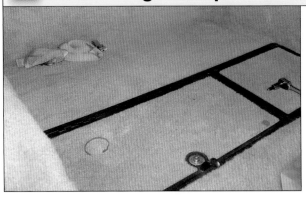

All 1978–1982 rear cargo compartments have two storage bins (1968–1977s have three). These bins are held in place with up to 10 Phillips screws. They must be installed after the rear carpet is in place. These storage bins help the carpet stay in place.

9 Install Center Cluster and Carpet

The center cluster on later C3 Corvettes have much-improved wiring systems. Each instrument is attached to a central connector with copper wiring that is impregnated into a plastic sheet. One main plug powers all of these instruments (shown).

After the cluster is installed attach the two side console carpet covers with three screws on each side. It is best to find their location before installing them. One easy trick is to insert a small piece of wire through the hole to help locate the attaching brackets. One screw is in the back, one is in the middle, and one is in the front.

10 Install Mirror Controls

All 1978–1982 Corvettes that are equipped with optional remote door mirror controls include an adjuster held in place with a metric setscrew. This setscrew must be tightened after the door panel has been installed.

Install the armrest and door pull cover and push the lower panel into the door clips to secure it to the door. A metal channel runs along the top of the door panel. Slide this into the top of the door frame, which allows the door panel to hang on the door. Use the clips (or screws on 1978–1982 models) to attach the panel to the door frame.

The seats are the last items that need to be installed into the interior. Attach a metal bracket with four attachment points to the seat. Each seat sits on top of the carpet and is bolted to the floor in the front and rear with four bolts. The cushions are held in their individual buckets with spring-loaded clips.

1968–1975 Convertible Top Installation

Corvette convertible production outsold coupes only in the first year of C3 production. Each year thereafter the coupe outpaced convertible sales. In its final production year in 1975 a total of 33,836 coupes and only 4,629 convertibles were built. Today C3 convertibles are highly desirable to own. Those that include both the optional hardtop and the convertible top are the most sought after.

Installing a new convertible top is not easy for a novice installer but it can be done. The top needs to be tightly mounted and stapled onto the steel frame, but still allow enough flexibility to fold efficiently into its storage well behind the seats.

Many aftermarket Corvette suppliers sell premade convertible tops. These tops include the rear window and panels that are fitted beneath the top to provide support. This material is attached to the existing metal frame with staples and screws; it usually takes an experienced installer about 3 to 4 hours to complete the job.

A leak-free convertible top adds a lot of driving pleasure to your Corvette experience. If you don't want to do the work yourself, shop around to find a competent professional installer. Don't be afraid to talk to some local Corvette clubs to get some recommendations before making your final selection.

Convertible Top Installation

1 Install Convertible Frame

Corvette convertible top steel frames are attached to the frame behind both seats with four bolts. The frame consists of ribs that are hinged on the sides so that they fold flat when the top is stored in its compartment.

2 Attach Vinyl Strips

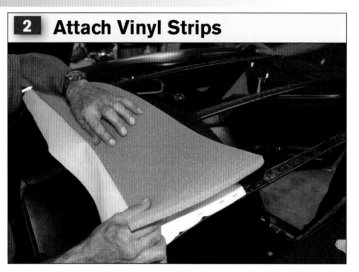

Before the top fabric is installed two panels are attached to the frame. These panels consist of vinyl strips that cover two large foam pieces. The vinyl is stapled to the frame and the foam is spray glued onto the vinyl. The vinyl is folded over to cover the foam and stapled to the frame.

3 Stretch Top and Remove Wrinkles

Premade tops are available from most major Corvette aftermarket suppliers. They are shipped preformed and designed to correctly lay over the car's steel frame top. The trick is finding an upholstery expert who has the knowledge to correctly stretch the material so that it is free of wrinkles.

4 Inspect Complete Installation

The completed top should fit tightly and be free from wrinkles when it is in the up position. A correctly installed top provides many miles of good service, such as the top on Ron Bray's 1971 convertible.

BODY INSTALLATION

The rebuilding of your Corvette's critical components has been a long process. After the body was repaired, painted, and sprayed with clearcoat, the new paint was wet sanded and buffed with compound. The entire interior was cleaned and refitted with its new interior. Once the work was finished the completed body was stored in a safe, low-traffic area. You properly supported the body to avoid putting any unnecessary stress on it and cracking any of its fiberglass body panels. You left the completed and painted body on a dolly because that provides the most secure support.

You are now ready to place the body onto the refurbished frame.

Power Brake Booster Installation

The power brake booster is mounted onto the firewall on Corvettes equipped with this option. Four nuts hold the booster in place and the master cylinder is attached to the front of the booster.

Master Cylinder Installation

Bench bleed the master cylinder before installing it to the firewall. First clamp the cylinder to a vise by using one of the two ears that are used to attach the unit to the firewall. Then remove the cover and fill it with clean brake fluid. Work the pushrod back and forth to force air from the outlets. Be careful not to damage the piston during this operation.

Once the body has been painted and the trim has been reinstalled, it is time to reunite it with your restored frame. Be very careful when you mount the body on a lift and make sure you leave plenty of room to lower it onto the frame rails. Be patient as you are getting close to completing your project.

Remove all of the air before installing it into the car; using vacuum is the most effective way to do this. You can buy a master cylinder bleeder tool at your local auto parts store. With your tool in hand remove about 2 tablespoons of brake fluid from one of the discharge ports. Be sure to keep the reservoir full during this operation. When you are finished, seal off the ports with a cap or bolt to keep dirt out and fluid in during installation.

Mount the master cylinder onto the brake booster. If you do not have power brakes attach the master cylinder directly to the firewall.

The master cylinder is operated when the brake pedal is pushed. Force is transferred via a pushrod to the master cylinder piston, which moves forward. This force is applied to the primary piston spring, which moves a secondary piston forward at the same time. When these pistons move forward they cover the bypass holes and hydraulic pressure builds up actuating the pistons in the brake calipers.

When the brakes are released the piston return springs force the fluid back through the brake lines into the master cylinder. At the end of the brake release excess brake fluid is returned to the reservoir through the bypass ports inside the master cylinder.

Steel lines connect the brass block to both sides of the master cylinder. A distribution block is not a proportioning valve; its function is to distribute the master cylinder fluid to all four wheels. It also measures line pressure difference under braking conditions to two separate braking systems. A warning light is connected to the block that illuminates a warning lamp on the dash if one of the braking systems fails.

Body and Frame Preparation

The frame has now been completely repaired and is free of damage and rust. The powdercoat finish will keep it this way for many miles. The suspension, brakes, and driveline components have all received attention and have been refurbished or replaced. All of the brake and fuel lines are new. With proper care, such as yearly flushing, they should provide excellent service. The gas tank and steering system have been installed, which completes the frame preparation process.

The frame is now ready for its Corvette body. This is where the industrial steel casters that were installed onto the dolly pay off. They rotate 360 degrees and make moving the body a breeze.

If you don't have a lift, it is time to get some friends to help maneuver the body. One person at each corner of the car should have enough muscle

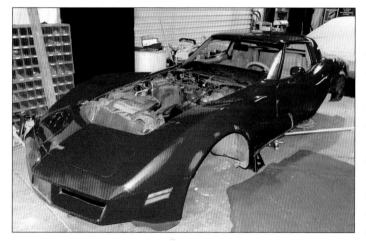

Work on the body, engine, frame, suspension, and paint on this 1980 Corvette has been completed. While the frame was being restored, the body was repaired, sanded, and given a new paint job. After the trim and interior were reinstalled the body was stored on a floor dolly. Great care was taken to support the long nose to avoid putting it under stress.

The frame measurements were checked to make sure it meets factory specifications. All rust and road damage was fixed. After the frame was powdercoated, new or refurbished suspension components were installed. The frame received all new brake and fuel lines. The front and rear suspensions were completely refurbished. The original engine and automatic transmission on this car were in excellent mechanical condition. Both were returned to the frame without any service. The gas tank was inspected and no rust or damage was found so it was reinstalled. The completed unit is now ready to accept the body installation. It will be removed from the lift area and set aside until the body is in place and secured onto the lift.

power to lift the body and guide it into the correct position on the frame.

As I mentioned, both the coupe and convertible bodies are fitted with a steel frame called the birdcage. The fiberglass body panels are attached to this frame. The coupe is more rigid because a steel hoop is installed behind the passenger compartment that is secured to the windshield frame with a center steel support. This support is used to attach the twin roof panels.

Convertibles do not have this feature and great care must be taken when lifting these bodies. Having the

doors installed on a convertible does provide some additional body support, but it's best to take extra care.

At Van Steel the body was rolled into the lift area to begin the reassembly of the body to the frame. We used a four-point lift to complete this procedure. The four pads on the lift provide enough support to the birdcage to safely raise the body high enough to roll the frame under it.

It's very important to position the lift pads on the very outside edges of the birdcage because there must be enough room for the frame rails to fit when the body is lowered onto the frame. Once the body is

firmly resting on the lift pads, slowly lift it off its dolly. At this time, closely inspect the body to make sure it is sitting securely on the lift. If it is not secure, lower it back onto the dolly and reposition the lift pads until you are satisfied that it is secure.

After the dolly has been removed, roll the completed frame under the body. Double-check to make sure it is lined up correctly as you do not want to damage the newly painted fiberglass during the lowering procedure. Once the frame is in its correct position, place the body mount doughnuts into their correct location onto the frame.

1 Move Body into Assembly Area

The steel casters that support the car are very maneuverable. It is always good to have friends on alert during your restoration process because you may need some help from time to time. Make sure the body is properly positioned and equally balanced on the dolly. Carefully and cautiously move the body across the shop floor on the dolly; everyone needs to work as a team. Be sure that the body does not slip off the dolly because you would not want to damage the body and crack the body work or the paint surface. Use extreme caution when using this method because of safety concerns.

2 Locate Lift Arms

If using a lift, place the four lift arms onto the steel birdcage that surround the body. This birdcage is strong enough to support the body as long as the lift arms are placed correctly. It is important to lift the body evenly to eliminate any stress to the body panels during this procedure.

3 Position Body Over Chassis

The bottom of the Corvette's steel birdcage is under a lower panel that is usually covered with a trim piece or sidepipes. This panel must be removed prior to lifting the body back onto the frame.

Notice how close to the edge of the birdcage the lifting pads are placed. This was done to leave enough room to allow the body to be lowered onto the frame. If the pads are moved too far inward they hit the frame and have to be repositioned.

4 Check Body Position

Make a final check to ensure that the body does not shift when it is lifted and to leave enough room to roll the frame under it. Once you are satisfied, roll the completed chassis into place beneath the body.

Body Installation

Confirm the body is securely sitting on the lift pads and then slowly raise the body high enough to clear the frame. Position the frame under the body and make sure all of the wires are out of the way. If a wire gets snagged, reassembly becomes more troublesome as you try to locate the broken connection. Make sure the body-mount doughnuts are still in the correct location. After this has been rechecked and everything is in order you can start lowering the body onto the frame.

1 Identify Body Mounts

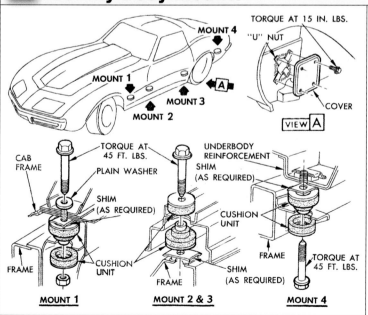

This diagram explains where each individual C3 body mount is fitted on all coupes. (Convertibles have an additional connection between mount No. 2 and No. 3 that is indicated by View A on the drawing.) Pay close attention to how the doughnuts and shims are located as each one is slightly different. The correct torque specifications are also indicated here. (Photo Courtesy Van Steel)

This 1973–1982 Van Steel body mount kit includes all necessary parts and instructions to safely secure the body to the frame. Van Steel also offers a 1968–1972 body mount kit.

2 Connect Electrical Wires

It is very important to follow the GM body diagram when placing the mounts into their correct location on the frame. Some have their washers on the top while others do not. It all depends on the location. All of them must be installed onto the frame correctly prior to lowering the body.

This body mount is fitted to the driver-side front bracket located under the front door. The attachment bolt is installed inside the body footwell where it is secured to the frame bracket after the body is lowered onto the frame. During the lowering process it is a good idea to routinely check to make sure that these doughnuts have not shifted. If they do, raise the body and reset the doughnuts.

The left center body mount is identical to the one that is located in front of the door. If you have a convertible you need to install one additional doughnut on the frame. This one is located under the center of the door between mounts #2 and #3. Review Step No. 1 on page 161.

When the frame is in the correct location, lower the body slowly onto the frame. Only lift the body high enough to clear the highest obstacle on the frame to minimize the risk of the body falling off the lift pads.

Make room in the tight engine compartment by removing the air cleaner assembly. If you do, make sure the air intake on the carburetor is sealed so no stray part falls into it. This would be costly and time consuming to fix.

As the body is being lowered onto the frame pay particular attention to the clearance in the engine compartment. The engine compartment on this generation Corvette is a very tight fit and any contact with an inner fender or firewall could cause extensive damage. Make sure no wires are hanging or have gotten caught on something that might rip or tear them from their mountings.

We used a long-handle broom to snag the transmission shift cable that was laying underneath the car. We wanted to make sure it was on the driver's side of the transmission as the body was lowered onto the frame. Failure to do this can crush or bend the cable so it is unusable. Do not be in a rush to complete this step. It is a good idea to lower the body a few inches and then stop to make sure the wiring and mechanical parts are clear.

Connect the Steering

As the body is lowered onto the frame, pay particular attention to installing the steering column flexible coupling onto the steering gear. When the steering column reaches the steering gear, stop the drop while you line up each end of the steering column and the steering gear.

The shaft on the steering gear has a flat flange on one side. It must be lined up to the flange inside the flexible coupling on the steering column. Work the two flanges back and forth until they are matched. Use a small hammer to gently tap the steering gear flange onto the steering gear shaft. When both units are coupled correctly tighten the bolts and resume lowering the body onto the frame.

1 Align Steering Collar to Spline

Line up the steering column collar so it can be attached to the steering box spline. In addition position the brake lines to be installed onto the master cylinder.

It helps to have two people working on this task. One can turn the steering wheel while the other lines up the steering box with the steering column. These two parts need to be matched up as the body is being lowered onto the frame.

The steering box spline has a flat spot that helps it line up with the steering column collar.

2 Seat Column on Spline

Once everything is lined up correctly, lightly tap on the steering column to seat it on the steering box spline. Make sure the flat spot on the steering box spline is lined up correctly with the steering box collar before tightening the four bolts. These are 12-point 7/16-inch bolts that require the use of a 12-point socket to tighten them.

Turn them until they stop. You want them tight, but be careful to not snap the heads off the bolts.

Install the Headlight Doors

Every C3 Corvette utilizes vacuum-operated headlight doors that retract into the nose when they are not in use. The engine provides pressure to the actuators. A manual override system is located underneath the steering column and the doors can be kept in the open position at the driver's command. The vacuum system requires many lengthy rubber hoses to operate and a cracked or broken hose or connector can cause a vacuum leak in the engine.

Aftermarket Corvette suppliers, such as Lonestar Caliper Company, sell replacement headlight door parts.

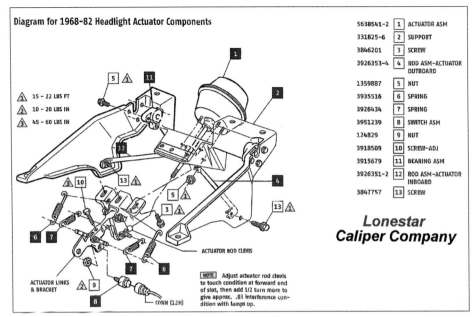

Diagram for 1968-82 Headlight Actuator Components

5638541-2	1	ACTUATOR ASM
331825-6	2	SUPPORT
3846201	3	SCREW
3926353-4	4	ROD ASM–ACTUATOR OUTBOARD
1359887	5	NUT
3935516	6	SPRING
3926434	7	SPRING
3951239	8	SWITCH ASM
124829	9	NUT
3918509	10	SCREW-ADJ
3915679	11	BEARING ASM
3926351-2	12	ROD ASM–ACTUATOR INBOARD
3847757	13	SCREW

Lonestar Caliper Company

△ 15 – 22 LBS FT
△ 10 – 20 LBS IN
△ 45 – 60 LBS IN

ACTUATOR ROD CLEVIS

ACTUATOR LINKS & BRACKET

CONN (12H)

NOTE: Adjust actuator rod clevis to touch condition at forward end of slot, then add 1/2 turn more to give approx. .03 interference condition with lamps up.

This exploded view diagram shows the headlight actuator system. (Photo Courtesy Lonestar Caliper Co.)

Remove the Front Bumper Cover

If the bumper cover was installed onto your 1973–1982 car after it was painted to prevent it from wrinkling, remove it now. You need this extra working room to install the front bumper assembly that is hidden by this outside cover.

This step is not necessary for 1968–1972 Corvettes as they are equipped with a small bolt-on chrome bumper that can be installed easily.

If your car is a 1973–1982 model, remove the front rubber bumper cover and then remove the bumper bar that is secured to the subframe. If you have painted the Corvette, leave the bumper covers off until the body has been attached to the frame. This bumper cover was left in place during storage so it would not distort. But now is a good time to remove it. Put the front bumper cover in a safe location until it is time to reinstall it. Keep this part away from any excessive heat because it might warp, making it difficult to reinstall.

Align Frame to Body

The frame and body have holes that are located near body mount #2 (see step 1 on page 161). To aid alignment place a rod through the hole in the lower door jamb and into the hole in the frame. This procedure keeps the body and frame in their correct front and rear locations. It also helps prevent any mechanical components from hitting various parts on the body as it is lowered onto the frame.

Once the body is on the frame measure the gap between the body and the frame. Both front and rear measurements should be the same on both sides of the car. You can shift the body by gently pushing on it until all of the measurements are the same.

1 Lower Body onto Frame

Once the front bumper is removed, finish lowering the body onto the frame. Make sure that none of the rubber doughnuts have shifted out of place. If they have, slightly raise the body, readjust them, and lower the body back onto the frame.

2 Align Body and Frame

Every frame has an alignment hole located behind mount #2 (see illustration on page 161). Its purpose is to line up the body, front to the back. (It also enables the fan and gas tank to align correctly during the body installation.) When these holes cleanly align, the body is properly aligned. Insert a socket extension into the hole to move the body forward and back or left and right depending on the adjustment required.

Measure the body/frame gap behind each wheel on both sides of the car. This helps verify that the body is square on the frame. The right and left sides should have the same measurements. They do not have to be precise but they should be very close.

Front Bumper Installation

As federal crash standards became progressively more stringent during the 1970s, Corvette engineers had to make the 5-mph crash bumper stronger. The 1973–1974 models are the lightest, while later models are stronger because they are fitted with more material.

The front bumper plays a vital role in securing the fiberglass nose to the frame. A metal support on the bumper is bolted to the nose on the underside of the body. This part of the front body is very heavy because it supports the weight of the headlights. The bumper brace helps to prevent cracks in the fiberglass. You might be tempted to omit this heavy metal part, but that is not recommended for street use as it does provide effective front-end protection in case of an accident.

1 Assemble Crash Bumper

Corvettes built from 1973 to 1982 have some form of crash bumper attached to the front frame rails ahead of the engine and suspension. The bumper is concealed under a rubber cover.

This 1980 Corvette uses a rubber eggcrate material that serves as an energy-absorption barrier in case of a sudden impact. It is attached to a steel frame with four bolts. Use a 5/8-inch socket to tighten and torque them to 60 ft-lbs.

This unit bolts directly to the front of the frame to provide maximum strength. The center of the fiberglass nose is secured to the large black piece of metal in the center of the front bumper. Do not forget this bolt because the front overhang on these Corvettes is very long and breaks quickly if it is not attached to the bumper.

2 Position Front Bumper

The bumper is an awkward component to install. It might be helpful to have a third person available to install the frame bolts while two people hold the bumper in place.

3 Attach Front Bumper Brackets

Secure the bumper brackets to the frame with six bolts, use a 3/4-inch socket to attach them.

Here, two of the three 3/4-inch bolts and nuts per side are installed into the front frame rail. The missing third bolt will be inserted into the round black hole. Each one should be torqued to 75 ft-lbs.

One bolt attaches to the front bumper bracket from beneath the nose of the car. Be sure to include the rubber doughnut on top and a washer under the bolt. This bolt is very important to install because it prevents the nose from shifting or sagging. Use a 5/8-inch socket to secure to the body and torque it to 60 ft-lbs.

Secure the Body

When the body is resting on the frame and you have confirmed that the alignment is correct, insert the body bolts. (See step 1 on page 161 for the correct placements and torque specifications.) Before tightening them, it is a good idea to insert each one and turn it several times into the

This is what the passenger-side rear No. 3 mount bolt looks like prior to being tightened into the frame (see step 1 on page 161). Torque each bolt to 45 ft-lbs.

This body mount bolt can be reached through the removable panel inside the rear fenderwell. The mount should be torqued to 45 ft-lbs, which is enough to secure the body to the frame. This spec helps reduce body flex and minimize frame-to-body squeaks. All 8 coupe bolts (10 for convertibles) should be secured the same way.

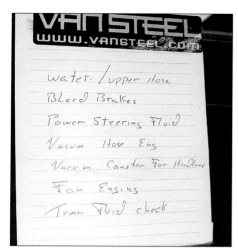

A good time to check your notes is when you are filling fluids and hooking up vital components. Before proceeding check and double-check each item on your startup list, such as fluids and correct hose hookups.

nut to make sure it lines up correctly. Once all bolts are started, tighten them beginning with No. 1 and moving toward the rear on each side of the car until they are all secured.

Fluid Level Check

You want to add the right fluid/ oils to the radiator, power steering,

Start adding necessary fluids, such as coolant, brake fluid, power steering fluid, and transmission fluid. This is also a good time to check the engine oil level to make sure none drained out during storage.

engine, brakes, automatic or manual transmission, differential, etc. Make sure these are all filled to factory specifications before you attempt to start your engine. This is also a good time to revisit your checklist to verify that all hose attachments and electrical fittings are connected correctly.

Brake Bleeding

The most common method to bleed your brakes is gravity (manual) bleeding. It is simple and effective but it requires two people.

The other method is pressure (or pedal) bleeding. This requires using diaphragm-type, mechanical pressure bleeding equipment that is usually found in repair shops.

All 1968–1982 Corvette are fitted with four-piston brake calipers that have bleeder valves on each side of the rear and one on the front caliper. Always be sure to use the correct brake fluid and never let the master cylinder run out of fluid or you will have to start the process all over again. When the system is finished bleeding, the pedal should be firm and not drop when you push it down.

Start the brake bleeding process by removing the brake master cylinder cover. Raise the car into the air and remove the wheels. Keep the fluid topped off during the procedure

Exhaust System Installation

All 1968–1974 Corvettes came from the factory with true dual exhausts. Each side of the engine had its own dedicated exhaust system that feeds into two large mufflers underneath the bumpers. Only 1969 Corvettes were available with the optional factory side-mounted exhaust system (N14) that exited under each door.

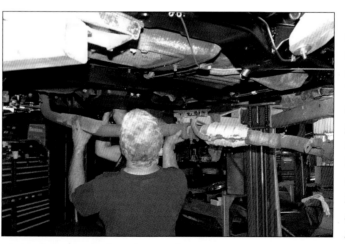

This 1980 exhaust features a catalytic converter for emissions control. The long tube is attached to the air pump in the engine compartment that blows air into the converter to make it more efficient. It's a very restrictive system, but many states have emissions inspections and this equipment must be installed to pass the test. The exhaust is connected to the two front headers on the engine. The rear pipe is connected to a pipe that is routed to both mufflers.

Brake Bleeding Methods

Here's a quick overview of the procedures for bleeding brakes.

Gravity Bleeding

One person can complete bleeding of the Corvette brake system with this method. Place the car on safety stands and remove the wheels. Open all bleeder screws and disconnect the vacuum booster check valve on power-brake-equipped cars. Verify that both rear calipers are 15 inches off the floor. Do not pump the brake pedal. Watch the bleeder valves until fluid begins flowing and then close them. Reconnect the power brake booster hose, reinstall the tires, and lower the car to the ground. Remember to always keep fluid topped off in the master cylinder during this procedure.

Pedal Bleeding

With this method, bleed the brakes in the following sequence: driver-side rear inner, driver-side rear outer, passenger-side rear inner, passenger-side rear outer, driver-side front, and passenger-side front. Have someone sit in the car and pump the pedal until it is firm. Apply a 5/16-inch wrench to the correct caliper bleeder valve. Attach a bleeder bottle with a long piece of brake hose that is submerged into old fluid. Turn the bleeder valve and keep it open until the brake pedal is fully depressed. Have your helper hold the pedal to the floor while you tighten the bleeder valve. Once the valve is closed, pump the brake pedal until it is firm. Repeat these steps at each bleeder valve until all of the air is evacuated from the system. Remember to check the master cylinder fluid level and refill as necessary.

Re-center Pressure Differential Switch

After the bleeding is complete turn the ignition switch on. Have someone depress the brake pedal to build up pressure. Slowly loosen the nut at the outlet port of the differential switch that is on the opposite side of the brake caliper (passenger-side front) that was bled last. As soon as the warning light goes out tighten the nut.

Brake Fluid

Maintaining clean brake fluid is probably the most ignored maintenance item. The fluid provides the hydraulic pressure from the master cylinder to the braking system when the brake pedal is applied.

Factory-supplied brake fluid is a modified form of ethylene glycol (DOT 3); it is an alcohol-based fluid that absorbs water. Moisture is absorbed into the brake fluid from vents in the master cylinder. The fluid absorbs about 2 percent of moisture every 12 months depending on the humidity in the air. This amount of water greatly lowers the boiling point of the fluid.

Silicone brake fluid (DOT 5) does not absorb water and the condensation that builds up in the system. Using this fluid can cause corrosion over time unless it is flushed frequently.

This is the correct way to bleed each brake caliper. Use a box-end 5/16-inch wrench to push a piece of brake hose up against the bleeder valve. The hose should be submerged into brake fluid inside a clear or semi-clear container. Be careful; brake fluid is very caustic and causes damage to any painted surface.

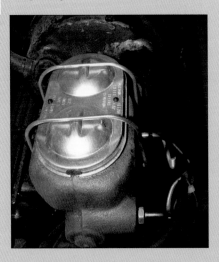

Once the bleeding process is complete and the fluid is topped off, reinstall the master cylinder cover and check for leaks.

Each of these pipes had a built-in muffler to help reduce the exhaust noise. You will know if sidepipes are installed on any other year except a 1969; they are not factory original. However, these pipes are very popular with C3 owners and a lot of cars have them installed. If the noise doesn't bother you and your car is not being judged at an NCRS meet, enjoy them!

Corvettes built from 1975 to 1982 have two pipes that feed into one catalytic converter under the passenger compartment and then split back into two pipes that lead to the mufflers. These cars are equipped with an air pump that feeds air into the converter to help emissions. If you live in a state with emissions inspections, this system is necessary to pass the annual test.

Vacuum Line Connections

It is very important to carefully inspect every vacuum line that exits the engine. These lines should be soft and flexible when squeezed. If they are hard and brittle, they are old and prone to fail, so you need to replace them.

The basic system is fairly simple to troubleshoot. It uses vacuum from the engine to open and close the headlight doors. If your car is a 1968 to 1972 this system also operates the hideaway windshield wiper door.

Both doors actually have two subsystems: control and operating. After your car is reassembled and these systems do not work, troubleshoot each one separately. The control system opens and closes the headlight and windshield wiper door. The wiper door system (which was eliminated starting in 1973) contains the wiper door safety

switch that is between the override and the wiper actuator relay. This relay prevents the door from closing until the wiper blades are in their parked position.

Wiper Doors

The wiper door system is very similar to headlight door operation. The main difference is that the headlight door system has two actuator relays and actuators compared to one for the wiper door. The other difference is that the headlight system does not need a safety switch to protect another system in case of failure.

Operation of the wiper system begins at the vacuum source, which is located on the intake manifold. The line goes through a filter and a check valve, then out of the lower fitting on the valve to the windshield wiper switch that is in the off position. When the wiper door is opened, vacuum is not allowed to reach the wiper actuator relay valve without vacuum present. A spring in the actuator valve pushes a diaphragm to open the wiper door. In effect all it is doing is routing the vacuum from the intake manifold to the actuators (vacuum motors) to open and close the doors.

If you have a vacuum leak that does not allow you to open your headlights or operate the wiper door your engine is probably running rough. You will have to find the leak and repair it.

Headlights

This system consists of vacuum hoses, vacuum hose filter, one-way check valve, headlight switch, manual override switch under the steering wheel, vacuum accumulator (storage tank), relays, and two actuators (vacuum motors). You need a

vacuum gauge to troubleshoot the system.

Disconnect the headlight/wiper door vacuum line where it connects to the intake manifold with the engine running. Connect a vacuum gauge directly to the manifold outlet. The engine should produce 18 to 20 inches of mercury according to the gauge. If you discover a 2- to 3-inch drop anywhere in the system, you have a leaking hose. If your car has a high-performance cam with excessive valve overlap, your vacuum reading is much lower; as a result the headlights slowly open if they are working correctly.

If your lights or wiper door is not opening, isolate the system to find the leak. If you have both wiper and headlight systems unhook the wiper door circuit and plug it with a golf tee or something similar. If it is too hard to reach, lower the panel under your steering column and plug the wiper override hose by disconnecting it from the switch.

Be sure to check the amount of vacuum coming into and out of this switch before proceeding. Make sure there is only one path back to the source of the vacuum (intake manifold) when testing an individual line.

If a reading is within 2 to 3 inches, that particular vacuum line is fine. If there is a significant drop, troubleshoot that line to find the leak. If all the vacuum lines are close to specifications and the doors are staying open, it indicates that a diaphragm has a hole in it and is leaking.

The actuators have a spring-loaded diaphragm inside and operate with vacuum. If the actuator is not getting vacuum, that relay stays in the up position at all times. A C3 Corvette with one light up and the other one down has a leaking diaphragm.

Reservoir and Actuators

The reservoir is easy to test. Remove both of the lines that go to the actuators. Plug one of the outlets where you just removed the lines and put your vacuum gauge on the other side and check the reading. If it is below the normal operational range, the reservoir is leaking.

On all 1973–1979 Corvettes the vacuum reservoir is in the round crossmember underneath the headlights. This crossmember has three fittings: one on the driver's side and two in the center to provide vacuum to the headlight relays.

If the reservoir is within specification, check the two headlight

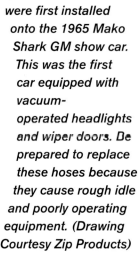

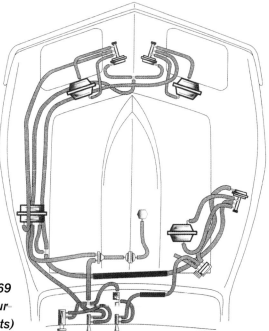

The 1968 included many of the power-operated features that were first installed onto the 1965 Mako Shark GM show car. This was the first car equipped with vacuum-operated headlights and wiper doors. Be prepared to replace these hoses because they cause rough idle and poorly operating equipment. (Drawing Courtesy Zip Products)

Here is the early 1969 system. (Drawing Courtesy Zip Products)

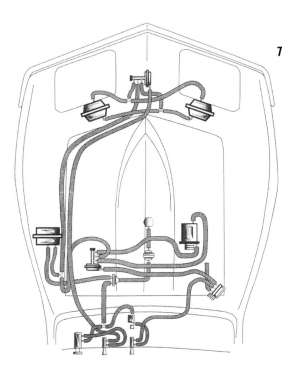

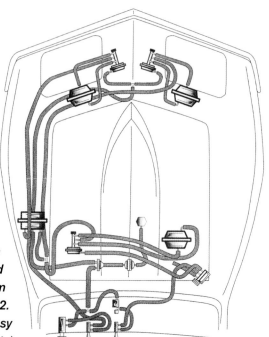

This is the late 1969 system, which used a different kind of actuator for the windshield wiper door. (Drawing Courtesy Zip Products)

The vacuum system stayed unchanged from 1970 to 1972. (Drawing Courtesy Zip Products)

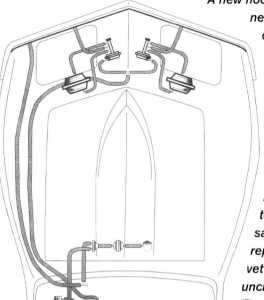

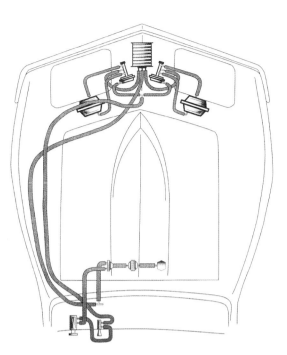

A new hood design eliminated the need for a windshield wiper door in 1973, much to the relief of Corvette mechanics and owners. The doors were prone to not opening on time and snagging the windshield wiper arms and burning out the motor. I always used the manual override that was located below the steering wheel to leave the door open if I saw any hint of rain. I never replaced a motor. This Corvette vacuum system remained unchanged from 1973 to 1979. (Drawing Courtesy Zip Products)

actuators. Test them the same way you checked the rest of the system until the part that failed is located.

Air Conditioning System

If your car is equipped with air conditioning and no seals were broken during disassembly, return the compressor to its bracket on the

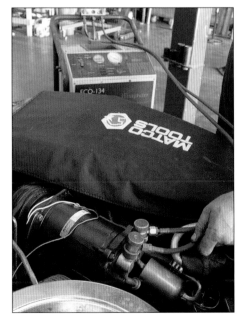

This 1969 Corvette air conditioning system has been converted from R-12 to R-134 to comply with new environmental regulations.

engine. Take the system to a shop that specializes in air-conditioning services and repairs if you are not familiar with it.

Most of the parts are available from Corvette aftermarket supply houses. Many auto parts stores stock rebuilt compressors at a reduced price. You can even buy duplicate factory stickers to paste onto rebuilt compressors.

C3 Corvettes were produced with two types of air conditioning systems. The original A6 compressor was an axial-flow unit that used R-12 freon for refrigerant. R-12 was banned due to environmental concerns and was replaced with R-134 refrigerant.

Later C3 Corvettes began using a rotary A/C compressor that was lighter and more efficient but still used R-12 as refrigerant. If the system was left intact when the car was dis-

The simplest vacuum system installed on a C3 Corvette was used from 1980 to 1982. The engineers used a large fruit can to serve as a vacuum can to operate the lights and it proved to be pretty trouble free. (Drawing Courtesy Zip Products)

mantled, it can be quickly reinstalled onto the engine.

However, if the system was removed and has been open to the atmosphere for an extended time, a number of parts must be replaced before it is recharged. Some of these parts include the drier/accumulator, expansion valve, condenser, and maybe even the compressor.

Older C3 Corvette A/C systems must be converted to use the new R-134 refrigerant.

Odds and Ends

Now it is time to connect the battery and turn on the electrical system. It is a good idea to test anything that is powered by electricity by turning it on. This includes dash lights, interior lights, headlights, taillights, and radio. You need to make sure your tunes work.

Look closely at all hoses to make sure they are tight and all fluids are filled to factory specifications. Leave the hood off until you have run the engine for a while so you can check for leaks or loose connections.

Add some gasoline and turn the engine over a few times to make sure no gas is leaking anywhere.

The only remaining items to be installed are the rear bumper, hood, and the trim rings on the wheels.

T-Top Adjustments

C3 Corvette coupes were fitted with two removable T-tops. They were designed to be stored behind the seats or on an optional luggage rack. From 1968 to 1977 only fiberglass roof panels were available. In 1978 new laminated glass roof panels were introduced (option code CC1) and became a popular addition.

The 1968–1977 T-tops had dual pull-down latches to hold them in place. One latch was located at the front of the top and one was at the rear. Two pins were inserted into the T-bar and the outside latches secured the tops to the birdcage. In 1978 the rear latch was eliminated and replaced with a movable pin that was part of the standard antitheft alarm system.

The roof panel gap (down the center of the T-bar) should be no more than 1/2 inch wide. The tops should sit 1/16 to 1/8 inch from the roof behind the seats. Loosen the retaining bolts and move both tops until you get the correct measurements. Tighten the attaching points with the roof in place.

The glass roofs are designed to sit 1/8 inch higher than the rear

Now it is time to reconnect the various wiring harnesses marked during disassembly with stickers or tape. By matching the numbers or writing on each side of the wiring harness the reconnection process should go very smoothly. Check each connector carefully to make sure none are missed during reassembly. Each connector plays a vital role in the smooth operation of your Corvette. Check and double-check this part of the installation.

Carefully check all of the various hoses to make sure they are not leaking before the engine is started.

With the hood off, start the engine and recheck all the hose connections. Leave the engine running for a few minutes to make sure nothing is leaking. Check all lights and accessories to be sure they operate normally.

Waxes, Polishes and Sealants

You should choose a leading brand for car care products. The brand chosen is often based on personal preference. At the end of the day, most modern products are high quality and do protect new paint. If your car was painted without the help of a heated paint booth, avoid waxing it for at least 90 days. Just to be safe, go onto the website of the paint company that you used and follow the recommendations.

Polish and Cleaner

In general, products that have the words polish or cleaners have a mild abrasive to help clean the roughness and oxidation from the surface of the paint. They remove paint, but the amount is very small. Epoxy-based clearcoats are very durable and usually stand up well to using these products. If your paint is glossy and smooth, there is little reason to use them on your car.

Abrasive

If the side of a product container says "no abrasives," it is of limited value. The problem is that manufacturers differ on what they consider abrasives. Even water is abrasive when it hits a surface under high pressure. The best option is to talk with people who have used the various products and get their feedback on what they have had the most success with.

Wax

Cleaner waxes are a faster one-step solution to shining and protecting your car's new finish. Purists, however, like to go through the effort of applying carnauba wax that is made from a Brazilian palm tree, which many believe is the longest-lasting wax. Again, it all boils down to how much time and effort you want to spend to get your ride sparkling.

Sealant

These are generally more expensive than wax and can be applied by hand or buffed into the paint. Most pros report that sealants last longer than wax, but after about six months, most sealant protection disappears.

Clearcoats

Many believe that clearcoats need more delicate handling because of their glass-like finish. The reality is that clearcoats are very hard and durable, especially those with epoxy hardeners. Products that are labeled for clearcoats usually contain no abrasives or fewer abrasives than other finish protectors.

Washing and Drying

Using a washing mitt makes the job much easier. You are able to cover a large area quickly, and can easily get into small spaces to maximize your cleaning. One trick is to mark your mitt to indicate which side you use to clean the dirtier, lower side of the car. This keeps the upper portions of your paint from getting scratched.

Don't forget to pop up your lights when you are washing the car. Clean lights are much brighter at night.

Using a chamois is a great way to dry off your car and prevent water spotting or streaking. A synthetic chamois soaks up 50 percent more water than a typical chamois and you can store it damp, so it is ready to use the next time you wash your car.

Finessing Paint

Every time your Corvette is taken out of your garage or storage area it is subject to unexpected hazards. Say, for example, you parked your 'Vette in a safe corner of the parking lot to have a nice lunch. You come back and to your horror find that the sprinkler system has come on covering your car with mineral-laden water. Unfortunately the sun was shining and baked all of these chemical stews onto your paint and the water was dry when you returned.

Fortunately these types of blemishes are quite shallow and can be carefully eliminated by a process called finessing. Professionals use this method to remove surface issues without repainting the car. Today's harsher environment and the growing number of clearcoat finishes have made this process vital to increasing the life of your paint.

This process involves using micro-fine wet sandpaper, such as 3M in 2,000- or 3,000-grit or a clay bar kit. You are not trying to remove deep blemishes on your paint; just surface spots.

If you use wet sandpaper, use plenty of water and very light strokes on small areas. Don't forget to rinse the sandpaper to prevent paint from building up on its surface and scratching the paint. Constantly check your progress by drying and inspecting the area. Keep some fresh water with dish detergent in a bucket and clean the paint surface as necessary.

Clay Bar is a soft putty that is used with the liquid polish that comes in the kit. It is used to rub the surface of the paint to remove water spots and restore smoothness.

Hopefully you will not encounter this situation, but if you do, don't panic; a little elbow grease can correct it.

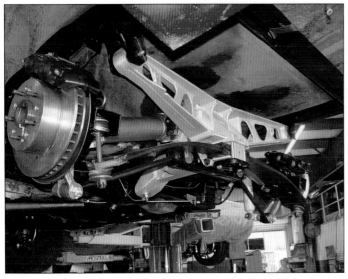

The rear suspension on this 1980 Corvette has been completely refurbished. Some of the new parts include brakes, trailing arms, spring, universal joints, brake lines, strut rods, differential, and halfshafts.

The back bumper has been reattached and adjusted to minimize the seam between the body and the bumper. The trim has been mounted on the wheels and the hood is the only remaining part that needs to be installed to complete this body/frame procedure. All of the mechanical and electrical checks were passed and after the hood is installed this Corvette will be road tested.

roof. They should not be adjusted lower than this as they might break from stress.

Use an 8 x 10-inch sheet of paper to determine if your tops are fitting snugly onto their gaskets. Put the paper on the gasket and install the roof. If the paper slides out easily from between the two, the top needs adjustment. Repeat this process until the paper cannot easily be pulled out.

Road Test

Art Dorsett's completed 1980 Corvette was given a 20-minute road test to check its brakes and fluid levels, and to verify that the transmission shifts correctly. The engine temperatures and oil pressure were all normal. This car passed the road test successfully and it was sent to the alignment shop to receive a four-wheel alignment.

Final Cleaning

You are joining a unique club as a Corvette owner. The majority of owners take pride in how their car looks,

and it is not unusual to see them cleaning their cars on a Saturday afternoon. Detailing your Corvette can be a very complex task, starting with deciding which products to use. There are a large number of brands being sold over the counter, and each

one claims that it is the best on the market. The final decision on the best one to pick rests on you. Talk to your friends and other Corvette owners to get their opinion on the best products. Today simple waxes have expanded to glazes, cleaners, polishes, sealers, etc.

The hood has been installed and the Corvette has passed its road test successfully. The completed car was sent to the alignment shop to have its suspension set to factory specifications. It is now ready to do what it was designed to do: put a smile on the owner's face.

S-A DESIGN

SOURCE GUIDE

3M Products
www.3m.com

American Powertrain
2199 Summerfield Rd.
Cookeville, TN 38501
www.americanpowertrain.com

AutoNation Chevrolet
15005 US Hwy. 19 N.
Clearwater, FL 33764
www.clearwaterchevrolet.com

AutoZone
www.autozone.com

Barrett Jackson Auctions
www.barrett-jackson.com

Bloomington Gold
705 E. Lincoln, Ste. 201
Normal, IL 61761
www.bloomingtongold.com

Carlisle Events
1000 Bryn Mawr Rd.
Carlisle, PA 17013
www.carsatcarlisle.com

Circle Products
4303 46th St. N.
St. Petersburg, FL 33714

Corvette America
100 Classic Car Dr.
Reedsville, PA 17084
www.corvetteamerica.com

Corvette Black Book
P.O. Box 1966
Gambier, Ohio 43022
www.corvetteblackbook.com

Corvette Central
13550 Three Oaks Rd.
Sawyer, MI 49125
www.corvettecentral.com

Corvette Forum
www.corvetteforum.com

Corvette Instrument Service
9627 Begonia St.
Palm Beach Gardens, FL 33410
www.corvetteinstrumentservice.com

Corvette Repair Inc.
132 East Fairview Ave.
Valley Stream, NY 11580
www.corvetterepair.com

Corvette World
www.Corvette-World.com

Cutaway Creations
703-425-8886
www.cutawaycreations.com

DeWitts Radiator
1275 Grand Oaks Dr.
Howell, MI 48843
517-548-0600
www.dewitts.com

DPS Powder
4980 110th Ave. N.
Clearwater, FL 33760
727-573-2797

Eckler's Corvette
www.ecklerscorvette.com

Ebay Motors
www.ebay.com/motors

Evercoat
6600 Cornell Rd.
Cincinnati, OH 45242
513-489-7600
www.evercoat.com

Gear Star
132 N. Howard St.
Akron, OH 44308
330-931-7311
www.gearstar.net

GM Performance Parts
www.gmperformanceparts.com

Harbor Freight Tools
www.harborfreight.com

Holley Performance Products
1801 Russellville Rd.
Bowling Green, KY 42101
www.holley.com

Lectric Limited
6750 W. 74th St.
Bedford Park, IL 60638
www.lectriclimited.com

Lonestar Caliper Co.
11299 Interstate 20
Canton, TX 75103
www.lonestarcaliper.com

Lowe's
www.lowes.com

Maher Chevrolet
2901 34th St. N.
St. Petersburg, FL 33713
www.maherchevrolet.com

Mecum Auctions
445 S. Main St.
Walworth, WI 53184
www.mecum.com

Mid-America Motorworks
17082 N US Hwy. 45
Effingham, IL 62401
www.mamotorworks.com

Mid-Southern Restorations
2113 Cane Creek Rd.
Cookeville, TN 38506
www.midsr.com

Mobil 1
www.mobil1.com

National Corvette Museum
350 Corvette Dr.
Bowling Green, KY 42101
www.corvettemuseum.org

NCRS
6291 Day Rd.
Cincinnati, OH 45252
www.ncrs.org

Paragon Corvette Reproductions
8040 S. Jennings Rd.
Swartz Creek, MI 48473
www.paragoncorvette.com

Richmond Gear
1001 W. Exchange Ave.
Chicago, IL 60609
www.richmondgear.com

Sears
www.sears.com

Southern Style Racing Engines
4921 73rd Ave. N.
Pinellas Park, FL 33781
727-546-7000

SSBC Performance Brake Systems
11470 Main Rd.
Clarence, NY 14031
800-448-7722
www.ssbrakes.com

Tackley Auto Body
12330 49th St. N.
Clearwater, FL 33762
727-572-4303

Van Steel Corvette Parts & Service
12285 West St.
Clearwater, FL 33762
www.vansteel.com

Vern's Chevy Service
1649 S. Missouri Ave.
Clearwater, FL 33756
www.chevyservicecenter.com

Volunteer Vette Products, Inc.
3103 E. Gov. John Sevier
Knoxville, TN 37914
865-521-9100
www.volvette.com

Zip Products
8067 Fast Ln.
Mechanicsville, VA 23111
www.zip-corvette.com